CW01023975

THE SMUGGLING STORY OF THE NORTHERN SHORES

Other books by the same author also published by Wyre Forest Press:

The Isle of Man in Smuggling History
Scottish Customs & Excise Records, with particular reference to
Strathclyde
Strathclyde's Smuggling Story
Dumfries & Galloway's Smuggling Story
Family Histories in Scottish Customs Records
The Smuggling Story of Two Firths (Montrose to Dunbar)
George Moore and Friends (Letters from a Manx merchant 1750-1760)

THE SMUGGLING STORY OF THE NORTHERN SHORES

[Oban to Montrose, including the Islands]

Frances Wilkins BA

Wyre Forest Press

© Frances Wilkins 1995

Published by Wyre Forest Press
8 Mill Close, Blakedown, Kidderminster
Worcestershire DY10 3NQ

Printed by The Bath Press
31 Lower Bristol Road
Bath BA2 3BL

ISBN 1 897725 05 1

Contents

Illustrations

Tables

Notes on Illustrations

Figure 1 is extracted from the Robert Morden Map of Scotland in the 1695 edition of Camden's *Britannica*

Figures 2 and 10 are reproduced by kind permission of Dennis Wilkins

Figure 3 is from the Letter-book of Bailie John Steuart

Figures 4 and 5 are from the Watt papers (D3/110 and D3/72) reproduced by kind permission of the Orkney Archives

Figures 6, 8 and 11 are from *King's Cutters and Smugglers* by E Keble Chatterton

Figures 7 is from *A New Geographical Grammar* by Charles Vyse

Figure 9 and the insert in Chapter One are from the custom house letter-books, both Crown copyright reproductions reproduced by permission of the Keeper of the Record of Scotland with the agreement of the controller of HMSO

Figure 12 is reproduced by kind permission of Duncan Brown, photographer of Fraserburgh

The cover is reproduced by kind permission of Imray, Laurie, Norrie and Wilson Ltd and of Admiralty Charts and Hydrographic Publications

Tailpieces

PREFACE

The scene is set by quoting from various sources describing the attitude of the locals towards smuggling in the area of the northern shores.

'Besides this, there are such strong resolutions and endeavours to crush the importation of brandy that it is disparaging to a man's character at this juncture to be known to meddle that way ... the Duke of Argyll and Marquis of Seaforth have engaged in the strongest manner to allow no brandy to be bought or drunk in their several counties. And ... Culloden and the Advocate [Forbes of Culloden and his brother, Duncan, Lord Advocate] expect McLeod and Sir Alexander McDonald to come to the same resolution'. [Bailie John Steuart to John McLeod, Glenelg, 20 August 1730]

During 1744 William Gordon ran a cargo of brandy and tobacco into Spey Bay and landed it at various places along the coast. The Board of Customs, hearing of this, applied to the local justices to take a precognition. The justices refused, alleging that they might be compelled to interrogate witnesses, who could turn out to be implicated. The Board consulted the Lord President of the Court of Session [the same Duncan Forbes as mentioned above], who sent the chairman of the local bench the following letter:

'The Christmas holidays, which have emptied the town and adjourned the Board of Customs, have prevented my being able to write to you on the subject of your smuggling, as I once thought I should; but lest what I may write you after consultation with others should come too late for your meeting on the 15th inst, I have taken the part in the meantime of dropping you this line.

'I have not been more surprised for a great while than when I heard that a majority of justices at your last meeting put off the precognition on a doubt whether they lawfully could take the information from the witnesses upon oath and thereby, however innocent their intentions were, flung some cold water upon the enquiry. As to the doubt itself, I confess I am at a loss to guess on what it is founded. Precognitions have at all times been taken on oath in

Scotland, and hence the established practice in the court of justiciary of cancelling, at the trial, the oath formerly emitted on the precognition, before the witness emit his deposition in Court, if he desire it. No occult crime, however dangerous to the commonweal, or to the crown, could be detected or punished, if witnesses were in the least backward, without a power in those whose duty it is to enquire, to examine upon oath ... so that, as I apprehend the scruple is without any just foundation, I doubt not at your next meeting, after gentlemen have time to inform themselves duly, it will evanish.

'I cannot suffer myself to suspect that, considering the notoriety of the mischief that smuggling does to this poor unhappy country, and the forwardness lately shewn by all ranks of men to express their detestation of it, to bind themselves to one another and to the public, by resolutions and engagements of honour, to discourage that villainous traffic, any gentleman or number of gentlemen will in broad daylight and in an open court (whatever their connection with, or tenderness for the unhappy smuggler be) be so impudently profligate as to attempt to screen the cutthroats of their country, and thereby expose themselves to the universal contempt and abhorrence of mankind. Such an attempt requires more than an ordinary degree of courage and wickedness. The guilty person cannot hope to remain unknown. The minutes of the court must record his infamy. Nor is it to be expected by him that the character, which by such practice he may purchase, shall remain confined to his own country. The common post can, by an extract from the minutes, convey his fame to Edinburgh, from whence it may be communicated to the whole kingdom.

'Now, though for these reasons I hope you will be unanimous at your next meeting, yet, if contrary to my expectations and very much against my wish, the smugglers should find protection and the national justice, as well as interest, should be defeated, I hope you will be so good as to transmit the minutes, distinguishing how each justice voted. Besides furnishing me as a private gentleman with information who I ought to detest and avoid as a scoundrel, that I may be able to inform my fellow subjects, as far as that may be done within the laws, who they ought to look upon as enemies to their country. Other rebukes they may possibly meet with but it is not necessary to speak of that at present. I write, you see, with great freedom, as I am very much in earnest. But what I have said are the dictates of my heart and you are at full liberty to make what use you please of what I have wrote. This mean, shameful course of destruction must be prevented, or our unhappy country must be undone. Make my compliments to everyone who can lay his hand upon his heart and say he does not deserve the title of rascal'.

The goods in return No 7 dated May 1770 forwarded to the Board in Edinburgh by the collector and comptroller at Aberdeen 'being seized in a house for holding fish belonging to Alexander Wishart at Sandend and among the bents near the seaside, there was reason to hope that a discovery might be obtained of the proprietors and the persons concerned in running and also that the ship from which it was run would be discovered so as to make examples of all because the gentlemen in this and two neighbouring counties had entered into the most positive resolution to prosecute with the utmost rigour and attention every one person whosoever that was concerned in smuggling upon this coast, had made advertisements to this purpose and appeared perfectly keen to do it. The collector therefore called upon the sheriff and several of the justices and acquainted them of this smuggle, that the fishing boats at Newburgh, as he was informed, had refused to board the ships or take out anything but that the smugglers had found means notwithstanding to get the goods put ashore from the ship on the sands near Sandend and there run the whole cargo, part of which was seized, that we and the officers of the revenue had it not in our power to point out to them the proper proof to have all concerned punished and that there was no other step to be taken but for them to summon in every man in the neighbourhood of the place where the smuggle was made, examine them by way of precognition upon oath, by which means there was all the probability ... that we should get to the bottom of the whole smuggle and all concerned, so as to strike a terror by punishing them.

'The justices to a very considerable number met to consider this matter and resolved at the expense of the county to order their fiscal to cause summon the whole inhabitants in the neighbourhood of the smuggle to be examined by them by way of precognition and which was accordingly done and no less than about eighty people brought in. But after the utmost pains used to make them tell truth there was no discovery made of the proprietors, of the ship's name or of any person concerned in the smuggle excepting only Alexander Wishart's servants and horses, and George Willcox, merchant and farmer at Newtyle, his servants and horses being employed. A scene of perjury appeared evident but nothing further could be made of it. The justices brought in Alexander Wishart and George Willcox upon Friday last and it seems ordered their procurator fiscal to give in to them a complaint against these two people for their conduct in giving their horses and servants. They thought proper to submit themselves to the justices, who fined each of them in £300, as treble value of the goods they were concerned in smuggling. Upon which they petitioned the justices, representing their poverty and inability to pay anything except a small sum. Their appearance of perjury when they were examined, especially Wishart, as they had denied they had given any orders to their servants, made them send

Wishart to prison. But finding their inability to pay any considerable sum they restricted it to £12 10s each, which they obliged them to pay immediately for the use of the infirmary [for George Willcox see also Chapter Four].

'The justices of the county of Mearns where the seizure of spirits was made among the rocks by Mr Vitty have determined to try also a prosecution if they can find out how to do it in order to have their fishers punished, who brought these spirits ashore. Whatever is done your Honours shall be acquainted of but they seem all surprised at the perjuries they meet with in these enquiries'.

The collector at Aberdeen also wrote to the Board on 13 December 1780 'Having by no means a good opinion of the procurator fiscal for Banffshire ... as we are well informed that the rioters [who attacked Andrew Blair and James Davidson on 26 October 1780] keep proper spies to get information of what may be done against them at Banff and are all on their guard so that the most effectual way of securing them is by sending from this a trusty man to take them up upon a justiciary warrant and which we are humbly of opinion will be the most effectual means of success in apprehending them. We are also informed that they keep a lookout upon the shires of the county and have been in Moray so that there has been little chance of apprehending them from any procedure of the sheriff of Banffshire. We have therefore thought it our duty humbly to represent this to your Honours and to send the enclosed precognition as a foundation for a justiciary warrant which, if your Honours approve of ... every means in our power will be used to get the persons guilty apprehended'.

Against this background the smugglers appear to have acted at will while the customs and other revenue officers struggled to undertake their duties with any degree of success. This is the basis for the smuggling story of the northern shores.

ACKNOWLEDGEMENTS

It would have been impossible to undertake at long distance the research necessary for a book of this type without the willing assistance of a large number of people. The author is very grateful to the Archive and Record Centre, City of Dundee District Council; West Search Room, Scottish Record Office, Edinburgh; the Orkney Archives, Kirkwall; the Shetland Archives, Lerwick, and Strathclyde Regional Archives, Mitchell Library, Glasgow, who provided the photocopies and microfilms and likewise to David Dobson of St Andrews, Michael Dun of Dundee and Sue Mowat of Dunfermline for chasing the 'loose ends'. Many thanks are also due to the Public Record Office, Kew, Northamptonshire County Record Office, the Manx National Heritage Library, HM Customs & Excise Aberdeen and Edinburgh and the *Aberdeen Press and Journal*, and to Eric Graham of Essex, who identified Isle Martin, and Duncan Brown of Fraserburgh, who provided photographs of a modern smuggling wreck. Once again mention is made of Ainsley Monger, postman of Blakedown, who had the uneviable task of delivering all this material.

This seems to be an appropriate opportunity to thank all the others, mainly based in Scotland, who have provided support and encouragement throughout the research into Scottish smuggling history. It would be invidious to select individuals from such a large group so that this attempts to encompass you all. However, special mention should be made of my husband, Dennis, whose photographic expertise produced all the illustrations and my son, Steven, who was the essential computing expert.

Finally sincerest thanks are due to John Gibson-Forty, practitioner of cranial osteopathy in Ross-on-Wye, without whose understanding treatment it would have been impossible to complete the physical task of research let alone the writing of this book.

Since August 1993, when the author was told that it would be physically impossible to continue a writing and publishing career, three further books have been completed. We did it.

This book is dedicated to Archibald Watt and other members of the
Stonehaven Heritage Society with thanks for your support and
encouragement on 30 November 1993

INTRODUCTION

'Would you say that this area has the most exciting smuggling history in Scotland?' [Journalist, Stonehaven Heritage Society lecture, 30 November 1993]

Such comparisons tend to be somewhat otiose: it is all too easy to say that x is better than y when one is in x but y is better than x when one is in y. The smuggling history not just of Stonehaven but of the whole area covered by this book does stand out as very different from that of the other regions studied to date. But then each of these regions: Strathclyde, Dumfries & Galloway, the Two Firths had its special 'magic' which made it unique within the overall Scottish framework. So can it be claimed that the present book describes 'the most exciting smuggling history in Scotland'?

The area covered is extensive - the mainland from Oban on the west to Montrose on the east and the offshore islands ranging from the Outer Hebrides and Skye to Orkney and Shetland. Is this a cohesive whole or just a convenient classification: add to the North-East 'the rest' where the custom houses were comparatively few and far between so that there will not be enough information to justify a separate book? Earlier doubts soon proved to be unfounded. Eighteenth century merchants in Inverness supplied high duty and prohibited goods to the west coast from Argyll northwards, including Stornoway and Orkney, while merchants in Thurso supplied Inverness. In 1775 the Board of Customs in Edinburgh forewarned the collectors at the northern outports that they had 'received information that on the 25th of this month a large lug-sailed smuggling vessel passed the harbour of Peterhead steering for Duncansby Head bound for the west coast of Scotland, the wind that day and the day following being at south by west, blowing fresh'. From the viewpoint of the present study such information provides the necessary links between the boundaries of this area.

As 'there was a notable lack of customs surveillance in the north-west Highlands and Islands' [Cochran], would there be enough material to write a comprehensive story? The custom house letter-books still exist for Oban, Stornoway, Thurso, Kirkwall and Lerwick. But what about the gaps in both time [some of these letter-books only exist from the late eighteenth century] and on the ground? These gaps are filled by the letters to three merchants based in Kirkwall, Thurso and Wick and the letter-book of bailie John Steuart of Inverness. When all the locations mentioned in these sources are plotted on a map, they cover an ewxtensive area. To this is added the more comprehensive letter-book coverage for the north-east.

Another nagging doubt has been whether there was the market for what might appear to be yet another 'formula' book on Scottish smuggling history. Surely everything had been said already. In fact the rich source material has made it possible to approach this smuggling story even more from the viewpoint of the individuals involved: Walter Sime, notorious smuggler of Bervie, James Philip et al, tidesmen of Gourdon, William Watt junior, merchant of Kirkwall etc. As a result the layout of the chapters is subtly different - instead of separate sections on goods and their origins this information is provided 'along the way'. There is so much detail available that in addition to individual chapters on smuggling vessels, pretended bound voyages and wrecks Appendix II includes an almost complete alphabetical listing of 'smuggling' vessels found in the records.

Previous critics have suggested that the books would be of wider interest if the primary sources were used not for factual smuggling history but as background for fiction. The author believes that this would spoil the original stories, many of which rival fiction in their vivid portrayal of larger than life events. In fact the primary source material has been used to write the smuggling story from a 'they saw it happen' viewpoint.

In the interests of readability the transcripts have been modernised in terms of spelling and punctuation and various 'superfluous' words such as 'Mr' [when repeated several times in a short space], 'said', 'and' and 'that' have been omitted, unless this altered the meaning of the quotation.

Where not actually known on the ground, attempts have been made to locate the many places mentioned on the Ordnance Survey 1:50,000 maps. In most cases these have been corrected for modern spelling - Miltoun or Milntoun of Mather or Mathers is referred to as Milton of Mathers. An exception is Inverbervie, where the name Bervie has been retained, partly to save space. Some places defied identification. Birchen Isles stand out in particular - though there are enough clues as to their location. Where other places have not been found, this is indicated in the text. The overseas ports - many of which cannot be identified today - have been standardised to their most common spelling. The names of vessels posed a familiar problem - was it the *Peggie* or *Peggy*? Once again the commonest spelling of each individual vessel has been used. As brackets appear in the original texts, the author's comments are enclosed in [] brackets.

The first chapter, describing the sources of information, is followed by two chapters based solely on the contemporary merchant correspondence. Smugglers mentioned frequently in the custom house letters lead on to three chapters about smuggling vessels. The revenue officers are described in another three chapters and the final chapter looks beyond the eighteenth century. In an attempt not to clog the text with important yet overlong quotations such extracts have been reproduced as tailpieces at the end of each chapter in the form of 'A Story of ...' Similarly shorter stories have been used as a commentary on the illustrations. Three Appendices describe the revenue in the northern shores, as seen in 1656, smuggling vessels and Jacobite connections. There is an index of the individuals mentioned in the text.

The end-product is certainly an 'exciting smuggling history'. As a result a diorama in the new Phase II of the HM Customs & Excise National Museum at Albert Dock, Liverpool records a beach landing taken directly from this book [see Chapter Four]. This is the ultimate triumph - the recreation of an eighteenth century event based solely on the contemporary records of those who actually 'saw it happen'. The story lives on.

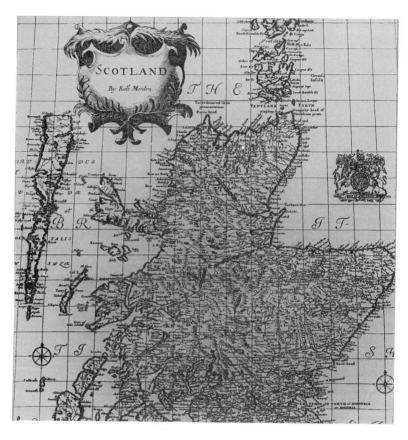

Figure 1: The Northern Shores, excluding Shetland

CHAPTER ONE: SOURCES OF INFORMATION

'I have this moment received certain advice that Captain Ogilvy's yacht is at Stromness and has seized some ankers from R Sandison and from Mrs Burney. They have got a great seizure in Caithness. Destroy this'. [Letter from TB [Thomas Balfour of Edinburgh] to William Watt junior, Kirkwall, no date]

When attempting the reconstruction of the smuggling history of an area, the first concern is: how many documents have survived? The miracle is that there are any, be it the correspondence of the Board of Customs to and from the collectors at the outports or that of [smuggling] merchants, which was preserved rather than destroyed, as instructed in the letter quoted above.

There is often an unwillingness to believe what is written by the merchants, as if the secrecy of their correspondence means that the facts cannot be trusted. As a result it is especially rewarding when an event discussed at length in this correspondence also appears in custom house letter-books, so giving it authenticity. One example of this, the seizure of the *Peggie* of Stromness at Montrose, was also mentioned in *The Smuggling Story of the Two Firths*. Other examples, where individuals and events mentioned in the merchant correspondence appear elsewhere, are quoted in this book.

A related problem is the relationship between 'folklore' and 'fact'. In the northern shores area there is the well documented story of the death of Philip Kennedy, the smuggler. This story, as told by James Dalgarno in *From the Brig o'Balgownie to the Bullers o'Buchan*, is the basis of Figure 2. A slightly different version is told in John B Pratt's *Buchan*. This time 'Anderson was observed to hold up his sword to the moon, as if to ascertain whether he was using the [sharp] edge'. The version which appears on the custom house letter-books is reproduced in the tailpiece at the end of this chapter.

Figure 2: The Death of Philip Kennedy, the Smuggler

'Philip had on that night [19 December 1798] secured sixteen ankers of Holland gin at the shore of 'Cransdale', Collieston, and employed women to carry it off in creels to the hiding-place on his farm at Ward, a distance of three miles, while he and his brother John went off to protect the property from two gaugers and a tide watcher, who were on the way to Collieston from having made a seizure of gin at Sandend, Cruden. The Kennedys had scarcely gone a mile when they came in contact with the gaugers, two of whom were armed with cutlasses. They had not exchanged many words when a desperate struggle ensued. Philip, with his oak cudgel, in which there was sunk a lump of lead, warded off the cutlass, and tripped up two of them, and held them down in his giant grasp, calling on his brother to secure the other. John was in combat with the other gauger, and in parrying off the cutlass with the stick got a severe cut on the forehead, piercing through his thick bonnet, the blood flowing over his eyes and face rendering him helpless. After wounding the brother, the gauger roared out to Philip to let go his grasp or he would sever his head from his body, but he still kept his hold. Anderson then, uttering an oath, brandished his weapon, and with one fell stroke laid open the head of poor Kennedy. He immediately started to his feet and shouted out 'Murder!' Although severely wounded he walked the distance of three quarters of a mile to the farm of Kirkton, and seating himself heavily on a chair in the kitchen, said, 'If a' had been as true as me the prize wid a' been safe, an' I widna' a' been bleedin' to death!' After which he expired with a groan. It was said a finer, broad-shouldered, stalwart fellow never entered the Kirk of Slains, and that he was always known among his fellows on the Kirk road by his uniform home-spun blue suit, staff in hand, and broad blue bonnet with red tap. He might have been useful in the sphere in which he moved for other fifty years, but for the wiles and deceit of two informers under pay, who betrayed him into the clutches of the gaugers. The skull of Philip Kennedy has been repeatedly turned up in excavating the graves of others of the name buried in the same spot. His brother John, who died in 1842, bore the marks of the cutlass as long as he lived.

'Anderson, the exciseman, who inflicted the fatal blow, was tried on the 28th September following, on charge of murder, but was acquitted by the jury on a verdict of 'Not Guilty!''

From: *From the Brig o'Balgownie to the Bullers o'Buchan* by James Dalgarno, 1897.

In contrast a detailed inspection of the customs and excise records has failed to corroborate the stories surrounding Malcolm Gillespie, the excise man who was reputedly the first revenue officer to use a dog [see bibliography]. The lack of evidence does not mean that the stories are untrue. They may exist in other letter-books not consulted as yet or the relevant records may have been destroyed. This book is based on the extant contemporary records - the letter-books and minutes of the Board of Customs in Edinburgh, the letter-books of the local custom houses and the correspondence of merchants based in Kirkwall, Thurso, Wick and Inverness.

Custom House Letter-books

The most valuable source of the smuggling story of an area is the custom house correspondence that is found in the letter-books containing transcriptions of the letters from the collector and comptroller at the local outport to the Board (Class 1) and the letters from the Board to all collectors (general letters) or the specific collector (Class 2). The letters from the collector were written to 'Honourable Sirs' and ended 'Respectfully etc'. In contrast the Board addressed their letters to 'Gentlemen' and, even when delivering an admonition, tended to sign themselves as in this letter dated 1735:

Table Ia lists the original outports in the area, as defined shortly after the Union of 1707. Over the next hundred years additional outports were created, as indicated in Table Ib.

TABLE I: The Outports of the Northern Shores

a: **The outports and creeks as defined in 1707**

Ports	Creeks
Montrose	Arbroath, Auchmithie, Lunan Water, Usan, Ferryden, Mathers, Johnshaven, Gourdon, Bervie, Tod Head
Aberdeen	Catterline, Crawton, Dunnottar, Stonehaven, Skateraw, Findon Cove, Old Aberdeen, Newburgh, Slains, Boddam, Peterhead, Rattray Head, Cairnbulg, Fraserburgh, Rosehearty, Banff, Portsoy, Cullen
Inverness	Garmouth, Lossiemouth, Burghead, Findhorn, Nairn, Alness, Cromarty, Portmahomac, Tain, Dornoch, Dunrobin, Helmsdale

Note: This list was obtained from *The King's Customs* by Atton & Holland. In May 1786 the magistrates, town council and community of the Royal Burgh of Banff, the other noblemen, heritors and freeholders of the lands and estates on the north-east coast of Scotland sent the Treasury a memorial 'praying to have a custom house established at Banff'. Peterhead also became an independent outport.

b: **Later Outports**

Fort William (Maryburgh); Isle Martin - Ullapool; Lerwick; Macduff; Oban; Stornoway; Thurso and Wick

Note: This list is based on references within the custom house letter-books.

Not all the correspondence for these outports has survived until the 1990s. Some of the losses have been comparatively recent: Masterton in *Jurisdiction in Marginal Seas* [1929] quotes from letters written by the collector at Wick to the Board on 8 November 1742 and 13 July 1763 and by the collector at Macduff on 26 December 1804 and 14 August 1811. Yet no records for these ports exist today. Similarly Masterton quotes letters from the Aberdeen collector dated 28 August and 31 December 1721 [the earliest letters now extant are dated 1728] while Atton and Holland in *The King's Customs* [1908] refer to a letter from the collector at Inverness dated 18 May 1733 - see p 157 [No Class 1 letters].

Table II lists the records that do exist, together with details of the earliest date of the Class 1 and Class 2 letters respectively. Details of the customs and excise [CE] records studied while researching for this book are listed in the Bibliography.

TABLE II: The Custom House Letter-books studied for this Book

Ref No	Port	Class 1	Class 2
CE53	Montrose	1724	1707
CE54	Thurso	-	1791
CE55	Kirkwall	1799	1823
CE62	Inverness	-	1781
CE64	Banff	1820	1801
CE65	Peterhead	1850	-
CE75	Oban	1838	1823
CE85	Lerwick	1795	
CE86	Stornoway	1765	1765
CE87	Aberdeen	1728	1720

Note: Other customs and excise records available for outports and creeks in the northern shores area include CE36 Elgin, CE66 Fraserburgh, CE78 Elgin, CE83 Stonehaven, CE89 Buckie, CE94 Drumnadrochit and CE97 Grantown. None of these were consulted by the author.

This is not the first time that the letter-books have been used to describe the smuggling history of the area. Duncan Fraser's *The Smugglers* tells the story of Montrose through the custom house letters while Hance Smith has used the customs records for Lerwick in his definition of 'smuggling rings' in *Shetland Life and Trade*. This book is recommended for further reading. The present author would like to emphasise that there is still an important source of Scottish history untapped in the letter-books for the northern shores. Possibly the most rewarding are those for Aberdeen and Montrose but none of the others should be discounted.

As there are so many custom house letters, the previous method of research was to sample every fifth year, chasing any 'loose ends' in order to complete a story, either in previous or successive years or in another Class of letter-book. Because of the apparent hyperactivity in the Montrose district and because the letters for 1770, 1775 and 1780 had been studied for the *Two Firths* book, with any *Northern Shores* material appropriately indexed, it was decided to 'fill in' the gaps by also studying 1771-1774 and 1776-1779. The result was interesting. Some of the major stories which had been identified already were expanded, in particular the tidesmen of Gourdon [see Chapter Nine] but there was little 'new' or 'surprising' information, so justifying the five year sampling approach. As there were comparatively few Class 1 letters for Stornoway between 1765 and 1805, these were all studied.

Merchant Correspondence
Several of the [smuggling] merchant letter-books are transcripts of letters from a particular individual to his overseas suppliers, partners, shipmasters and local customers eg Bailie John Steuart [see Figure 3], George Moore of Peeltown on the Isle of Man [see *George Moore and Friends*, letters from a Manx merchant 1750 to 1760], Oliphant & Co, Ayr and Walter Lutwidge, Whitehaven. The extensive Carteret Priaulx collection in Guernsey includes letters to the merchant house, so giving a

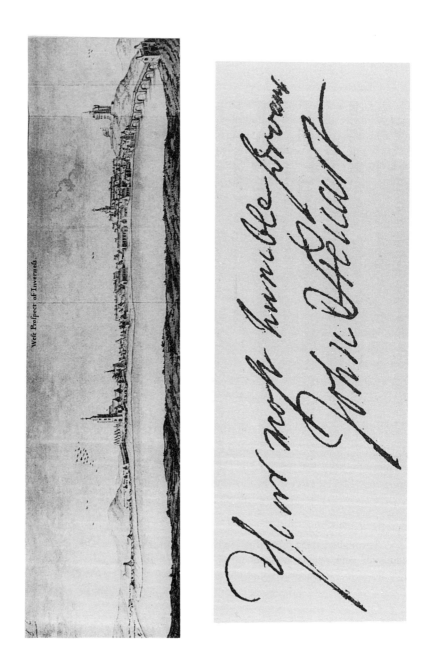

West Prospect of Inverness

8

Figure 3: Bailie John Steuart of Inverness

John Steuart was born on 2 September 1676, the son of Alexander Steuart, merchant of Inverness. John started his business in 1700. For several years he was a prosperous merchant and factor to the Earl of Moray. He was on the Inverness Town Council from 1703-1716 and a magistrate from 1713-1715 - after this he was always known as bailie Steuart. His Jacobite connections drove him to exile but he returned to Scotland to die in virtual poverty on 20 April 1759.

The letter-book, which covers nearly forty years from 1714 to 1752, was published by the Scottish History Society in 1915, so making the correspondence comparatively easy to study. The letters include many detailed insights into the problems facing a smuggling merchant.

'I spoke to my partners in the *Alexander* (which ship is not yet reached Cork in Ireland, her port of delivery, by reason of contrary winds). They are willing to accommodate you in lastadge, but think forty quarter casks too much, seeing it will pinch themselves; however I have prevailed, and by the next post shall give commission to Mr Gordon, of Bordeaux, as you have ordered; only, if you please, that if [you and I] be a third concerned in this adventure of brandy it will be a favour, since otherways I can have no separate concern from the cargo; as to which send me your answer by the bearer. If you incline, I will order forty-five quarter casks, so there will be thirty for your account and fifteen for mine. I'll likewise take care of the wine for your own use ... Mr George, who is master of the *Alexander* for this voyage, has orders to call at you when he returns from France. The signal is his mainsail hurled up and his ensign out; so I judge you'll get more goods to trouble you than your own'. [To William Gordon of Farskan, near Cullen, a merchant in Elgin, 18 November 1717]. These problems are further developed in Chapters Two and Three.

Throughout the research into smuggling in Scotland during the eighteenth century the same question has recurred: how did the smuggling links develop? Previous attempts have been made by the author to link the smuggling partnerships to a political underpinning. This is the first time that some of the smugglers have been positively identified as Jacobites - bailie Steuart and his friends [see Appendix III].

subtly different viewpoint of report and complaint rather than instruction. The Watt collection in Orkney includes letters to Alexander Watt and William Watt junior & Co in Kirkwall and also to Alexander Bain junior in Thurso and Thomas Baikie in Wick. These have been used by other writers [eg W S Hewison in *Smuggling in Eighteenth Century Orkney*]. But a wealth of material still remains.

An example of this correspondence is a second letter from Thomas Balfour to William Watt junior & Co, dated Edinburgh 25 May 1772. 'At present I cannot lay my hands upon your two last letters. In the first you advised that you had ordered a certain quantity of brandy to be shipped on board the sloop *William* of Kirkwall [see Appendix II], Thomas Balfour master, at Bergen deliverable at Orkney as also that you had ordered a certain quantity of geneva from Rotterdam by a ship in which Mr McPherson of Shetland was concerned, of both which adventures I hereby agree to stand the risk and hazard of my shares thereof agreeable to the conditions of both your letters above referred to. Please to acquaint Mr Traill of Westness that his bill on me to you or order for £154 payable at one month from the 6th current is accepted by me and the payment is ordered how soon it falls due'.

As a result of the detailed indexing of the Watt papers by the Orkney Archives, it has been possible to identify the significant 'smuggling' letters, which, together with those from bailie Steuart, form the basis of Chapters Two and Three.

Sometimes it is impossible to trace what seems like an obvious national or international event referred to in the records. For once the Gentleman's Magazine did not produce the answers, either to 'what you mention of having seen in the news about the smugglers here [Dunkirk] is not true' [see Chapter Two] or to a comment about the death of the lady Steuart of Ardshiel, whose gravestone has not been traced, yet, in Northampton [see Appendix III]. But, overall, it is wrong to complain when so much can be reproduced to tell the story of smuggling on the northern shores.

All the primary, and secondary, source material used in this book is listed in the bibliography.

A STORY OF THE DEATH OF PHILIP KENNEDY, THE SMUGGLER, CUSTOMS STYLE

'We beg leave to refer your Honours to the enclosed letter from Gilbert Leighton, tidesman at the Ward of Cruden, dated 27th instant giving an account of a smuggle which happened lately in the neighbourhood and of a disagreeable accident ensuing there anent of a man being killed. We believe the account he gives of it to be just with this addition that Mr Anderson, officer of excise, has been apprehended in consequence and a precognition having been taken by the sheriff he was admitted to bail. On first hearing of this matter we immediately dispatched Mr Medcalf, assistant tidesurveyor, to the spot with four of his boat's crew, who came too late to secure any of the goods. We submit Leighton's request to be removed to some other place to your Honours determination, his reasons for it appearing to be well founded, and we take the liberty of suggesting that if your Honours shall be pleased to grant the same there will be a necessity for filling his place with a stout and active officer and in that view we beg to refer your Honours to the list of officers and their characters and ages as at 5 July last'. [Collector at Aberdeen to the Board, 28 December 1798]

Copy of a letter from Gilbert Leighton to the collector and comptroller dated Aberdeen, 27 December 1798

Gentlemen,

Upon the 19th December 1798 Mr Anderson and Mr Trail officers of excise and myself went on information of a smuggle being at Collieston and seized three ankers of gin, carrying without a permit near to said place, and seeing more people carrying ankers at a little distance we left the ankers of gin we had seized with Mr Trail and Mr Anderson and I went to seize them. Coming up with the people carrying those ankers, two men came out from amongst them with bludgeons in their hands and one of them attacked Mr Anderson and the other attacked me in a cruel and ferocious manner, dashing me to the ground and knocking me down and did all in his power to throw me headlong down a bank I was lying near, which if he had affected would have dashed out my brains, and he so much grasped and pressed me I could scarcely speak and expected every minute to be murdered. In the oppressed situation I was in I was unable to know whose strokes or if any were given. contd

11

A STORY OF THE DEATH OF PHILIP KENNEDY, THE SMUGGLER, CUSTOMS STYLE contd

'The two officers above named relieved me from the man that attacked me and as he was above me I could not discern what occurred, finding myself much indisposed from the cruel treatment I met with. I suppose their intention was to murder us all, as a number of people appeared at a small distance from us. The above occurred about ten o'clock at night on the 19th December 1798. After I was relieved, with difficulty I was able to carry one of the three ankers with the two officers and lodge them for safety. The two officers and I went next off from the coast up the way of Ellon and seized four horses and two carts, carrying nine ankers of foreign geneva without a permit, and lodged them at Ellon. The above occurred about two o'clock in the morning of the 20th December. In the course of that day we searched further and were joined by another three excise officers and searched through the parish of Ellon and seized in different places and lodged fifteen ankers of foreign gin without a permit and lodged said goods at Ellon. On the evening of 20th December we heard that one of the men who attacked us was wounded and since dead, which we were sorry to hear. There were, as I suppose, from twelve to twenty people carrying ankers that the two men were escorting, who attacked me and Mr Anderson. Neither Mr Anderson nor I know those two men nor did I hear them speak any word but have since learned their names to be Philip and John Kennedy, both residing in the parish of Slains.

'From the circumstances that have happened I have great reason to believe the smugglers may bear malice to me in the further progress of my duty and from the situation of the place I am stationed at I may have reason to go along the coast by night as well as by day and therefore may be exposed to the smugglers in danger of my life. I humbly beg therefore that you will be pleased to state the case to the Honourable Board to get me removed to some other creek in the district as you may judge most proper to direct, which is humbly submitted to your consideration'.

Margin Note: 'Reference of 31st December answered thus: 'We beg leave to recommend John Blackhall, tidesman at this port as a proper person to succeed Gilbert Leighton at Ward of Cruden'. 3 January 1799'.

CHAPTER TWO: THE SMUGGLING BUSINESS PART ONE: THE ORDERS

'You are to proceed without loss of time to St Martins and you are there to address yourself to Alexander Gordon, merchant ... who will furnish you in what quantity of salt your ship can take in, and with the liquor which Robert Gordon of Bordeaux is to ship for our account, which will be about twelve tuns ... and notice that when, please God, you return, in case you meet or is taken up by any custom house yachts, to declare yourself bound for Riga in the Baltic; and be sure you be well furnished with clearances accordingly'. [Bailie John Steuart of Inverness to Alexander Tod, master of the *Katherine* of Leith dated 22 June 1726] [see also Chapter Six: Pretended Bound]

The next two chapters are based on over three hundred letters from both the Watt collection held by the Orkney Archives and from the letter-book of bailie John Steuart. These letters give a detailed, often day by day account of the many transactions necessary to ensure that a cargo of brandy, geneva, wine, tea or tobacco reached the customers in some remote part of northern Scotland [see Table III]. This chapter concentrates on ordering the goods from overseas while the next chapter describes their delivery.

The letters include those to Alexander Watt and William Watt junior & Co in Kirkwall, Alexander Bain junior in Wick and Thomas Baikie in Thurso and from John Steuart in Inverness. The Watts, Bain and Baikie were interlinked by marriage - the Watts took an interest in Bain's vessels and tobacco manufactory after his death. The Watt correspondence has been described by Hewison [see bibliography]. The importance of both Bain and Baikie is that they were based on the mainland. Alexander Bain's vessels included the *Lady Anstruther* and the *Tartar* and his joint ventures brought contraband goods from Gothenburg, Ostend and North Faro [see Figure 4]. John Steuart has been discussed in Chapter One.

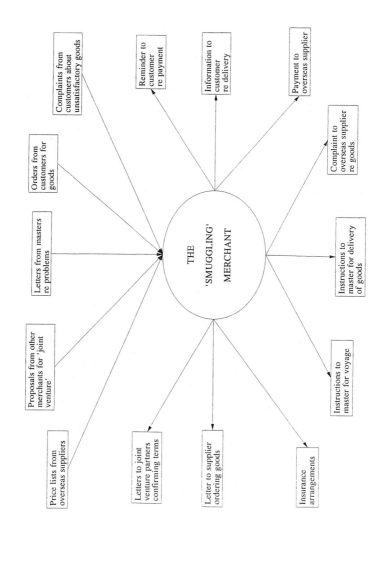

Complaints from customers about unsatisfactory goods

Orders from customers for goods

Letters from masters re problems

Proposals from other merchants for 'joint venture'

Price lists from overseas suppliers

Reminder to customer re payment

Information to customer re delivery

Payment to overseas supplier

Complaint to overseas supplier re goods

Instructions to master for delivery of goods

Instructions to master for voyage

Insurance arrangements

Letter to supplier ordering goods

Letters to joint venture partners confirming terms

THE 'SMUGGLING' MERCHANT

Table III: The Smuggling Business: Correspondence

Contact from Other Merchants for a Joint Venture

Although one would imagine that a complicated overseas voyage could only be undertaken if the home markets were secure, there is a strong suggestion that the cargoes were based on non-confirmed orders: 'I'll take some, if you have any'. Once a merchant had the goods on board ship or stored in Scotland the situation was different. On 13 June 1771 Andrew Cruikshank at Stromness wrote to Alexander Watt 'You may send as many ankers gin as you possibly can, under twenty, but fail not to send as many in halfs as you can'.

In 1753 John Sutherland at Gol Tower wrote to Thomas Baikie 'I am much straightened for want of some things I promised to send to my friends in Loch Broom so must beg the favour of you to leave for me a hundred and fifty of white sugar, two ankers rum and six gin. I shall give you to the value of my salmon to bring more from Holland ... So for my sake let me have this as the greatest favour you can do me. If you have no gin I'll take brandy and as I'll satisfy you to your contentment I'll expect you'll not disappoint me'. This was a more positive approach. There were often other merchants who would be prepared to take part in a joint venture.

Alexander Brodie, merchant in Fort George, was interested in freighting Alexander Bain's *Lady Anstruther* to Gothenburg [1780]; a small sloop to North Faro [1781] and the *Tartar* to Ostend [1783]. His partners included John McPherson, merchant in Inverness and bailie Paterson and Mr Miller, possibly from Fort George. Brodie spelled out the conditions: 'You must fix upon the exact time you will send her off', 'if you accept this offer [for the *Tartar*] we will only allow you to ship goods to the amount of the freight [two hundred and fifty to three hundred ankers] but that will make no difference to you as the freight will be the same' and 'the goods to be shipped by one house'. The goods were to be landed in the west Highlands or on the Sutherland coast.

Donald Smith, merchant in Inverness, was also in contact with Bain. He wrote on 15 February 1783 'Mr Tulloch at Campbeltown called here Thursday last when he showed me your letter soliciting him to come in to this place to procure orders for your sloop for Gothenburg and that you would allow his expenses to this town with 5 per cent upon the freight. He has got some orders which he will forward you this post ... as I am sure that you will in every respect conduct this matter with prudence and secrecy, I here enclose you my commands with some others that I procured from friends of mine with a note of their marks and packages, which I doubt not you will care of as your own. My friends here and I have ordered no insurance and as you know your vessel best and the man that navigates her let me have your opinion and the precise time she sails for my future government. I hope you will order her away upon receipt of this. I am told your brother [Harry] goes supercargo, which is well ... If you execute this business with propriety you may depend that your vessel will never want employment ...

'PS Since finishing the above I have prevailed upon two friends to take a concern whose orders are here enclosed ... as that is the case I have a good right to be cheaper served than my neighbours in freight. I have therefore directed my friends Messrs Low & Smith to pay but 3d for my teas, bohea and congo and 20s per hogshead, which you will attend to direct. Adieu'.

In November 1783 Smith reported 'I have been talking to my friends Messrs Inglis & Cumming with another that we can depend upon to freight the *Tartar* to go to Dunkirk for a parcel of combustibles [consumables] there, none to be concerned but yourself and us nor none on earth to know anything of it'. But in June 1786 he complained 'my correspondent at Rotterdam ... writes me the 23rd May that your brother was not arrived. I fancy he has not yet proceeded. If not, I shall certainly countermand my orders. It is very wrong in you to apply people for orders and disappoint them afterwards, which is too often the case. If you had executed this voyage speedily I might perhaps help you to a Gothenburg freight about the middle of next month'.

Another proposal came to Bain from one of his masters, Andrew Irving [see below], who was at Stornoway in September 1781. 'I heard by a man belonging to Tain, which is now in this place, that if you thought proper yourself to risk the sloop to North Faro and if you would write to George Simson, merchant at Tain, and bailie George Miller at Tain and Alexander Manson [postmaster] at do. and John McCloud at Cromarty that these people would make up a freight, as they always have, their goods landed at Loch Lochsford [not located], which would answer very well'.

Despite the fact that Steuart frequently complained about Somerville flooding his Scottish market with cheap Marseilles brandy, he turned to the Renfrew merchant for advice in October 1736. 'I had lately a proposal made me of getting a large quantity of roll tobacco from your parts to be entered for exportation, and landed in a certain island nearby, which my friend tells me there might be 50% got. I am utterly a stranger to such matters, and would by no means meddle unless such a friend as yourself would a third concern in it. The gentleman, my friend that writes me, says he would get gentlemen of very good credit would take it at a tolerable good price, suppose it were delivered them in February next, and grant their bills, payable for the same at Michaelmas market of Creif thereafter. I am well aware that dealing in this manner is a much greater risk than formerly, and therefore I submit to you how far such a project is practicable or not, or if you would incline to be concerned, and furnish the goods on our joint security, as to which I entreat your answer in course. I would not venture to write on this subject but to a sure friend like yourself, and therefore beg you preserve this from being exposed ... If the tobacco affairs would do I would send a friend, a young man, to go along the ship, and take in a 150 bolls foreign salt, to be entered likeways for exportation in the same barque. I mean one boll of 4 bushells. But all this I submit to your better judgement. Meantime, let me know how the tobacco and salt would be purchased for this purpose with you; and I am determined not to meddle in the above project but according as you'll advise me'. There is no further reference to tobacco in the bailie's letter-book.

Sources of Goods

Figure 4 lists the overseas contacts with whom the Scottish merchants corresponded. As the London-based East India Company held a monopoly over all trade with the East Indies - the source of tea, spices and several different types of materials etc - the smugglers looked to East India companies based on the continent for their supplies. This explains the number of contacts in Sweden, Denmark and Holland etc.

Currency of Goods at Bergen in Norway of Anno 1774

Imports.

Imports		
White Wheat		p. Barrell of 4 English Bushells.
Red ditto		
Best Barley		
ditto Bigg or Bear		
Middle ditto		
Meaneft ditto		
Dantzick Rye		
British ditto		
Best Barley Malt		
Bigg or Bear ditto		
Oats ditto		
White Peafe		
Gray ditto Spilkins		
Oat Meal p. Bagg of 56 lib. Amfterd.		
Small Coals p. laft of 12 Barls or 60 Bushells		p. Barrell of 5 Bushells.
Flour p. Wogh or 36 lib.		
Grindftones P. Chalder		
Leaf Tobacco P. Wogh or 36 lib. Amfterd.		
Roll Tobacco		
Loose Tow of Flax p. Mart of 112 lib. English		
Barr or Pigg Lead p. Wogh of 36 lib. Amfterd.		
Large Spanish Salt		
Lisbon & Small ditto		
French ditto		
Exchange on { London, Amfterdam, Humb. }		

Exports.

Exports		
Large Spanish Salt		p. Barrell of 5 English Bushells.
Lisbon & fmall ditto		
French ditto		
Lisbon white Wine		
French ditto		
ditto Claret ditto		
Red Port ditto		
White ditto ditto		
French common Brandy		p. Anker or Vertier.
ditto Coniac ditto		
Thick Tarr		p. Barrell.
Thin ditto		
Pitch		
Norland Herrings		
ditto Meaneft ditto		
Waar Herrings		
Strahl ditto		
Barreled Codfish		
white Train Oyl		
Brown ditto ditto		
Round Stockfifh		p. Wogh or 36 lib. Amfterd.
Split ditto		
Sey or Colefish		
Smoakt Salmond		
Tallow		
8 feet double Deals		p. Dozen.
ditto fingle ditto		
Trees		
West India Rum		p. 5 Verties.
Bohea Tea		
Congo ditto		
Sufong ditto		
Imperial Green ditto		p. lib.
Hyfon ditto - ditto		

Figure 4: The Overseas Suppliers: A Bergen Price List

1. Some of the Overseas Suppliers used by Steuart, William Watt junior & Co and Alexander Bain junior & Co

Bailie John Steuart
Stockholm: Nelleton & Campbell, Montgomery Mould & Fenick and Campbell, Gerrard & Dobson
Gothenburg: Hugh Ross
Danzig: Marjoribanks & Coutts and Francis Grant
Hamburg: David Barclay and Bartholomew Bludworth
Copenhagen: Alexander Ross
Amsterdam: Jackson & Bradley
Rotterdam: Alexander Andrew, Robert Gerrard, John Gordon, and Robert Mackay
Campvere: David Gregory
'in Holland': John MacDonald
Boulogne: Charles Smith
Rouen: Robert Arbuthnott
Havre: Jacob Ferray
St Martins: John Souper and Alexander Gordon
Bordeaux: Robert Gordon and John MacLeod
Bilbao: Ivan van Duffel
Barcelona: Shalet, Vonder & Ferrant, otherwise Winder and Ferrand
Leghorn or Livorno: Aickman & Winder, and Godfrey & Hudson

William Watt junior & Co
Bergen: William Farquhar and Jesper de Fine
Rotterdam: William Murdoch and George Gibson
Frederickswaag, North Faro: Rosenmeyer, Flor & Co

Alexander Bain junior & Co
Gothenburg: Low & Smith
Dunkirk: Alexander Hunter

2. The price list was sent to William Watt junior & Co by Jesper de Fine of Bergen on 18 April 1774.

There was considerable competition for orders. As William Murdoch in Rotterdam wrote to William Watt in 1771 'It may be some would make you believe that some merchants here would have given a discount ... I look upon what any would have had you believe that way to be with design to gain your custom from me and I doubt of any serving you in such easy terms as I have done'. Murdoch wrote to William Watt Junior & Co again on 9 June 1772, clearly referring to a further order and hoping for more in the future. By 1784 they were dealing with George Gibson in Rotterdam.

Another solution was for the smugglers to use an entrepot - somewhere that the goods could be stored ready for shipping to Scotland. In August 1777 Rosenmeyer, Flor & Co of Frederickswaag, North Faro wrote to William Watt junior & Co 'Our Mr Flor, who arrived here some days ago, informs us that you and some of your friends intend to make a trial to this place, when you see a good opportunity, and that the most of your order would be for geneva. We therefore find it necessary to advise you that we have lately had such a demand for gin that we are almost run out of that article - we are now expecting another cargo from Rotterdam. As soon as it arrives we shall not fail to advise you and in the meantime have ankers made of the size and after the Dutch manner'.

Although the 'uncustomed and prohibited goods' formed a high proportion of a vessel's cargo, there were often legal goods on board as well. At the same time, the merchants needed to establish a trade that would help to pay for the homeward cargo. The main exports from the northern shores tended to be fish: herring or salmon. Steuart wrote to Robert Gordon, Bordeaux in June 1717 'Please advise me what goods from Hamburg, in one of this country's ships, would sell best with you, and the duties such goods do pay with you. The reason why I want to know this is because we send from hence a vast many herrings to said port and would be glad to make return your way if [you] thought it would do'. In March 1721 he asked Alexander Andrew, Rotterdam for advice. 'Some friends and I have a cargo of herrings going to Danzig or Konigsberg. We have thought of returning said ship to you with a cargo of wheat and rye; therefore write to Mr Coutts of Danzig of the prices of grains with you when this comes to hand, for his government, and what advice you think needful'.

The overseas suppliers frequently sent price lists of their goods [see Figure 4].

Orders

All orders for goods were both detailed and included many special requirements. In December 1718 Steuart ordered from Alexander Andrew in Rotterdam 'four hogsheads of tobacco in matts, providing it be had of a good, large, fresh, strong leaf, and not exceeding 4 or 4½ stivers. We must earnestly entreat that the tobacco be right chosen and good, or that you send none, for some came lately from your parts hither proves very naught'. In March 1721 Steuart asked Andrew to ship on the *Christian* of Leith, George Cockburn master, 'four chests best burgundy wine, each chest to contain fifty flasks; one chest of best Champaign wine of fifty flasks and four half hogsheads of best Spanish sake, to be bought new off the quays if possible; eight reams writing wheat paper of such as is commonly shipped for this place from 50 to 60 stivers per ream; one hundred and twenty single and ten double ankers best French brandy; and one chest of burgundy and one chest of forty flasks for James Russell and me in company; for my proper account 50 lib best Cork fee [?] indigo and a tun of best strong French claret to be bought off the quays; a warming pan and a waffle ditto; and a large black bear's skin dressed on the inside ... as I told you in my last the price of these goods will be made good to you once in the month of May next. All that I have to add now is to buy for my by advice of Mr Cockburn a new main top sail for my ship the *Margaret* of this place, 50 tons burthen, such as will serve Mr Cockburn's own ship, I think, will do exactly for me, if not somewhat too large'.

Steuart wrote to Robert Gordon, Bordeaux in November 1722 'In the meantime I most earnestly entreat that what wine you ship for me be good and strong and all rack of the lees; and the brandy to be shipped be put in quarter casks or ankers to contain 5 vertes'.

In April 1727 he was looking for a tea supplier. He wrote to Francis Grant in Danzig 'Alexander Tod, who went with you last winter, informs us that he could have bought with you very good bohea tea at 4 guilders the pound. If such can be got that you know is truly good at that price, we hereby desire ... that you ship for our account ... 100 lbs in

21

pound canisters ... but we entreat, if you are not sure that it's very good, not to buy it. May likeways buy 30 lbs weight of green tea if can be had proportionally cheaper ... we doubt not of your good endeavours for our interest, which will encourage a further correspondence'. As Donald Smith wrote to Alexander Bain in 1783, tea was not always a good speculative venture. 'I find that those who deal capitally in importing teas from Gothenburg are already engaged, as are all my neighbours in this place, in a sloop of Mr C Cg [Cumming?]'s that sails soon. On that account I am afraid you could not make a freight worth your notice to that port'.

In September 1722 the *Margaret* sailed from Findhorn with salmon for Havre. Steuart's son, Alexander, was involved in this voyage and he reported to his father from Havre on 22 February 1723 that one hundred and fifty barrels of salmon had been sold at 125 livres per barrel. It was doubtful if the rest could be sold that season and in fact the final payment for the cargo was not received until June 1725. As the *Margaret* was then to proceed to Bordeaux for wine and brandy, Steuart warned his son 'not to lench deep in credit ... I would not be easy to answer bills, having abundance of money to pay at Whitsunday'.

The merchant would report on the goods received. Steuart wrote to Alexander Steuart in May 1735 'the parcels of tea you shipped for me [are] in good order; the price and charges as per invoice amounting to £178 17s Hollands, which sum will take care to remit you very soon. I have tried the several qualities of the several kinds of tea sent. The bohea and soatihan are exceeding good, and the green tea is pretty good, for which I thank you'.

Frequently there were complaints. In January 1719 Steuart wrote to Alexander Andrew 'Pray notice that the Holland and muslin be well chosen and bought for the last I got about two years ago was too dear bought, and I made nothing of it'. And in May 1720 he referred to 'the invoice of goods per Andrew Watson and John McKenzie's barques, which goods came safe to hand except that one of the chids of burgundy had wanted one flask and had another old broken flask, which looks as if put in not full; and the half piece of Holland per said Watson measures 17¼ yards whereas it should measure 19 yards or thereby, being charged at 25 Dutch yards; so you'll enquire into these mistakes and let them be redressed'.

Steuart wrote to John Gesse in London on 30 November 1730 'Now I must inform you that all our French wine in this country is gone quite wrong, being picked this year; but in March or April next I expect a parcel of good new strong wine'.

Other problems related to different systems. Low & Smith of Gothenburg wrote to Alexander Bain in April 1783 'There has been a good deal of confusion with the freights, some desiring to pay only 5s per anker and the others 45s per hogshead, which your brother rejected, all which he will better tell you himself. We would recommend at another time to be on a more certain footing with them and if you grant any favours to particular friends don't let it appear here, as it is productive of no good consequences'.

Instructions to the Shipmaster
The master of the vessel would be given detailed instructions. On 5 April 1722 Steuart wrote to David Stevenson: 'Loving friend, You are to proceed with the ship *Margaret* of this place to Rotterdam, where you are to address Alexander Andrew and Alexander Castares, merchants there, who will have orders to load the ship with Lisbon salt and wine; and from thence you are to proceed for this place, and bring letters and bills of loading as from Lisbon'. The accompanying letter to Alexander Andrew stated 'I entreat that, in case any of cruising sloops should meet the barque, you make up invoice and bill of loading for the salt and wine as from London, borrowing some merchant's name living there since the ship is to report here as from Lisbon, and the wine to be entered as Portugal wine'.

Sometimes, as a result of unforeseen circumstances, the master would have to make his own decisions. The story of the *Alexander*'s voyage is told in the privateer section. Steuart wrote to Thomas Greig in January 1718 'since now it will be too late to prosecute your intended voyage for Cork ... embrace the first opportunity of a convoy to proceed to Danzig, where you are to address yourself to Marjoribanks & Coutts, to whom you are to deliver the cargo of herrings, and who will have the needful instructions anent disposing your cargo and reloading your ship; and you shall be paid according to the ordinary freights have been paid to others that have gone from this to that place this year, and caplagen [a small fee paid to the master for his care of the goods] conform ... if a convoy does not offer to Danzig ... you can make a market the place where you are, and the places adjacent, and from the nett proceeds of the herrings you are to reload the ship with barrel staves from Arundale for this place or from any other parts there about where they can be got. Should it happen that you can not sell your herrings where you are, but to loss, and cannot find convoy in the spring but for Danzig, then, and in that case only, you must proceed the herrings first for Hamburg, where you are to address yourself to Mr Robert Barclay, but reload the ship with Spanish salt, and return directly here; for which you will be likeways paid the current freight ... We recommend you to the divine direction and protection ... Acquaint us how soon this comes to hand how you determine yourself'. Greig returned to Inverness in 1718, having sold his cargo in the Baltic [exact location unspecified].

Insurance

Insurance was a constant concern. The vessel and outbound cargo could be insured in Edinburgh or London. But only the overseas merchant would know the value of the homeward cargo so that they would arrange this insurance. Because of the cost of insurance it often barely covered the replacement costs. An example when insurance cover was needed is quoted in the tailpiece to this chapter.

Problems at Sea
The Weather

Examples of storms will be discussed in Chapters Six and Seven and in Appendix II. In 1719 Steuart wrote to Alexander Andrew 'I am afraid your rivers will be frozen up and she [the *Alexander*] cannot get to Rotterdam; so that I have but a very melancholy prospect of a market for the salmon, though I depend on your best endeavours, I wish you a good new year'. In February 1721 the *Marjorie* was frozen up at Copenhagen.

War

The number of European wars during the eighteenth century caused the merchants continual problems. Steuart wrote to Robert

Gordon in October 1718 'This serves to advise you that your friend Alexander Steuart and the ship *Alexander* of this place were designed to have gone your way for a loading of wine etc but the surprising news of war with Spain has deviated that project and therefore now he proceeds for Rotterdam ... Therefore we desire that how soon this comes to hand you'll enquire if [you] can find any occasion of any ship on freight to Holland, bound for Rotterdam; and, in case such an occasion should immediately offer at a reasonable, easy freight, then you are to ship for our accounts ten tuns of excellent good strong claret wine, two tuns white wine, which is to be marked *AS*. You are to take bill of loading for the same for to be consigned to Alexander Andrew, merchant in Rotterdam, a double of which you are to transmit him per post, and at the same time advise him to insure the value of said wines for our accounts'. The following January he wrote to Alexander Andrew 'I ordered Mr Gordon to ship the wine in a Dutch ship and advise you to insure the value. If he has not obeyed these orders accordingly it is a fault, but I hope he has. Now this comes chiefly to desire that if the *Alexander* do not arrive in time to overtake the season for selling his salmon, you ship no brandy or tobacco for my account'.

On 22 December 1780 Alexander Hunter, merchant in Dunkirk, wrote to Alexander Bain junior, Wick, that he would have replied to his letter dated 11 October sooner but he had been 'in daily expectation of procuring a pass [allowing them to enter Dutch ports] for both ... of the vessels you wrote of to me. But after all my trouble I find it impossible. There is no other mode than to come to Ostend and lay off there in the Road and the captain take a horse and come to me. Then I could get him a pass. When he once had it, it would ever serve him after. I am heartily sorry but I will never wish to advise until I am certain there is no danger ... should they come to this port, they must not come in the night but in the day time and anchor in Bushells Bay, where all the smugglers lay. If asked any questions, say from Scotland consigned to me for gin and when the captain has moored let him directly come to me. The whole risk is before the vessel comes here. All prize vessels sell here extravagantly dear, much above their value. What you mention of having seen in the news about the smugglers here is not true'. [No appropriate comment has been found in the Gentleman's Magazine]

Taken by a Privateer

In October 1717 the *Alexander*, Thomas Greig master, took on board four hundred and forty-six barrels of herrings for Cork in Ireland. She was then to go to Rochelle for wine and brandy but she was taken in the English Channel, off the North Foreland, by a Swedish privateer commanded by an Englishman, Norcross. The privateer planned to take the *Alexander* to Gothenburg but called at France, where Norcross was apprehended and sent to England. The crew continued to Sweden without him. The rest of the story is told in a letter to the master from Steuart dated 17 January 1718.

'We have seen your very acceptable letter of 29th November last from Porter in Norway, wherein you advise that you have brought the ship into said harbour, and, after you have turned the Swedes who commanded the ship ashore, and taken possession of her yourself, that a Danish man, [which] lay in harbour near you, had sent a part of his men and taken possession of your ship to Lerwick [in Norway] and from thence to Copenhagen, which we wish they may do, having reason to believe by our advices from Mr Ross of Copenhagen [see also tailpiece] the pretensions of the Danish man-of-war are very groundless, and will very soon be determined to your advantage. But however matters may happen we are very sensible of your good conduct in the affair'.

Andrew Irving was taken by a privateer in September 1781, as he explained to Alexander Bain. 'I am sorry to inform you that on the 14th instant I sailed from the Birchen Island in order to go round to Loch Seaforth to take in the remainder of the kelp to make up the cargo. It was about two in the afternoon and at four about two miles distance from the harbour mouth, being becalmed, I was boarded by the *Fly* of Dunkirk's boat, commanded by Captain William Hall the privateer, about 5 leagues distance, bearing north-east. At five it sprung up a breeze and at ten I was carried aboard of the privateer and two of the men along with me. As soon as I come on board Captain Hall asked me if I would ransom, which I told him I would provide in that his demand did not exceed the value of vessel and what part of the cargo there was shipped. He told me his demand was 350 guineas, which he immediately demanded an answer to. I told him in return that the vessel and what kelp was aboard was not worth the half of the money. He told again that there was no time to be lost and that he would send the boatswain to ship the rigging and the carpenter to scuttle her, which I took no notice of ... I told him that I would give him 160 guineas. He instantly tore up the letter and ordered all to plunder the sloop and afterwards sink her, upon which the boat was immediately manned and went aboard and begun to cut the sails down and the running rigging, which I found then that there was no time to be lost I desired his clerk to acquaint him that I would give him a 180 [guineas] which returned and told me that he would not take it. I desired him 'Go and tell him that I would give him 200 guineas'. As soon as he heard that he ordered the people to give over plundering. He then came down and filled up the ransom bill for the sum of 200 guineas. There was then 29 tons 8 cwt of kelp aboard. At twelve I came aboard, where I found there was not a wearable belonging me or the men left and the square sail cut from the yard and the running rigging cut. The boy William Dunnet is gone ransomer, which I hope you'll acquaint his parents of and give them all the comfort you can, as I hope you'll lose no time in corresponding with Sir John [?] concerning the ransom and write me to Liverpool, as I mean not to discharge any of the cargo till I hear from you ... I hope you'll not blame me for what's happened as I am the greatest suffer myself and is sailed this summer for nothing. I will not trouble you with any more'. [His next paragraph was quoted in the section about joint ventures - see above]

Wrecked or Lost at Sea

The story of the *Marjorie* is told in the tailpiece. Several other vessels belonging to the bailie were wrecked/lost at sea: October 1725 the *Ann*, with wine from Bordeaux, sank thirty miles off Ushant. The crew were saved by an Arbroath ship, David Spink master; December 1725 the *Margaret*, John Reid master, was lost on the bar of Montrose and nothing was saved except a barrel of pitch and September 1728 the *Agnes*, Donald Stuart master, was wrecked 'on a blind rock among the North Isles of Orkney, being three days before being forced by Lochinver, where he was to load salmon for my account'. There are also suggestions in the other merchants' correspondence about vessels that had been lost, including Alexander Bain's *Lady Anstruther*. Alexander Brodie of Fort George wrote on 26 January 1781 'I am really sorry for the unlucky fate of the *Lady* and her crew, and especially for the loss you have sustained'.

Loss of Goods

Despite insurance, money was still owed for goods whether they had been lost at sea or seized. The story of Jerom Setter's vessel, the *Peggie*, is told elsewhere. The goods that were seized had been supplied to William Watt junior & Co by William Murdoch of Rotterdam. He wrote to them on 19 July 1771 'I observe the concerned for the owners of Jerom Setter's ship and cargo have compromised the matter with the seizure makers by accepting of £140 with the sloop in full of all claim, which I believe may be better than if had come to trial. The expense of £60 cuts deep into the sum and I hope you may soon find ways to make up the loss. By the annexed sketch of your account you are now due me £112 2s besides interest thereon for at least seven months'.

The replies from William Watt, dated 19 July and 10 August can be guessed from Murdoch's letter dated 17 September 1771. 'If I had thought any longer delay would have been agreeable to you it should have been readily granted. Nor did I expect otherwise than that you would have been very well satisfied with the time I waited after the money was due without making charge the interest'.

The next chapter traces the problems over delivering the goods to the Scottish customers.

A STORY OF THE *MARJORIE*, DANIEL FRASER MASTER

This story is taken from the letter-book of bailie John Steuart and includes extracts from <u>some</u> of the letters relating to the 1720/21 voyage of the *Marjorie*, Daniel Fraser master.

According to a letter from Steuart to Messrs Marjoribanks & Coutts, Danzig, dated 22 August 1720 the *Marjorie*'s outward cargo included thirteen small packs lamb skins, containing one thousand and ninety dozen mort lamb skins; three hundred and sixty larger lambskins, commonly called small slaughter skin; one hundred and thirty-five fox skins and sixty half otter skins. According to the charter party Fraser's freight was £22 sterling and 20s caplaken. The cargo required was sixteen ship of iron: 1/3 'champaleon' and 2/3 'midlin' iron; one 'lentren' steel; four and a half chests of Brimar window glass of best kind; one hundred and fifty spruce stone flax in six packs of the best; <u>six barrels washing soap in four and eight parts equally about 500 lbs</u>; sheet copper done up in two sheeted bundles, the coils white rope from 6 to 12 threads; if any space left a great hundred barrel staves for salmon casks about 32" long. This was to be insured by Alexander Andrew of Rotterdam. The other partners in the venture were Lachlan McIntosh and William MacKay.

'So, friend, you are to proceed directly for Danzig, where you are to address yourself to Alexander Coutts, and deliver him my letter, who is to receive your cargo and pay you outward freight, and to ship your homeward loading. When you receive your freight at Danzig, and [have] paid own and men's half wages, you are to buy for my account ... [ropes, linen, two caves of best double strong Danzig waters, a barrel of best white peese 'for the barque's use and mine' and 'a shuffle of Carline peese for present eating']. Be sure to write wherever you happen to touch; and if should, as God forbid, your barque should meet with any misfortune by storm or otherways, you and your crew are to make affidavit before the first magistrate you can find ... let all soap and saleable goods be stored out of the way; and be sure you allow no brandy to be shipped by any of your crew ... let my goods be first shipped at Danzig and my soap keeped at hand for running; and take notice that you come not above Chanonry Ness or Chery Road [not located] till all your soap be out'. [Daniel Fraser, 22 August 1720]

contd

A STORY OF THE *MARJORIE*, DANIEL FRASER MASTER contd.

A letter to George Auchterlony, London, dated 9 September 1720 confirmed insurance of the *Marjorie* to Danzig for £130.

'About the 20th December the *Marjorie* in her way homeward from Danzig was forced by a violent storm to anchor three Danish miles southward from Copenhagen, in which place, the storm increasing very violently, and sea being full of ice, the master and the crew, it seems, despairing of safety for their lives in the barque, betook themselves to their boat in order to get ashore, being five in number; but, misfortunately, falling in among ice and broken water, the boat was overturned, by which the master and two of the crew were drowned, and only the remaining two narrowly escaped. But the barque being left at an anchor happened to ride out the storm ... and some days thereafter, the storm being over, one Jean van Oste, a Danish sea captain, went on board the barque, having our two surviving men and some Danish sailors along with him, who on the 25th of that month brought the barque safe into Copenhagen harbour, where, for ought we know, the barque and the cargo remain still safe ... as it appears by your several advices ... that William MacKay had got insured on said barque and cargo F839 bol and John Steuart F1950 bol upon the barque and cargo, both policies being signed by your company, we think as the company will be liable for our damages, it will be their interest to adjust the salvage and charges that falls on the ship and our proportions of the cargo with van Oste ... we hope you will ... advise Mr Alexander Ross of Copenhagen what it will be necessary for him to do ... For your government we send you doubles of our invoices from Danzig, attested, and our bills of loading, as also John Steuart's declaration anent his property on the ship ... the money we insured upon the barque and cargo comes so near the full value of our interests, that should the insurance masters demur in paying of our demand in Copenhagen, we are willing to assign them our interests in ship and cargo upon payment of our money insured; but we leave it to you to do for our interests as seems you best'. [Messrs Andrew and Gerarrd, Rotterdam, 13 January 1721]

'Though we must own that we cannot think of being ingrait or ungenerous to any that has given assistance in preserving our interests on such an occasion but on the contrary that they shall be handsomely rewarded, we

contd

A STORY OF THE *MARJORIE*, DANIEL FRASER MASTER contd.

are mightily surprised that any men pretending to charity or honesty would make such an extravagant demand as the third of the ship and cargo ... we hereby empower you so to notice and secure our interests in said barque and her cargo to all intents and purposes as if we were personally present, that is, by securing the cargo that none of it be embezzled or damnified, paying reasonable reward to the Danish captain and others who concurred to bring the barque to Copenhagen, and, by inventoring and securing the papers and effects of the defunct Daniel Fraser ... and lastly by encouraging the two surviving men, Alexander Clark and John Grant, to remain with the barque, and notice her and cargo until a master arrive with them ... what money you deburse in this affair please value on us for the same, as also for your own trouble and pains'. [Alexander Ross, Copenhagen, 13 January 1721]

'I must own this to have been a charitable, kind action, and I have writ to my friend, Mr Alexander Ross of Copenhagen, merchant, to reward thankfully your pains, trouble and charges. But I am surprised to find you mention in your letter as if you was in design to unload the barque. I do not know but you doing so may be found too rash an action, since I suppose your claim of salvage will not arise so high as that you need meddle with the cargo'. [Jean van Oste, Copenhagen, 13 January 1721]

'This principally is to desire how soon this comes to hand you'll call for David Stevenson, or, if come off, for his mate, Charles Pape, and try if [you] can prevail with either of them, particularly David, to go to Copenhagen without loss of time to take charge of my barque the *Marjorie*, and to bring [her] home hither. In case he condescend to ask of, you are to agree for his wages, not exceeding £7 sterling, with the needful allowance of money for charges to Copenhagen, where please recommend him to Mr Ross'. [Alexander Andrew, Rotterdam, 13 January 1721]

'You have compounded for the salvage of the barque *Marjorie* of said cargo at 240RD as also have paid 70RD as charges for burying the dead, and that the bark was now in your possession, and the cargo unloaded entire and in safe custody, which is all well; and I thank you for your care though cannot help to think the salvage charges very high, yet no doubt you have done the best for our interests'. [Alexander Ross, Copenhagen, 25 February 1721]

contd

A STORY OF THE *MARJORIE*, DANIEL FRASER MASTER contd.

'I have yours of 25th February and do note that my barque is frozen up, and all the cargo unload and entire, and that Clark and Grant ... are going to law for their wages and to leave the barque. I hope David Stevenson ... is with you ere now and that these lads will come to better temper. But if they do leave the barque or give you trouble about their wages they need not think of returning to this country again, for they were certainly paid their half wages at Danzig and I know not what claim they can have by any law to the other half until the voyage is ended. Your bill of £100 sterling has appeared here from London which indeed is much more than was expected ... the others that wrote with me, will not accept [it] because no account is come for what this money is. Yet in honour to you I accept it for all, not doubting your integrity and that you will do no injustice'. [Alexander Ross, Copenhagen, 27 March 1721]

'The barque *Marjorie* is arrived here ... I find I am first in advance for all, and that the others concerned and I are not so easily to adjust matters as I expected. David Stevenson tells me he has drawn on you 128RD so that I find the whole damage will amount to near £140 sterling. I find likeways that Mr Ross is a very sharp man, to say no worse, for he charges 120 dollars commission, and I find a good deal of the rest goes to his own pocket. All I shall say is God forgive him, and keep me hereafter out of such hands'. [Alexander Andrew, Rotterdam, 22 May 1721]

CHAPTER THREE: THE SMUGGLING BUSINESS PART TWO: DELIVERY

'Having been informed that the ship *Relief*, Dougal McGregor master, from Hamburg lately arrived at Dunstaffnage in the precinct of the port of Oban was a considerable time among the Western Isles, where sundry goods were clandestinely landed, the commissioners direct you to use your utmost endeavours in order to discover the particulars of said fraud. For which purpose it is judged expedient that you should write upon the subject to the ministers and gentlemen of those parts, whom it is apprehended at this time of danger from such practices will exert themselves to procure the necessary intelligence'. [Letter from the Board to the collector at Stornoway, 22 December 1770]

Having survived wars, privateers, loss at sea or shipwreck 'on foreign shores', the next problem faced by the masters of the vessels was that of running the goods without their being seized. A vessel needed to identify itself to those waiting on the shore and then small boats had to be available to transfer the goods to the shore as quickly and secretly as possible. Payment was preferred within a short time period, always remembering that other merchants could attract the customers by offering better terms and longer repayments. Finally any complaints about the quality of the goods delivered had to be settled satisfactorily.

The Vessel's Arrival

In April 1722 Steuart wrote to David Stevenson 'before you come directly up here [Inverness] you are to make a signal with your ensign off Helmsdale, if the wind serve, where my orders will wait you either there or at Tarbat Ness'. However, the signalling system was not necessarily foolproof, as explained in a letter from Andrew Strang at Lopness to William Watt junior on 24 September 1772.

'The vessel we expected came up with this land Friday 19th inst and has ever since been stretching from the westward of North Ronaldsay to the northward of the Start Point. Immediately on his making his appearance David Drever and I took a boat and made for him, at same time keeping up a signal in the boat the whole time, which we naturally imagined would have made him watch for us, as we had every reason to believe he could not fail to see us. When we were within a quarter of an hour's pulling of him, he wore his ship and stood to the northward. Next day, being very fine weather, we saw him to the eastward of North Ronaldsay at a very great distance, standing for the land. With this encouraged and with the fairness of the weather we rowed for him, I dare say six miles to the northward and eastward of North Ronaldsay. When he just served us in the manner he had done the day before by wearing the ship and starting directly to sea. With difficulty against wind and tide we reached North Ronaldsay in the evening and late at night got over to Sanday, having left word with John Tulloch to board him with other necessary directions to him how to proceed. Sunday and Monday he was out of sight. Tuesday evening he made his appearance off Ronaldsay, just in the sunlights. Wednesday evening he came up again off Burness and David Drever with four men went off and pulled close to the vessel but as usual he immediately stood to sea. We cannot be mistaken in the vessel as the appointed signal was made upon her coming up with the land.

'I am, I must confess, at a loss how to behave and thought proper to advise you of his misconduct, which may prove fatal at this season to ship and cargo or otherwise may be the cause of losing the whole, if no accident should befall the vessel, as now his intentions must be evident to every person. I therefore write you, who are acquainted with business, that the proper steps may be taken and that I may have your advice on the above with all possible dispatch'.

Unloading the Vessel
Unloading the goods was one of the more dangerous operations. Before agreeing to a joint venture with John McLeod of Glenelg in August 1730, Steuart wrote 'if such a project be undertaken, it must be done in the most clandestine manner possible, and the ship can only touch at one remote port, and only lie while the goods can be unloaded and immediately thereafter to come off without letting anybody know the ship or master's name, or where she belongs to'.

Steuart instructed Donald Steuart in July 1728 'Before coming up here, be sure you stop in the night time in Connage Bay [near Ardersier], where boats will wait you to get ashore what brandy you may have aboard, which I hope will be but little by the time you come there. However, it is fit you advise me by express from Lochinver before you sail from thence what quantity you have aboard'.

When it came to getting the goods on to the boats, opinions differed. Donald Smith of Inverness wrote to Alexander Bain in February 1783 'When she comes upon your coast, if the wind and weather serve and that you think the Firth is clear, I would have you run her up at once under silence of night to this place. Your brother [Harry] knows how to act and you and I can correspond about it. This would serve us materially and the risk is not so much as putting the goods into boats on your or the Sutherland coast. We would cheerfully pay something extra for coming up the Firth with the vessel'.

In September 1785 Inglis, in partnership with Donald Smith, wrote to Bain 'Should this reach you before our friend makes his appearance I have to request that in place of mixing the goods, as was first proposed, that you put my eight hogsheads claret into one boat, sending John Fraser as trustee in her and directing him to make for Cadboll Bay, where he is to land the hogsheads and send away the boat immediately. After landing the hogsheads he is to go to Geanies and call for George Duffus, the grieve, who will bring carts immediately to carry away the goods. You will direct him to take care to be at Cadboll about ten or eleven at night but not sooner for fear go being seen from Cromarty'.

Not all the arrangements were successful, as Smith wrote in September 1783. 'I by no means blame you for the loss that happened. How could I charge you with that which never was recommended to your care? But you must allow that I could not help being a good deal [hole in letter] at the conduct of Mr Miller, who when he came here to solicit for orders promised Messrs Reid, Inglis and me that he would take special care of our goods and send his own two large boats with proper trustees to convey them with safety. Otherwise we would not have taken the concern. Instead of which he never gave himself any trouble about them but ordered a vessel to Clyth, as he says for our accommodation. Then

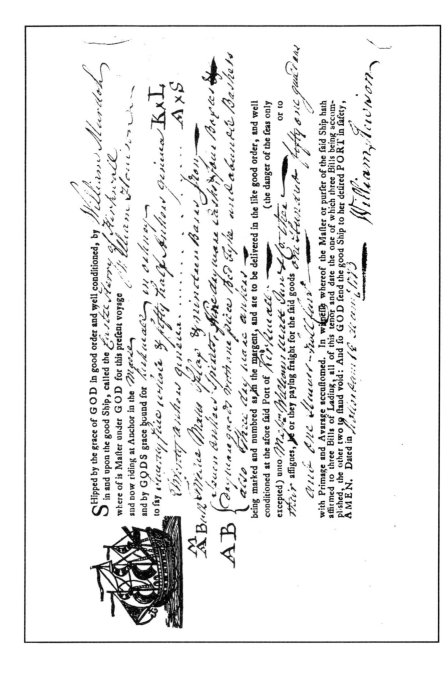

SHipped by the grace of GOD in good order and well conditioned, by _William Murdoch_ in and upon the good Ship, called the _Grace Henry of Portsmouth_ where of is Master under GOD for this present voyage _Wm Howison_ and now riding at Anchor in the _river_ and by GODS grace bound for _Kirkwall_ ... being marked and numbered as in the margent, and are to be delivered in the like good order, and well conditioned at the afore said Port of _Kirkwall_ (the danger of the seas only excepted) unto _Mr ..._ or to _their_ assignes, he or they paying fraight for the said goods ... with Primage and Avarage accustomed. In witness whereof the Master or purser of the said Ship hath affirmed to three Bills of Lading, all of this tenor and date the one of which three Bills being accomplished, the other two to stand void: And so GOD send the good Ship to her desired PORT in safety. AMEN. Dated in _Portsmouth 18 March_ 1773

Figure 5: Marks on the Packages

'I have however dispatched the bearer, John Fraser, a very honest, careful man, with two boats to receive all the goods on the other side noted* and to whom I doubt not you will lend every assistance in your power ... John Fraser and his crews will in every respect be guided by you and follow any directions you give them and wishing the matter to a happy issue ...

'PS Should John Fraser have occasion for any money please supply him and I shall thankfully reimburse you for it'. [Donald Smith, Inverness to Alexander Bain, 23 September 1783]

*one hundred or seventy-five ankers rum marked *CDK*
six boxes congo and six casks bohea under the same mark, if not they will be marked thus *DS*
one or two boxes *PWP*

This must have been successful because on 4 November Smith wrote 'I own I was wrong in not writing you immediately upon the goods' arrival but one hurry or other put it out of my view and indeed at the time they made their appearance I could not well expect them, considering how the wind blew there ... If you can depend upon your shipmaster, which I really think you may, the best plan would be to run up the Firth above Fort George and there to unload his cargo. But he must first call of your place for intelligence to know how the Firth stands and never to attempt coming up but under silence of night and with a fair wind. In that case things could be done quietly and prudently without any material risk. Of this let me have your opinion fully in course with the lowest freight you would take'.

The document lists twenty-five whole and fifty half ankers geneva, marked *K x L*, twenty ankers geneva marked *A x S*, twelve matts flax and nineteen bars iron marked *M / AB* and seven ankers spirits etc marked *AB* to be shipped by William Murdoch of Rotterdam to William Watt junior & Co in the *Castle Kerry*, William Hewison master, in December 1773.

Mr Corn sent them in yawls that a christian would be afraid to venture his life cross the pack in and there the misfortune lay. However as they had the good luck to come the length of Cadboll, where they discharged their cargoes. Not considering the property Mr Corn's, they were so genteel as to go to the tidesman at Portmahomack to inform upon the goods, which made me write you that I never would trust my property with any of these vagabonds in future'. The rest of this letter is quoted in Figure 5.

Similar arrangements were being made in May 1785. 'Now that the winds have been easterly for these three days past and have a chance of continuing so we think it prudent to send the bearer, John Fraser, with two boats your length but to stop with them at Berriedale and proceed to Wick with our letters and wait your orders there. I do not think it would be prudent for me to risk the letter by boat as conveying them by land they run no risk of being seized. You can send them by post to the care of my partner Mr Benjamin Ross ... Be sure to divide the goods equally, putting the half of every man's property in each boat. If we succeed here I am not sure but Mr Reid and me will give you a freight to Hamburg'.

An order from Robert Sandison, Stromness, to Alexander Watt, 1776

Robert Sandison's order was for two ankers and one half of gin and three halfs of brandy. On 28 October 1776 he wrote to Alexander Watt 'I observe what you say in coming round by Birsay but the season of the year is so advanced and the sea up that it will be dangerous so that [I] suppose it will come dearer by the way of Scapa. Yet it's the surest way'. Three days later he sent a man hoping that 'You'll dispatch as fast as possible in order that he may return this night, as there is great need for it for fear of suspicion if he is missed from the town. He will follow your orders in every respect'. But 'I am sorry the man came back without success, the night being bad. I am told there is a good boat at Scapa. If so be and good hands I think it would be better to employ her ... This you are the best judge of and you'll please acquaint me accordingly. Tomorrow is the last day of the week, which is not a proper day if not got done in time. Monday the custom house boat is coming to Scapa - I know not what about but it's good to have everything secured. You'll not let the bearer know that there was a boat in'.

At last the delivery was successful, as Sandison wrote on 7 November 'I ... am much obliged to you for your care and in dispatching the boat. There was no helping for it with regard the rude night coming on them but it makes the freight come dear. I paid James [?]ton 1s 6d and you'll please pay the other three the same and I shall account to you for it ... as to our officers I hear no reason for their going to your town, if it's not going to get their quarter pay. There is no word of any thing of the kind here as yet. I shall acquaint you when I shall take the next things which may be some time in the next week if it's good weather'.

Other orders were sent overland. Andrew Cruikshank wrote to William Watt junior in November 1772 'I have now sent you the half barrel salt put in a bag and then in the cass I was obliged to buy it for you in order to keep my word. You'll please send me the bag back and cass and deliver the bearer, John Sinclair, from ten to twenty ankers of gin, as many ... as you can conveniently and approves of, and let as many as possible be halfs. As to the brandy I am satisfied with what you think proper for your risk etc. Dispatch them as soon as you think possibly convenient and cause the horses go in sundries. I mean not all in one body'. On the back of the letter, in different writing it states: 'Mr Cruikshank got eight whole ankers geneva and twelve half ankers do sent the 14th November in obedience to the within order per John Sinclair, the Stress runner'.

Customs and Excise

The presence of customs and excise on land or at sea was a constant worry. They did not only effect the initial run but also the delivery of goods from one part of the coast to another. In 1767 George Gibson in Thurso wrote to his cousin William Watt junior 'I received the sixteen pounds tea safe and sound and believe it to be very good. I toasted it well before the fire before I opened it. It past the review of the custom house and excise who saw it without knowing what it was, having come on a friendly vessel to my brother'.

Andrew Cruikshank in Stromness warned William Watt in November 1772 'Ever since you wrote me last until yesterday there was a vessel lay out of our pier bound to the eastward with a cargo of tobacco which had always two officers on board, which stopped my sending a boat sooner. But yesterday they sailed and there is no vessels in the harbour just now at all but the old barque'.

In September 1783 Donald Smith wrote to Alexander Bain 'I see the *Tartar* sailed from Loch Inver the 1st current and that she may be expected the first northerly winds. I wish she may be lucky enough to escape the locusts there being no less than three yachts in the west coast, Kyd, Brown and Cook'.

Payments

Once the goods had been delivered, the merchants needed payment as soon as possible. Steuart was clearly worried about payments in July 1728 when he wrote to his son, Alexander, 'I have done all I could to sell our brandy in the west coast but I find there is no money to be had there. Though [I] am of opinion all will sell, if we trust the greatest part six months at 20d per pint or 30s per anker with a discount of 3 per cent for leakage, so that we are like to make little of this bargain, as I find the brandy will stand us very dear, no less, if I am not mistaken, than £1 5s 8½d an anker, prime cost [ie the profit was only 3s 4½d]. However, I am of opinion it will be better to make the best of it there than to be at the great trouble and expense of running it here, considering that we can sell it to very good responsible men on whom we may depend for punctual payment. And if Alexander Rose has shipped but a little brandy a good part of ours will go off about the Isle of Skye. But pray send me per first your thoughts of this affair. The countries about Lochaber and Appin was glutted with wine and brandy by little Somerville of Renfrew in the month of April last, and [he] has more still ... coming. But if we sell as cheap as any other, I find we will be preferred to any. If the Laird of Appin [Stewart] be at Edinburgh, as I hear he is, pray wait on him, and tell him I saw his children at his own house on Monday last. Try if you can deal with him for brandy, for he is a ready money merchant, and an honest, good man'.

A few days later he wrote to his cousin, Donald Steuart, master of the vessel, 'If said [George] Mackenzie or the Laird or Lady Assynt will call for any brandy let them have it on receipt or rather then bills payable at the current price in three months, or as much shorter time as you can. Fail not to sell both at Lochinver or where ever else you happen to touch, as much brandy as you can for ready money, particularly in the Orkneys. ... I am told, if you touched at Kylskow [not located unless Kylesku but this is still on the west coast] in Strathnaver, you could sell all your brandy for ready money; but this I leave entirely to yourself'.

In spring 1730 Steuart wrote to Donald McIntyre, his agent in the west, 'You are to trust no liquor but by the advice of Ardshiel or his son Mr Charles; and you are to take bills for the same, payable here or at Ardshiel's dwelling house, at as short time as you can, not exceeding six months after the delivery of the goods'. And 'there is a great penury just now over all the Highlands belonging to Seaforth'.

Complaints

One of the reasons for a delayed payment was complaint about the goods delivered. In March 1773 Will Tulloch in North Ronaldsay wrote to William Watt 'I had from you an anker of good gin and a half anker rum, which was not sufficient. You are not obliged to believe my word but I sincerely promise it was the most saltiest, disagreeable taste of any kind of spirits I ever tasted. I could not drink it in punch without double sugar and was content to sell it mixed among gin and sell it at the same price. I have sent you 40s for the gin. I think 20s too much for the rum'.

Robert Sandison in Stromness seemed to complain frequently to William Watt. All these letters were dated 1777. 'William Allan ... tells me your clerk delivered him fourteen ankers of gin and no brandy ... he likewise tells me they are in bad order and that no persons will buy them till they are filled up and the ankers in bad condition, which he told your clerk. So that you'll let me know what I shall do with them as none can buy them till they are filled up'. And 'I am sorry that I am obliged to return your half anker geneva, being so much mixed with salt water that there is no using it. Had it been any way passable I assure you I would have kept it ...

'NB Your servant knows it wanted a good deal of the measure also'.

'I received yours of the 17th inst acquainting me that if I wanted a few ankers of gin you would send me some. I wish you had sent me none of what you did for I was entirely affronted with it. After I had sold it and sent most of it off I was obliged to take it ashore again, owing to the badness of it, for which I send you a little in a small bottle by the bearer. It has a bad taste and muddy.'

In 1810 Watt himself complained to James Milne in Edinburgh. Milne's reply stated 'Sorry truly ... I am that the rum has not pleased. Nor can I account for it since the rum I sent was good. Upon enquiry I find one of my young people had filled it into a wine anker, which no doubt would give it a bad colour and even do no good to the flavour. But since it has happened will rather give you a small discount to keep it than to let it lie ever unused and since our next order you may be pleased to give me I have fully compensated you for the several complaints you mention both on your account and for the sake of my friend Mr Gibson, whom I highly respect and have wrote him to make intercession with you for my account'.

Watt decided to return the rum but the cask was seized. 'These certify that I found in the possession of William Watt Esq of Breckness one cask containing 9 gallons of spirits accompanied with a permit denominating the same foreign rum, which spirits Mr Watt requested might be covered with a permit in order to return it to James Milne of Edinburgh from whom it had been sent. Finding upon due examination that said spirits appeared in my opinion to be a mixture, the greater part whereof consisted of aqua vitae I therefore considered it my duty to seize the same as having come into Mr Watt's possession under a false description to the great detriment of the revenue'. [Robert Pringle, Collector of Excise, Skaill, 25 July 1810]

Seizures
Larger seizures were a greater problem. Harry Liddell wrote to Thomas Baikie in Thurso on 25 February 1752 'You have escaped fairly at this time but take care you do not follow such practices for the future, when probably you may be catched with a greater prize to your utter hurt and ruin, as has been the fate of many that has followed the smuggling trade. Good had it been that all such practices had been suppressed. But some individuals have little regard to the public welfare, if they make gain to themselves, which is a very wrong maxim'.

In 1729 a quantity of brandy, landed for bailie John Steuart on the shore of Petty was concealed in Lord Moray's house. He explained what had happened in a letter to Moray dated 6 June 1729. 'The disaster of the seizure lately made at Castle Steuart gave me a vast deal of pain, though I declare I was in a great measure innocent in it, having trusted the key of the house to a foolish servant who was imposed on in that affair. The supervisor of excise, Mr Hopson, who most barbarously broke in on that house, and allowed the military guard was with him to plunder and rifle all that was in that house to a considerable value of things belonging to me, is now pushing an exchequer process against me because I asked payment of the damage in modest terms; but I hope his masters, the commissioners, will not think fit to countenance him in such proceedings, and I'll take care hereafter that no such misfortune happen at that house. And in the meantime humbly beg your lordships pardon for what is past'. No prosecution took place.

John Sutherland at Gol Tower wrote to Thomas Baikie in February 1754 'You'll I dare say be sorry to hear that poor Sandy Ross's sloop was taken up Monday last was seven night by some excise scoundrels upon finding the ten half ankers and three more on board. He is just now at Inverness so that I cannot tell you what they may do but you shall be acquainted in course. If you have not sent the things for me do not send them till further advice. I hope in the worst event he may proceed on his voyage on bail'.

In 1772 Alexander Mowat at Stromness wrote to William Watt junior '[I] am sorry and very much doubtful that I cannot be of any service to you at present as there is so strict lookout that nothing can be gotten into this place. There has been a seizure made this day by the boatmen from Clestrain side but to whom the same belongs I know not nor from whence it came or can learn. Am sure from the sharp look out that they are keeping it will not be possible to get any into this place in safety until the NW ship be away and I make no doubt but the markets may be as good then ... I wish it may be in my power to serve you'.

Sometimes there was enough forewarning to put the goods 'out of the way'. Thomas Smith on Westray wrote to William Watt junior in September 1772 'As to the disposing of your goods, I took care that very day after the sloop came here to put it all out of the way, so as that if any of the rest had been made a seizure of (as it is surprising that it was not) you would have been safe and secure. It was at the places appointed before the officers came here. The expenses of transporting the above things amount to 12s 2d besides carrying from the vessel to the shore 3s 9d total 15s 11d.

'I am due you for a pair of black stockings valued at 3s 6d likewise for 6 lbs of lump sugar, a very bad pennyworth. Be so good as pay yourself and send me the balance by the first convenient opportunity, as I need it just now. If you allow me anything for the trouble and care I have been at I must beg the favour of you to send me a piece of single refined sugar. Since the fever abated I can take nothing for a breakfast but a little tea, very expensive to small circumstances such as mine at present are. I should not have been so very ill-bred as to have asked anything from you by way of reward but I am a good deal straitened at this same time.

'If anything that concerns your interest at any time is in my power to serve and accomplish you may depend I'll use my best endeavours. As to the conducting and managing the above I shall be glad to have your approbation and I am with esteem and respect.

'NB In Jerom Setter's late affair perhaps some mercenary low lifed beings would have thrown themselves in the way of being subpoenaed. Had I been proposed with a £100 [I] would have rejected and despised a seeming gain where my neighbour and friend might have sustained injury'. [For more information about this see Chapter Two]

Several other problems could effect the success of a cargo. 'Since a quarter cask is not reckoned equal to two ankers, you are to discount about half a crown of the price of two ankers for each quarter cask. Be sure you get the quarter casks first disposed of, being generally not so vendable as ankers. You are likewise, in case the buyers do not think fit to fill up their casks on board, to allow 5% for the leakage, that is an anker or quarter cask to the score'.

The demand/markets could change because of the time taken on a particular voyage. As Steuart wrote to Donald McIntyre in 1730 'He

[Ardshiel] is not able to do us any service, in respect, as he says, that Captain Campbell had resiled from his bargain with me, as also that the whole country is overshadowed with brandy by Somerville, who sells at 10s per gallon, and trust from six to nine months'. It was no solution to take the cargo round to Inverness because, as he wrote to the master, Duncan Baillie, 'I do not incline that any part of it should come about here, [where there is] very little encouragement besides a great risk and charges'. A later letter to Somerville about a possible tobacco joint venture was quoted in Chapter Two.

Having attempted to outline the smuggling business through merchant correspondence, the next chapter describes some of the smugglers not from the viewpoint of their letters but of the custom house records.

A STORY OF THE *CHRISTIAN*, DUNCAN BAILLIE MASTER

In October 1729 the *Christian*, Duncan Baillie master, took a consignment of salmon to Alexander Gordon & Co at Bordeaux. The return cargo, owned one third each by Duncan Grant, Kenneth MacKenzie junior and John Steuart, all merchants in Inverness, consisted of two hundred and forty ankers brandy, one hundred and eighteen half casks brandy, nine hogsheads claret and six half hogsheads white wine. As a result of problems when the *Christian* arrived on the west coast of Scotland in April 1730, Bailie Steuart devised several plans for the disposal of her cargo, details of which were sent to both the master and his agent in the area, Donald McIntyre.

Plan A (April 1730)
The bailie's instructions were to make for the west coast by the Irish Channel. Stewart of Ardshiel had ordered eighty ankers of brandy at 25s per anker and Captain Campbell, governor of Fort William, five hogsheads of claret at £10 per hogshead. McIntyre was to offer brandy to MacDonald of Kinlochmoidart and then proceed to:

South Uist 'and sell what you can there for ready money for as we are not acquainted in that country we cannot advise to give any trust there, unless it be to Clanranald, to whom deliver my letter'; Dunvegan: 'from whence you'll direct my letters to Donald McLeod, the tutor's son, and William McLeod of Ebost [not located], who will assist you about the disposal of what may remain of the cargo' and Portree: 'where you will address yourself to Donald McDonald, the tutor's son and Alexander McDonald of Knockow [not located]'.

If the cargo was disposed of 'on that coast', the master was to load slate at Easdale for Inverness or Leith, for account of James Simm, slater at Edinburgh. Otherwise 'there will be a necessity that you proceed with the barque to the Kyle [of Lochalsh] where my father-in-law [John McLeod] and his son Alexander McLeod will assist you to dispose of a part'. If these were not at home then he was to contact Alexander Rose.

The *Christian* arrived in the Sound of Mull in the beginning of April 1730 and on the 18th the bailie wrote to the master 'I am apprehensive there may be great danger in your laying any time in the Sound of Mull, and therefore I hope my friends will order matters so that no time be lost. Let all

contd

A STORY OF THE *CHRISTIAN*, DUNCAN BAILLIE MASTER
contd

you are to unload there be put to shore together, so as your lying make no great noise. And I think fit yourself and sloop take borrowed names, and that it be not known the ship belongs to this place'.

Despite these precautions, McNeil, the collector at Fort William, attempted to seize the *Christian*, only missing her at Lochaline [in Morvern] by two hours. The bailie was furious with McNeil, 'in whose pocket I hope to break an egg very soon'. By the 26th May he had calmed down, writing to Ardshiel 'Now, as to securing Collector McNeil, I leave that point entirely to yourself, and if you think it necessary to be done, I am willing you give him five guineas'.

Plan B [early May 1730]
'John and Alexander [McLeod] think it very hazardous that the barque carry any of her cargo back through the Sound of Mull but that rather a large boat be hired, and a trusty agent along with what Ardshiel is to get. And [they] … makes mention of one Norman McLeod, who was lately here, to be sent along with it, and the liquor to be covered with packs of straw, as if the boat had in victual, or feathers, or wool'. However, it was soon apparent that neither Ardshiel nor Captain Campbell wanted their orders.

John McLeod, the bailie's brother-in-law was to help in selling half the cargo in Skye and the other half was to go to Simon McKenzie, Gruinard's son at Gairloch. 'But if you find that the cargo cannot sell on that coast, you must try all round with it to the Orkneys', where 'my good friend the Lady Burray [wife of Sir James Stewart of Burray]' would help. 'You may come to get what wine and brandy you have sold in that country to good responsible men; but, should that fail, you must run express, advising of what you have on board, and you shall meet the proper directions at Tarbat Ness'.

On 18 May 1730 Steuart wrote to McLeod at Glenelg 'Being advised of the 14th current that those I depended on in Argyllshire for taking a large quantity of the brandy per DB [Duncan Baillie] are supplied by Somerville at 10s per gallon, and nine months for payment, which are terms I cannot go into. Therefore I entreat how soon this comes to hand you forward the

contd

A STORY OF THE *CHRISTIAN*, DUNCAN BAILLIE MASTER contd

enclosed to Donald McIntyre, wherever you hear of him, and, if as yet on the Isle of Skye, I would earnestly entreat that you and your brother give all the concurrence your can to get what of the cargo is not disposed of at Gairloch sold with you to good hands, which can do no harm to your interest, as it will be but a small parcel to the whole island, only seven tuns. For I am now not inclined that the barque return to the Sound of Mull at this time, there being little good to be expected that way, besides a great deal of risk and charges. For you see Somerville has knocked that trade on the head by his Marseilles brandy, which can be sold much cheaper than that from Bordeaux. So, as I have said, if it be possible to sell anywhere about the Isle of Skye I do not incline to send the barque or any part of the cargo southward'.

Plan C [late May 1730]

Having received letters from his agent Donald McIntyre dated 21 May at Gairloch and 24 May at Glenelg, the bailie wrote 'First, I observe what you have given to Simon McKenzie, and by the last what you have still on board, which I assure you is a great deal too much for the country you are going to, and therefore its my positive opinion that you endeavour to sell as much as you can at Glenelg; and, whether you can sell or not, that you unload in that country at least fifty ankers to the care of my father-in-law, but in his absence to Alexander Watt till my father-in-law returns from Skye … I know not but he [McNeil] may still be on the catch for you. So it's fit, when you come to your livering port, which I reckon will be the Kyle of Shuna, let all the brandy be immediately put ashore, whatever happens, in order to secure the barque in the worst event … and I think it most convenient, if possible, that you stay some time in that country after the barque is livered, to get good chances for what may be unsold of our cargo before you come home, since you may be assured that none of what is left with Ardshiel on our risk will be sold while any of his own lasts. Besides the great disappointment, charges and leakage that would be upon it if you should leave any unsold, which I beg you do not if possible. But would advise you not to go near Maryburgh [Fort William] in your return on several reasons. We are designed to have a due regard to your trouble and pray God to direct you'.

CHAPTER FOUR: THE SMUGGLERS

'The enclosed is copy of a paper [not transcribed in the letter-book], which was sent me by Mr John Duncan, writer and postmaster in Stonehaven, in confidence, desiring I might transmit to your Honours an exact double of the same. Concerning which I shall only beg to inform your Honours that it's my firm belief, as well as is of many others in the country, who must know better than I can, if there was a possibility to persuade them to say truth on this subject, that the officers in Stonehaven, as well as John Buchan, who is stationed in the southern division of the district of Aberdeen, and James Philip, tidesman in this district stationed at Gourdon, and Peter Grant, excise officer at Johnshaven, are all too intimate and too much connected with Robert Napier and Walter Sime, in company smuggling merchants in Bervie, who are both sensible people and very cautious and circumspect in carrying on their illicit trade and beside are people of considerable influence and very popular with all ranks along the coast, which makes it more necessary to have officers whose honesty and fidelity are tried to look after them. I humbly beg that in case your Honours shall see proper to communicate any part of this letter that Mr Duncan's name may be concealed'. [Letter from Robert Hunter, collector at Montrose, to the Board, dated 4 July 1771]

This chapter describes several of the smugglers mentioned in the custom house letter-books. The main section, on Bervie, is atypical. It includes a large amount of detail on the individuals involved in the smuggling runs, plus additional notes on some of the major smugglers. It was the ready availability of this detail which inspired the subject of the diorama in Phase II of the HM Customs & Excise National Museum [see Introduction]. There are frequent other references to the Bervie smugglers throughout this book. The section on McGilligan and Willcox refers to two smugglers who also appear elsewhere [in Chapter Eight and the Preface respectively]. The section listing some of the people who were mentioned in the letters to Alexander Bain junior is of particular interest as it links the custom house letter-books and the merchant correspondence.

The custom house letter-books include several references to smugglers. Two examples are quoted, this time linking the west and east sides of the northern shores. On 16 March 1784 the collector at Stornoway forwarded to the Board return No 21 - four boxes containing 336 lbs congo tea and one cask containing 74 lbs bohea tea - seized by Mr Robertson, comptroller. He added 'upon suspicion of large quantities of smuggled goods being landed on the mainland coast opposite to this Island ... the comptroller set off the 28th ult and on the 2nd inst fell in with the tea above mentioned at the side of Loch Maree a fresh water loch of twelve miles in length ... This tea was brought from Gairloch by land and carried across the loch in a boat by William Fraser, Alexander McDonald and Murdoch MacPhail, tenants upon Sir Heston of Machmore's of Gairloch's estate, who only pay about 30s each yearly by rent and have not a subject [any money] should they be prosecuted. The tea was intended to be carried to the low country of Ross and Inverness-shire, where the comptroller was informed large quantities of tea had been carried about that time but for want of a proper party could not lay himself out to prevent it, a number of resolute people being employed for such purposes'.

In November 1790 the Board wrote to the collector at Inverness about three writs sent to the sheriff substitute at Skye to be delivered to Roderick McLeod, near Dunvegan, and Angus McDonald, fisher in Rowindunan, and Donald McSween, mariner in Bravnel [neither of these places located]. 'After making all private search for Roderick McLeod and Angus McDonald he could find neither of them and was informed that McLeod had gone to Argyllshire but the sheriff had pounded the whole goods that could be found belonging to Angus McDonald, which only amounted to £2 11s 6d. Donald McSween had been apprehended by the sheriff substitute and his party but forcibly rescued from them by a parcel of emigrants ready to embark in board a vessel to America'.

Alexander Bain's Correspondents
Only the Class 2 letter-books still exist for Inverness but in the period 1784 to 1786 it is possible to identify some of the individuals who were writing to Alexander Bain. In October 1784 one half pipe of white Portugal wine, the property of John McPherson, and one pipe, one half pipe and forty dozen bottles of white Portugal wine, the property of

William Inglis & Co, were seized. 'It being mentioned in the letter from Mr Grant, landwaiter, upon this occasion that the ship *Janet* of Portsoy, out of which the wine in question was imported, was two miles out at sea at the time the wine was discharged, we direct you to report the occasion thereof, it appearing very extraordinary that this discharge should have been allowed in such a situation'.

In September 1785 Charles Cumming of Inverness imported goods, including six hogsheads of French red wine, three casks and four boxes of prunes and ten bags of walnuts, on the *Gairloch*, William Mule master, from Bordeaux. Cumming 'failed to pay the duties, [so that] these goods were secured in the king's warehouse where they have ever since remained ... as Cumming is in bankrupt circumstances and the six months elapsed from the date of the importation' it was agreed in March 1786 that 'as they will be in danger of suffering if allowed to remain too long on hand' they should be advertised for sale in the Edinburgh newspapers.

Donald Smith also had some wine on the *Gairloch*. According to the paperwork, this was six hogsheads from Robert Bonic & Co of Bordeaux but only five hogsheads had been discharged. The Board instructed the collector to enquire into the discrepancy.

In June 1786 Donald McLeod of Geanies [see p 35] leased 'a spot of ground on his estate for building a house for the accommodation of the tidesman at Portmahomack to endure for two nineteen years after Whitsunday 1786 at the yearly rent of 10s'. The Board had ordered the lease 'to be deposited in the bond chest'.

Robert McGilligan & George Willcox

On 13 May 1775 William Mitchell, landwaiter, stopped two hogsheads of red French wine, which had been brought into Aberdeen and which he found 'upon a cart in the streets'. According to the carrier, the wine came from Robert McGilligan, merchant in Newburgh. 'As there was a probability that this wine was run, though Mr Mitchell could bring no proof thereof, we thought it right to lodge the same in the king's warehouse until proof should be made to your Honours' satisfaction that the duties were paid. Robert McGilligan came to the custom house and claimed the wine as belonging to George Willcox and himself upon the credit of 200 gallons transferred by William Brebner & Co from an importation by them in July 1768 on board the *Providence*, William Mills master, from Bordeaux to George Willcox and of 40 gallons remaining on Robert McGilligan's own credit of French wine condemned in the exchequer in Candlemas term 1769. We asked McGilligan if he and Willcox could make oath that the wine stopped was the identical wine he referred to but this he refused to do ... it appears to us that there is not ... the identical wine ... which is about seven years old'.

In November 1775 James Anderson, supervisor of excise at Ellon, stopped three hogsheads of French wine found in the possession of Robert McGilligan, who claimed this wine included 66½ gallons entered by him 16 May 1775 on the *Happy Return*, 63 gallons transferred to him by George Willcox, having been imported on the *James & Margaret*, John Mowat master, on 26 May 1775 and 11 gallons remaining from a cargo of wine imported by him on 15 August 1771. These credits totalled 140½ gallons but the hogsheads contained 151 gallons, leaving 10½ gallons unaccounted for'. There was little doubt in the collector's mind that all the wine had been smuggled.

The Bervie Smugglers
In May 1773 the collector at Montrose wrote to the Board 'In the town of Bervie and village of Gourdon eight miles distant from this there are three persons who are not only smugglers themselves but from their long experience and connections in that part of the country are employed as agents and trustees for all the illicit traders in this place and a considerable way to the westward, even the length of Forfar, Kirriemuir and Glamis, who consume and deal in large quantities of spirits, teas and tobacco, which are all instantly carried off the beach upon their being landed to their respective places of destination and for the most part without any loss on the part of the importers'.

On 29 October 1773 Duncan Aire, commander of the *Royal Charlotte* excise cutter, suggested to the collector at Montrose 'As Bervie is a place where great smuggling is carried on and as nature has situate Bervie Bay for a safe landing place ... I will make bold to say was there a good officer of the customs and another of the excise set down in the town of Bervie with a party of military to be at their command by night and day they would effectually prevent the Flushingers from landing in the way they do at present. It would also effectually put a stop to people buying their goods was the two Boards [Customs and Excise] to give strict orders to all their officers ... to be on their guard when they hear of any Flushingers being on the coast, that although they may not have it in their power to prevent them from landing yet they in great measure have it in their power, if they are diligent, to find out the persons who were aiding and assisting and receiving the goods. What a shame it is at the present that there is no officers of the revenue nearer Bervie than Johnshaven and Stonehaven. With respect to the man Rodger at Gourdon I look on him as nothing and the Bervie folks can do with him as they please'. Another part of the same letter is quoted in Chapter Five under the Flushingers section.

The collector commented to the Board 'It was judged more eligible to station one [officer] at Gourdon, as they are more out of the way of the merchants of Bervie and because of the vicinity of Gourdon to Bervie beach, upon no part of which can smuggling be carried on without being seen from about a quarter of a measured mile from Gourdon, and Bervie is a part of his division'. The tidesmen at Gourdon, including John Rodger, are discussed in Chapter Nine.

The *Peggie* of Johnshaven

The *Peggie* of Johnshaven was built in Montrose at the end of the 1760s 'for the purpose of smuggling'. Her owners were Walter Sime and Robert Napier and she was known locally as the *Bervie* sloop. Her master was George Largie of Johnshaven. She was employed continually in trade between Montrose and Gothenburg or Holland. After unloading any smuggled goods she would then return directly overseas or go to Sunderland, Newcastle or the Firth of Forth for coals. Sometimes these were sold overseas and sometimes delivered to Stonehaven [see Chapter Eight].

On Friday, 29 March 1771, John Keel, a mariner from the *Princess Caroline* revenue cruiser, Captain John Read commander, sent a verbal message to the custom house at Montrose by way of a fisherman from one of the Ulysseshaven boats, asking for assistance, as he was alone on board the *Peggie*. The comptroller, surveyor and two tidesmen went to his aid but when they arrived the *Peggie* was just sailing out of Lunan Bay. John Keel, who had been put on shore by the smugglers, made a statement, which was not transcribed in the letter-book.

The ship went straight on the Milton of Mathers, where she ran a cargo of goods. Three small boats went out to receive her cargo of three hundred and fifty ankers spirits, four boxes tea and some tobacco stalks. These boats belonged to Thomas Blews from Johnshaven and James Wilson and Robert Grieve, both from Milton of Mathers. John Gibson, farmer in Milton of Mathers, received the goods out of the boats, took charge of them and ordered them to be carried to the top of the heugh [cliff]. The porters employed in carrying the goods were John Welsh, James Taylor, Robert Carthrae and William Welsh. They were paid in the house of Alexander Anderson, brewer in Milton, by Robert Scott, merchant in Milton and David Duiers. At the top of the heugh Robert Dickie, farmer at Milton of Mathers, ordered the goods to be put into carts and directed where they were to be lodged. The carts belonged to Alexander Livie, farmer in Lauriston, John Gibson, farmer in Milton of Mathers, David Duiers, farmer at Mill of Woodston and Thomas Clark, farmer at Little Woodston. Walter Sime and James Greig, farmer at Gourdon, paid the hire of the carts to those mentioned above and John Carnegie, carter at Bridgeton in Robert Dickie's house - he was present at the time. The goods were believed to belong to Walter Sime and Robert Napier.

In May 1771 the *Peggie* was on the coast again. This time the goods were run at Skateraw and Crawton. Three boats from Portlethen went out to her when she was just off the coast. One went to Skateraw [now called Newtonhill]. It belonged to William Craig, fisherman in Portlethen, as could be proved by James Alexander, George Andrew and John Greig, who were presumably the crew. The skipper was only paid 40s by John Smart, farmer in Rollenich, which probably explains why such detailed information was given to the customs.

A second boat belonged to Alexander Webster, fisherman at Cove [near Aberdeen]. The crew were George Webster, George Morris, John Gavin, George Webster junior and Alexander Craig and they discharged the goods at Crawton. The third boat belonged to Alexander Allan. The crew were Alexander Allan younger, Alexander Robertson, John Robertson, William Livingston and George Bonner. They also ran the goods at Crawton and were paid £4 by John Smart. The porters employed were John Walker, James Walsh and John Jervise, all fishermen in Crawton, and they each received 2s each from James Law, farmer in Crawton. The goods were directly carried off in carts but there was no information about the drivers' names or the owners of the carts. These goods were also believed to belong to Walter Sime and Robert Napier.

The *Peggie* next went to Stonehaven to discharge some English coals, where she was seized by James Kennedy, the comptroller, and William Blews, tidesman at Arbroath [see Chapter Eight]. Captain Kyd's boat, commanded by Andrew Watt, was at Gourdon and the collector's clerk 'went to him and required his assistance and his boat's crew ... to bring the sloop about to this port, which he very readily complied with'. But the weather was so bad that it was several days before the *Peggie* could be taken into Montrose harbour, arriving there early in the morning of 31 May 1771.

At first Largie, the master, tried to claim her. Finally the Board ordered that she should be burned. The expenses paid to David Watt, shipbuilder of Montrose, totalled £6 9s 11½d, including:

six men taking out the mast and bowsprit etc; two carpenters one day taking out all the movables; five men and a boat towing the vessel to the place of burning; five men employed in taking out the ballast; the shore dues of fifty-eight carts of ballast out of the vessel; carters carrying the ballast from the ship to the links; four carpenters one night and one day burning the vessel; one barrel of tar; two cart loads of whins; six half empty tar barrels and warehouse rent for the mast, bowsprit shrouds and stays.

This was offset by the sale of 12 stone of old iron at 2/6 per stone, reducing the costs to £4 19s 11½d.

On 8 June 1772 Patrick Ogilvie, in charge of an excise sloop, en route from the Moray Firth to Leith, sent his boat ashore at Arbroath for water. William Blews went on board and told him about a Flushing cutter with George Largie on board. Ogilvie seized her on 10 June - 'this was the cutter on board of which two of the men were shot dead and two more were wounded and sent on shore to this place'. Blews undertook to prove that a cargo was smuggled out of her at Bervie in mid-May and by October he had found a list of evidences. Nothing further has been found about Largie, as yet.

Walter Sime, merchant of Bervie

Sime appears frequently in the Montrose letter-books from 1771 to 1776. The first mention is on 13 April 1771, as a merchant in Bervie, applying for the return of two hogsheads of white wine and a box containing iron screw nails and plates seized from the *Arbroath Smack*, James Inverarity master, from London at Montrose. By 28 May 1771 the collector was writing that 'Robert Napier and Walter Sime in company, merchants in Bervie, are well-known to be the greatest smugglers upon this coast and drive little or no other trade whatsoever'. In December 1771 Sime and Napier, who owned a tobacco manufactory near Gourdon, imported one hundred and five hogsheads of tobacco from Port Hampton in Virginia on the *Christian*, James Brown master. This concerned the collector as it was the first tobacco importation received at Montrose for some time. The cargo was still being disposed of as late as 1776.

In December 1773 evidence was given by David Duncan, labouring servant in Bervie, and Alexander Walker, tailor, about one hundred and twenty ankers of spirits and fifteen or sixteen wax cloth bags of tea which they had been employed by Sime to store in his barn. The goods had been sent on shore from a three-masted Flushing cutter and landed on the bing [beach] at Bervie on Monday, 25 October 1773. According to the collector, 'Walter Sime is in very good circumstances and is said to have made a considerable sum of money by smuggling, which the loftiness and boldness of his manner and his art in the seduction of the officers of both revenues from their duty does greatly contribute. Sime, as I am informed, rewards his friends in a very liberal manner. By this man's illicit and destructive trade the revenue is and must be greatly hurt and injured as well as the country in general and it is remarked that as he so bountifully pays the wages of corruption to his prostitutes in office so he is as boundless in his resentment against those who detect or oppose him. These two deponents, Walker and Duncan, have therefore requested me to emplore your Honours will be pleased to direct that their names may be kept as secret as possible till such time at least as they shall be called for to appear as evidences upon oath in the court of exchequer in any trial or prosecution that may follow'.

Further evidence was collected against Sime, who was due to appear in the Exchequer Court in Edinburgh on 13 June 1774. The trial was finally heard on 5 December 1774 and Sime won his case. As reported by the collector on 25 January 1775 ever since this 'his behaviour to the officers of the revenue and others who he thinks may have any connection with them or any attachment to the revenue by persons in his employment and over whom he has influence ... is quite insufferable'.

David Christie of Newbigging was suspected by Sime of having become 'too intimate with the collector and some other officers of the customs'. As a result Sime 'did instigate and hound out two ruffians to shoot Christie that he might not have it in his power to bring him to further trouble'. As these men were disguised, Christie could not recognise them. But the collector, still believing that he would give information against Sime, put him in the care of a surgeon. Christie made an affidavit on 15 February 1775.

By October 1776 he was in Montrose gaol and his daily allowance of 6d per diem was paid by the smugglers.

In December 1773 Sime still had credit for most of twenty-one hogsheads of French red wine imported in 1767, claiming that this was because of the small consumption of wine in that part of the country. Walker Campbell, sheriff depute of Kincardine, had purchased ten dozen bottles of this wine for the use of his own family in Edinburgh, to be sent coastwise to Leith. The Montrose officers refused to give him a permit. 'We imagined that a merchant of Mr Sime's extensive dealing might before now have sold a much larger quantity of claret or French wine than twenty-one hogsheads in a space of time exceeding six years'. Indeed 'a gentleman of undoubted veracity' who dealt in the wine trade in 1767 'within the hour' had stated to the collector that he purchased twenty hogsheads from Sime at that date.

William Blews seized thirteen ankers and one ullage anker of geneva, containing 125 gallons, ten in Bervie gaol and four in the house of Thomas Christie, the provost in May 1774. The Board instructed the collector 'to use our utmost endeavours for ascertaining the property of the goods ... and to compare the marks and numbers of both parcels. Upon inspection we find there are neither marks or numbers upon any of them ... there are no marks on the fifteen casks of tea seized by William Blews in the end of December last and we are informed that these goods, which are fraudulently imported on this coast by Walter Sime, never have any marks on them ... we are convinced that the fourteen ankers geneva lately returned for condemnation were the property of Walter Sime and not provost Christie, who according to our information never was a smuggler. Nor that he was in the knowledge of the four ankers which were got in his house being lodged there ... we beg leave to add in justice to provost Christie's character that he was always ready to assist any of the officers of this port, not only by giving them warrants to enable them to search for prohibited and uncustomed goods but also ordered his own servant to attend them as constable, who is made such occasionally by him at the solicitation of our officers, who assure us that without the assistance they receive from provost Christie they could at no time effectuate the seizure of any prohibited goods smuggled in that part of the coast. The key of the gaol was not in the hands of the provost but either in a town officer's custody or in one of the bailie's and the provost upon the first application did not hesitate to grant a warrant for breaking open the door in case of refusal of access'.

Robert Grieve, Milton of Mathers

In mid July 1773 a sloop smuggled a large quantity of goods along the coast. Early in the morning a boat belonging to Robert Gowan, a fisherman in Gourdon, went into Milton with fifty-four casks and cases [quality unknown] for James Inverarity, a bankrupt cooper in Arbroath. As nobody in Milton was willing to receive the goods, Inverarity put them into Robert Grieve's boat. They were taken along the coast to Skateraw, where they were landed and delivered.

Robert Dickie

In April 1760 the collector transmitted to the Board a letter from Benjamin Smith, tidewaiter at Johnshaven, reporting that he and William

Wilson, excise officer at the creek, had been deforced on 3 April at Milton of Mathers and in the ensuing 'riot' that he wounded Robert Dickie. As a result a warrant had been granted by a justice of the peace in Kincardineshire 'to apprehend and carry him to the county gaol at Stonehaven'.

A precognition was taken on 29 April at Johnshaven and on 30 April in Forfar. 'The collector begs leave to observe to your Honours that by what he could learn the mob which occasioned the riot and deforcement consisted of a rabble of the meanest and lowest of the commonality. It appears by some of the witnesses precognosced that some spirits in ankers had been landed near Milton that night and seems to have been carried off before the officers got up to the place where it was landed and the boat gone off. The witnesses precognosced would not answer to the interrogatories put to them distinctly and that in his [the collector's] opinion they were straitened to give evidence in this affair so as not to discover the real facts. Robert Dickie who was wounded with the shot is quite recovered and was in the church of Montrose last Sunday'. The collector's expenses totalled £2 16s 4d.

Alexander Thom

In early December 1773 the collector described Alexander Thom as 'a smuggler of inferior note with respect to Sime though I am credibly informed that he presently is in good circumstances'. On 28 December 1773 William Blews seized fifteen casks of tea (1071 lbs sound and 13 lbs damaged), four ankers of geneva (34 gallons) and one matt of tobacco (44 lbs leaf tobacco) together with an open boat, which had been used in running the goods ashore, lying at the Burn of Binholm. The smuggle had been carried on by Alexander Thom who, after the goods were landed among the rocks where they were found by Blews, went in the boat to board the vessel and sailed to Auchmithie, where the rest of the cargo was smuggled. This vessel was a pink-sterned sloop the sole property of Walter Sime. In June 1774 Blews identified her as the *Katherine* of Johnshaven, Alexander Law master, but he had not been able to seize her. When the seized tea was put up for sale at Montrose nobody came to purchase - the collector believed this was because Sime had made an agreement with the local merchants about it. The tea was sent to Leith to be sold.

In 1775 Alexander Thom was prosecuted for the sum of £1,650 being treble the value of goods: one hundred and twenty-six ankers geneva, twenty-six matts tobacco and eighty matts tobacco stalks, which he had assisted in unshipping. The prosecution was based on the information of William Blews relating to a run at land of Shield Hill in February 1772. Thom hired boats from Shield Hill to take the goods ashore. They went out to the ship, the *Ann*, loaded the goods but could not return to the shore because of the high seas. As a result Thom ordered the goods on board again, except for the loading of one boat which overset. He then went with the vessel to Johnshaven where another boat made three trips to unload the goods. Thom went ashore with the third load.

In October 1775 Thom submitted a petition to the Board. He wanted the trial postponed because several of this material witnesses were overseas. 'The petitioner has also the misfortune of being in very low circumstances in life. He has a wife and a numerous family of young children for whose subsistence it is with the utmost difficulty he can provide. In that situation he can ill afford the charge of defending himself against a prosecution of this nature, although in the issue he is humbly confident of success. He is therefore advised to make this application to your Honours in hopes that you will accept from him the sum of £70, with such costs as have been already incurred, being the utmost that he can raise by the assistance of his friends for as he has already said his own funds can afford nothing'. The Board agreed to accept £85.

On the Beach: Bervie November and December 1784

The story of the two Gourdon tidesmen, Sharp and Swan, is told in Chapter Nine. On 19 November 1784 they were deforced after seizing a cart carrying goods inland. Following a detailed enquiry, the collector discovered that those present at the smuggle or with the carts at the time of the deforcement were John Young, wright in Ferney Flatt, William Davidson, servant to George Scott in Temple of Kinneff, James Walker, farmer at Hillside of Bervie, John Rae, farmer at Newbigging, Robert Christie, farmer at Barkhill, John Fetteresso, servant to Robert Christie, Robert Duncan, carter in Bervie, James Will senior, carter in Bervie, James Will junior, carter in Bervie and Margaret Mearns, spouse to Robert Watt, shipmaster in Gourdon.

It was believed that James Hadden, merchant in Montrose, was behind the smuggle and that others involved either as principals or assistants were William Jopp, carter and dealer in Montrose, Robert Maver of Coble Boards near Skateraw and Andrew Scott, merchant in Temple of Kinneff. But no further information was forthcoming.

Then in February 1785 James Walker, carter in Hillside appeared privately before the collector. He stated that on 19 November 1784 he was engaged by Robert Lawrence, labourer in Bervie, to go to the beach and take up a load of goods to be carted to the country; he did not know the contents of the ankers; he did not see James Hadden, merchant in Montrose, on the beach; he didn't know if Robert Maver or William Jopp were there because he didn't know them; there were about six carts laden with ankers which left the beach. His cart was last and as he had dropped some ropes he went back to search for them and so got separated from the rest. When he caught up with them, he was told that there had been customs officers among the carts but as he was not present he did not know what happened or who deforced them; he had not been paid yet, although he had called on Lawrence repeatedly.

Robert Lawrence was frequently employed as a corn thresher by the collector at Aberdeen. He was persuaded to make a deposition before two magistrates, John Dinwall and Francis Leys, on 25 January 1785. Between seven and eleven o'clock on an evening in middle November 1784 Lawrence was asked by John Farquhar of Bervie to go to the house of William Cream, inn-keeper, to speak to Robert Maver, who was 'employed by James Inverarity, residing near that place, in smuggling transactions'. Maver asked him if he could procure two carts 'for a certain purpose'. Then William Jopp, carter or workman in Montrose, and two sailors joined them saying that the boat and goods were on the beach so that they needed immediate assistance. Lawrence asked James Walker in Hillside and Robert Christie's servant, John Fetteresso, at Bark Hill for a cart. John Rae and James Will junior at Bervie also produced two carts, as did George Scott at Temple of Kinneff. All these carts were loaded with six to eight ankers. After seeing the carts loaded on the beach, in the presence of Robert Maver and William Jopp, Lawrence accompanied them as far as Bervie. Later he was told that John Farquhar had accompanied the carts into the country.

About eight or nine o'clock the next morning George Swan and John Sharp went into the barn where he was threshing and said that they had been deforced the night before. They searched the barn and asked him if James Hadden had been present at the smuggle or deforcement or if he knew who had deforced them. Lawrence declared that he neither saw not heard of James Hadden on that occasion not did he know the names of the deforcers. Some weeks afterwards James Thom, a merchant in Bervie, gave him 2s 6d for his trouble.

Finally 'a person who is a friend of the revenue' and connected with John Rae would not be persuaded to appear privately before the collector and comptroller. But he did say that James Hadden had met the loaded carts on 19 November 1784, immediately after the officers had 'fallen in with them' and rescued then or obtained the officers' consent to let them pass.

In his statement before the magistrates, Robert Lawrence declared that on 13 December 1784 he was on Bervie beach with Robert Maver and William Jopp and several others, whose names he did not know. He was employed to get some carts to carry off the goods. He employed Robert Christie in Gourdon, who supplied two carts, John Rae in Newbigging, who supplied one cart and James Walker in Hillside, who supplied one cart. James Will junior and Robert Duncan, both from Bervie, each had a cart there but were not employed by him. Late at night a boat came ashore from a lugger loaded with tea and spirits. Eighteen parcels consisting of boxes, bags and casks of tea and two ankers of spirits were carried off by Robert Christie and John Rae's three carts. Robert Christie drove one cart and John Fetteresso the other, John Rae drove his own cart. The boat was prevented from getting back to sea by a surge, which explained why the other carts were not loaded. The goods were carried southwards by way of Johnshaven as every road in the country was impassable. That evening he saw James Hadden in Bervie but was positively certain he did not see him at the beach or receiving any goods.

George Scott and Robert Thom

On 26 April 1785 William Blews and William McGregor, customs, and James McBeg, excise, seized at Braidon Bay four horses and two carts belonging to George Scott, farmer in Temple of Kinneff and four horses and two carts belonging to Robert Thom, farmer in Miln Hill, conveying twenty-nine ankers of geneva and brandy. The horses were condemned by the local justices, Sir Alexander Ramsay Irvine of Balmain and George Carnegie of Pitarrow 'for the use of His Majesty'. William Lindsay and Thomas Mills, tidesman at Montrose, appraised the eight horses and four carts at £8 16s as follows:

one horse £1 5s; one horse, old, £1 1s; one horse, old, £1; two horses, old, 17s 6d each; one horse, very old and lame, 7s 6d; one horse, very old and lame, 5s and one horse, blind of an eye and lame also 5s; one cart £1 1s; one cart 15s 6d and two carts at 10/6.

Having been exposed to sale on 28 April 1785 they were all bought by Robert Thom for £12 12s. As the charges, including corn and hay for the horses for two days and two nights, totalled £2 9s, the officers' reward was £1 13s 10d each. Blews and McGregor signed their receipts for this payment but McBeg could only make his mark.

The tailpiece to this chapter is an anonymous 'incendiary' letter received by the collector at Montrose and believed to have been instigated by Walter Sime. There are frequent other references throughout the book to Sime and the Bervie smugglers. The next three chapters consider the smuggling vessels - including pretended bound voyages and wrecks.

A STORY OF A MONTROSE COLLECTOR

'The enclosed incendiary letter was, on Friday morning last the 3rd instant with the postmark of Brechin on it but not assigned by any person nor dated from any place, brought me from the post office here. From that part of the contents where the anonymous correspondent seems so anxious about the prosecution of his friends, who he says are in and about the place that I live in, particularly northward, I can entertain no doubt that the insolent epistle has been composed and sent by the same set who lately fell upon David Christie, farmer at Newbigging near Bervie, for being suspected of giving information of Walter Sime, a notorious smuggler in Bervie, his villainous and fraudulent practices to the great hurt and prejudice of the revenue whereby he, Christie, was shot with a musket loaded with slug and beat and bruised on the head and other parts of his body to the imminent danger of his life. Not only so but Mr Sime and his friends and adherents have ruined him by buying up his debts and rendered him and his family not worth a sixpence.

'This letter and all the menaces it contains I beg leave to assure your Honours shall have no effect nor intimidate me from going on in the execution of my duty in detecting every fraud I can possibly bring a proof of either against Sime and his co-partners or any other. Against the authors of this audacious letter I have no revenge nor resentment to gratify as they never did me any private injury. But I detest and abhor all smugglers as infamous persons, as defrauders and robbers of the public, as corrupters of the morals of the people and particularly of the officers of the revenue, many of whom they have seduced from their duty and fidelity and thereby brought them and their families to utter ruin and destruction. At this last mentioned traffic this Mr Sime before mentioned is most remarkably expert and by much too successful, a recent instance of which your Honours had lately before you [see Chapter Nine]. The number of smugglers here and along the coast is considerably diminished within these few years but there remains a list, of whom your Honours have underneath, who are a set of the most daring and abandoned ruffians regardless of the laws and acting in defiance of them.

'List of the persons in this place and the adjacent coast whose principal business is that of smuggling tea, wine and spirits: James Badenoch in Glamis, Walter Sime in Bervie, Alexander Thom in Bervie, James Greig in Gourdon, David Scott in Johnshaven, Robert Napier and John Milne in Montrose besides several others of an inferior degree.'   contd

A STORY OF A MONTROSE COLLECTOR contd

'Sir, The receiving this letter from an unknown hand and unsubscribed may no doubt be matter of wonder and surprise to you but as I always have a pleasure of being serviceable to mankind and of preventing mischief when impending to any person (although never so worthless) as much as lies in my power, is the reason for my making free to acquaint you with the following particulars the knowledge of which I only got not many hours ago if its well taken as a caution shall be infinitely glad which will best appear from your after conduct If otherwise I shall only think my trouble lost and whatever may be the consequences afterwards I shall be very indifferent

'Having occasion yesterday to be a few miles from home on business I happened to fall in with a small but sensible company after talking over a great many things the conversation turned at last upon a subject altogether foreign to me namely anent several prosecutions which have of late been commenced against different persons in and about the neighbourhood of the place you live in particularly to the northward and was entirely consummated to hear that you are the principal instigator and actor of such hellish schemes as commencing these prosecutions to prove these persons to be smugglers or importers of prohibited goods in order to which you with some other your accomplices have suborned a set of the most worthless, perjured, infamous, lawlessed rogues that perhaps Scotland nay the whole world cannot produce such like perfidious wretches consummate knaves ad the very dregs of mankind yea more generosity is to be had from the most savage tiger that roams in the wilds of Nabia.

'If this is the case, which God, you and your accomplices only know) I think you must undoubtedly be the most unhappy of all men. I naturally enquired what motive one in your office and rank could have in such wickedness it was answered your motives were thought to be partly envy and revenge but mostly mercenary and that for a very inconsiderable trifle to yourself (after paying your banditti) you pay no regard to the ruining of individuals or whole families. The men who you have injured so much now after coming to the perfect knowledge that you are the main spring of action, are and justly raised to a degree of rage next to madness and are determined that if you do not immediately stop procedure in these matters that you will be treated as a common enemy and were their case mine I would look upon you worse than a highwayman and treat you as such first opportunity which I

contd

A STORY OF A MONTROSE COLLECTOR contd

understand you have reason to expect and if that should happen (as God forbid) I am absolutely convinced the world would justify the action. And pray what fine reflections must your family and friends have when they think of the great Honours you have brought any on self and them. But allowing you still go on in your ordinary career and meet with no disaster or obstacle and that you get your wicked designs accomplished that you cause a few people leave their country, that you get them ruined to all intents, that you get their families made destitute and that by their destruction you get a number of those detestable knaves you employ into low dirty offices, to be alwise plotting swearing and perjuring themselves as tools to your inflexible barbarity and voracious appetite pray what mighty conquests do you make Yes you make a few men that might live peaceably with their families miserable vagabonds and send these ignorant fellows who are subservient to you directly to the Devil and yourself at their head. It might be thought that one of your sense could never have thought of degrading yourself so much by being engaged in so horrid actions and with such low paltry company which must render you infamous to the last degree and without a speedy amendment of your manners you must leave the world with an abominable character and how hideous must your reflections be to think that you cannot survive long I may say looking into the grave and such a load of iniquity on your back. Pardon me for being so tedious only let me add that if your years shall be lengthened out sometime it will be your wisdom to change your method to a better way of thinking which if done must soon appear otherwise blame yourself if the consequences are fatal'.

'Mr Chalmers the sheriff was here on Thursday last and took the declarations of several people in this place as to their knowledge of the writing and by whom it had been written but no discovery was made. Both the clerks in this office declared that they suspected one William Leslie, a writer in Edinburgh, and that the cause of this suspicion was the similarity of the handwriting of several letters from Mr Leslie and the unsigned one. My declaration was taken also. I acknowledge that the likeness of the writing in the last and those produced did not appear to me but that my suspicion was founded upon the zeal with which he serves these his clients and that there was not a man that I know was connected with the smugglers but himself capable of composing such an epistle, although it is not an extraordinary performance. In case of any thing occurring towards a discovery I shall certainly notify it to you'. [Collector at Montrose to John Davidson, Assistant Solicitor to the Customs, Edinburgh, 31 March 1775]

CHAPTER FIVE: THE SMUGGLING VESSELS

'(We) transmit without delay as accurate an account as we can possibly procure of the number of smuggling vessels now employed in carrying on an illicit trade in this district in answer to which the following is the best information we can obtain, an exact list viz *Jean* of Aberdeen, John Wallace master, about 40 tons burthen, carries spirits, tea and tobacco; sloop *James* of Newburgh, John Barber master, burthen about 22 tons, carries spirits etc as above; sloop *Charlotte* of Peterhead, James Grant master, burthen about 20 tons, carries spirits etc as above; a cutter, William Lillie master, burthen about 30 tons, carries spirits etc as above; a lugger, Collins master, burthen about 70 tons, carries spirits etc as above'. [Letter from the collector at Aberdeen to the Board, dated 8 November 1785]

The letter quoted above is the only one found in the custom house letter-books which replied to the Board's enquiry of 4 November 1785 with an actual list of the main smuggling vessels in the area. It suggests a degree of incompetence on the part of the collector and his staff. They knew that all these vessels were smugglers but they did nothing about it. Yet, instead of being dismissed on the spot, the collector continued in post. The Board fully appreciated the problem. It might be possible to name the smuggling vessels but catching them was another matter altogether.

More information had been sent to the Board about Collins' lugger in March 1785. 'On the 3rd current, having received information from John Boyle and David Fetters, tidesmen at Skateraw, that a large lugger commanded by one Collins had been upon that part of the coast with a cargo of spirits and tea and was chased out to sea by Alexander Cook of the *Prince Edward* cutter, as also that a boat with a considerable number of her crew was at that time ashore at Skateraw, we immediately dispatched James Fail, landwaiter, over land with a sergeant and ten soldiers and Andrew Blair with his boat and crew by sea, with five more soldiers, in order to seize and procure said boat. Upon the appearance of the military, a part of the crew proceeded immediately to sea with the lugger's boat but Mr Blair was lucky enough to fall in with her at the distance of four miles from the land, when he seized and brought her to this harbour, where she is scuttled and drawn up'.

Nothing further has been found as yet about either the Collins lugger or the other vessels mentioned in the collector's letter. However, an analysis of the material transcribed during the research for this book produced an almost complete (only Q and Z missing) alphabetical listing of vessels, the majority of which were definitely involved in smuggling while the others were probably smugglers [see Appendix II]. This chapter concentrates on the clearly identifiable smuggling vessels. Having considered the 'clues' available to the customs, suggesting that a particular vessel was probably a smuggler, two main types of smuggling vessels, the Flushingers and the fishing boats, are discussed before looking at three specific stories: the HMS *Dauntless*, the *Tartar* of Dublin and the *Happy Return* of Lerwick.

Information about intended smuggles was frequently sent from the Board to the various outports. On 4 February 1775 the Board forwarded 'an information of the ship *Minerva*, Patrick Torrie master, loaded with brandies, teas, cloth, linens, cambrics and laces bound for Yell Island. Also that George Brodie, master of the sloop *Dispatch*, with sixty casks and two hundred ankers of gin besides cloth, linen, cambrics, muslin, silk stuffs, laces etc is supposed to be bound to Yell Sound westward of Shetland, which information we immediately communicated to all the officers in this port enjoining them to use their utmost endeavours to prevent or detect any fraud that may be attempted or committed by the vessels and to give notice of the same to such of the commanders of sloops and boats in the service of the revenue or admiralty as are or might be in their respective divisions. But as yet we have heard nothing of them. If they arrive in this port they shall be detained till your Honours be acquainted'.

Smuggling Vessel? The Clues
Various clues made the customs officers suspect that there had been a smuggle: the vessel needed to take on board more ballast before she could put to sea, there was 'a light hung in the shrouds', straw

tenders and other smuggling equipment were on board or the legal cargo was of too low a value to justify the length of her voyage.

On 21 March 1747 William Brown [see Figure 9], tidesman at Stonehaven sent an express to Montrose reporting the arrival of the *Thomas* of Arbroath, Thomas Strachan master, from Holland. Theo Ogilvie, tidesurveyor, and George Lobban, landwaiter, went directly to Stonehaven where, with Mr Stewart, supervisor of excise, they seized several hogsheads of wine and other goods. It was suspected that William Brown 'has been guilty of connivance or neglect' because the wine could only have been run in the harbour, as the hogsheads were 'all covered with wet sand' indicating that 'they had been landed a little time before and rolled up on the sands'. 'It is likewise obvious that such a quantity of goods had been run out of the ship after her arrival in Stonehaven that they could not venture to bring her to sea again before they had put a great quantity of stone ballast on board her in that harbour'. Brown 'does not pretend to have been deforced or anyways hindered in the execution of his duty and his sore leg did not hinder his boarding the ship'. His excuse for not stopping the smuggle was that 'he behooved to be sometimes on board the *Cumberland* [Andrew Garrock master, from Antigua] and sometimes on board Strachan, which we humbly look upon as a mere pretence'. There was not 'the least ground ... to apprehend any fraud from the nature of the *Cumberland*'s cargo though there was a great deal to be apprehended from the other, especially as he himself acknowledges that he had no got access to the hold'. Other examples of tidesmen and 'collusion' will be found in Chapters Eight and Nine.

The *Jean* of Portsoy, Henry Wilson master, with a cargo of fifty-one hogsheads, two half hogsheads wine, six tierces vinegar, three casks prunes and six bags of corks, pretending bound from Bordeaux to North Faro [see Chapter Six] was boarded in Cromarty Bay in 25 October 1775. The tidesman who remained on board was landed at Portsoy and the collector ordered all the officers in the district 'to keep an out look for this vessel believing that the cargo was to be run for the account of the merchants in Portsoy. George Henderson, tidesurveyor at Cromarty, boarded the vessel again on 1 November 'at anchor in Spey Bay about twelve o'clock at night within a mile of the bar in the mouth of the river and when there was a light hung in the shrouds (the usual signal for boats) and that soon after a boat did come alongside the vessel'. She was seized and taken into Portsoy.

The *Free Briton* of Folkestone, Edward Hainet master, reported at Montrose in ballast on 2 January 1771. Nothing was found during the rummage but the collector suspected that a cargo of prohibited goods had been smuggled from her. He examined two of the hands and the master, separately, and they 'having given very contradictory accounts of the voyage, we judged it our duty to stop her from going to sea till we can find out if our suspicions are well-founded'. On 5 January he wrote to the collector at Aberdeen, explaining his concern. 'There being a number of tenders on board her of a particular construction made up with hay or straw to keep off the boats that receive their loadings out of her, with a considerable quantity of empty half ankers, which has contained geneva, nine pairs of boots and a mast for a large boat on her deck, all tend to confirm the truth of her being a smuggler'. He believed that 'she has run ashore her cargo at a creek called Collieston in your district and that there is a boat belonging to her with some of her crew in Aberdeen, though perhaps they may conceal themselves'. He needed help from the other port as soon as possible 'as the master has thought proper to take an instrument of protest against me for stopping his vessel'. The problems caused by straw packing from the continent are described in the tailpiece to this chapter.

As the collector wrote to the Board on 15 January, the collector and comptroller at Aberdeen 'by their letters to us of the 7th and 14th inst acquainted us that the result of such enquiry made by them was to no purpose for that though a Folkestone cutter was two miles off the land yet what she was could not be found out. But that nothing was done thereabouts as Mr Duncan Aire's boat was lying at Collieston that night. Neither were our own officers more successful in their enquiries'. As a result the vessel was released.

'Besides the two commodities [tea and spirits] ... some of our smugglers have got into the importing of wine from places not the growth in vessels freighted to Norway on a nominal voyage for wood, which could not bear the expense even of a low freight, especially if a supercargo is sent out with the ship, while the principal intention is to bring a certain quantity of French wine for the purpose of smuggling before the ship arrives in port and the vessel proceeds to some place where it is thought she is not known and there sells and discharges her wood cargo.

'By a letter from the collector and comptroller at Inverness, dated the 2nd January 1777, we were informed that the ship *Betty & Ann*, George Barclay master, had been put into Cromarty with a cargo of wood and thirteen hogsheads of French wine, pretending bound to Newcastle [see Chapter Six]. On the 11th January this vessel was put into Peterhead, where there were two tidesmen boarded on her with orders to attend her to Newcastle, as the officers there suspected a fraud was intended. On the 28th January this vessel sailed from Peterhead and when in the bay of that place Barclay, the master, and one Charles Strachan, the supercargo, told the two tidesmen that the voyage to Newcastle was altered and that now the vessel was bound to St Martins ... and desired them to go on shore, which they did and left the wine and ship. That very night, the 28th January, the wine was smuggled in Bervie Bay, and the vessel proceeded directly to Burntisland, where the master reported and entered his cargo of wood [but not wine] and then took in a loading of coals for this place [Montrose] ... The merchants concerned in this trade deal also in tea and spirits and are become opulent. It is therefore wished that they were curbed and we humbly submit it to your Honours consideration if a prosecution for the penalty of breaking bulk and making a false report may not be commenced against the master in the present case.' Andrew White was believed to have travelled from Montrose to assist at the smuggling of the wine but 'is gone from this some time ago and is believed to be on board a man-of-war'.

Charles Strachan had been supercargo on the voyage from Bergen and owned some of the wine, which had been secured in the king's warehouse in October 1777 'for the duties'. On 5 January 1778 the *Betty & Ann* was forced on shore to the eastward of the entrance to the south Esk and George Barclay 'against whom two several prosecutions at the suit of His Majesty's advocate was commenced in the court of exchequer was drowned'. Strachan paid the duties for five of the hogsheads of wine in the warehouse and the remainder, totalling 341½ gallons, was sold by auction in May 1778 to John Miln, a Montrose merchant, for £80 10s.

Figure 6: 'Sailed on a Smuggling Voyage'

On 5 October 1771 the *Mary* cutter of Leith, James Inverarity mater, a sloop of about 18 or 20 tons, square-sterned, with a stroke of blue paint round her with a battan at her mast head, which was rigged on the after part of the mast, sailed from Montrose on a smuggling voyage. She was in company with the *Jean* or *Johanna*, James Sutor master, of about 15 tons burthen, being red in her upper stroke and whose mast was all of one piece. Their cargoes were to be unloaded at Peterhead. 'Both these vessels are in the employment of one Davidson, in Silverdykes near Peterhead, an ancient smuggler, who has made a considerable sum of money in that illicit trade. In the *Mary* cutter there is gone a son of Davidson's as supercargo'. On 18 January 1772 the *Mary* 'smuggled her cargo, consisting of teas from Gothenburg, ... at night in Milton ... and afterwards put into Stonehaven and I am informed sailed from thence a day or two thereafter to some port in the Firth of Forth to take in a cargo of coals ... the tidesman in whose division the smuggle of the tea was committed was on duty at a distance from his residence'.

On 28 February 1775 the *Janet* of Johnshaven, Robert Law master, a small schooner of about 20 tons burthen and the *Ann* of Johnshaven, Robert Mearns master, sailed from Johnshaven to Holland. 'With the first there are gone two persons from Aberdeen and on board the *Ann* ... there are three persons, all belonging to the town of Aberdeen, as supercargoes'. A few days later the *Peggie*, Andrew Mearns master, sailed from Johnshaven to Gothenburg for a cargo of tea. In April a quantity of tea and spirits run out of the *Ann* was seized by Andrew Rutherford's boat's crew in the yards of William Walker, farmer at England, and Alexander Gerard, farmer at Portlethen. The vessel, with prohibited goods still on board, was seized by Captain Duncan Aire of the *Royal Charlotte* excise yacht and carried to Leith.

The *Peggie* was brought into Montrose by Captain Laurence Brown, commander of the *Princess Caroline* revenue cruiser in early May with two hundred and three ankers of spirits and ninety matts of tobacco stalks on board. 'Upon the score of his ancient acquaintance with Andrew Mearns ... William Blews had the interest ... to induce him to give a full explicit declaration and discovery of the bargain entered into by him with the smugglers, which contains a complete journal of the voyage and of the goods smuggled out of her, which will effectively prevent a claim being entered by the merchants in the court of exchequer and the uncertain consequences of a trial'.

In August 1760 Johannes Lyderson, master of the *Edward* of Christiansand, went into Aberdeen where he offered for sale a parcel of spirits and a hundred weight of tea. A boat was hired 'to go off to sea and run ashore' the goods. But information had been given to the collector about the proposed run and Andrew Blair, assistant tidesurveyor, [see Chapter Ten] boarded the vessel which, as it was within the limits of the port, was brought into harbour. 'The strictest search being made, the goods could not be found until the ship should be unloaded as she was quite full of wood, they being concealed. The master ... finding it impossible to run the goods, and we having received intelligence that it was his intention to destroy the teas by throwing them overboard to prevent the seizing of his ship, Blair with all the officers who could be spared remained on board ... but notwithstanding all their diligence Blair discovered some of the teas just as the mariners had thrown it overboard and took about a pound of it out of the water and found concealed in one of the anchor buoys and in other parts 31 lbs of tea and likewise twenty-two ankers and two half ankers of spirits ... but notwithstanding of all the search that possibly could be made there is no more tea found, the ship being now fully unloaded and it is probable that some method has been fallen upon to destroy it'. The vessel was seized and as 'several merchants here will give considerably above the appraised value for her the seizure-makers therefore pray that the vessel may not be admitted to bail in case application should be made to that purpose'.

Sometimes it was difficult to distinguish an illegal from a legal trade. The *John* of Aberdeen was seized in 1770 together with one hundred and fifty one matts of tobacco by Mr Finlason, collector of excise. Mr Vitty, tidesurveyor, explained that he had not boarded her himself as 'this vessel only sailed from this twenty-one days ago, was in the coal and lime trade, came into the bay in the morning, was spoke to by an excise yacht and had all appearance of a lime ship, the decks covered with lime and pumping lime water. One of the boatmen hailed him and was answered from Limekilns with lime and seeing the appearance of the ship to answer he had no suspicion it was not so and reported to him accordingly. Upon enquiry we find that what Mr Vitty sets forth as to the appearance of the ship is true and that no person could have suspected the vessel to be loaden with anything but lime but we have told him that the smugglers use so many inventions to deceive that nothing should hinder the examining every ship whatever and being perfectly satisfied there is no deceit'.

Any opportunity was taken to run goods. While the *Cabersea* of Stornoway, John Robinson master, from Alicante and other foreign parts was under quarantine at Stornoway in spring 1771 brandy and wine were run from her. This illustrates the problems faced by customs in finding witnesses for the trial, which in this case was over two years after the smuggle. The four the sailors on board, Donald Carmichael, Farquhar McCraw, Roderick Taylor and Ken McLee, had absconded. It was suggested that they might be found 'if the officers at the several ports were directed to examine into the crews of the different vessels that arrive into their precincts as no doubt they will endeavour to find employment elsewhere, it being reported that they have been sent off with a price of money in order to absent themselves from this place for the matter of six or eight months ... The sailor Malcolm McLeod, who formerly gave information on oath anent the above fraud, sailed from Stornoway on board the *Neptune* of Greenock, Humphrey Warden master, for New York in America in June last with emigrants on board ... and as we are informed will soon return to Greenock, where McLeod may be apprehended on his arrival'. Other possible witnesses who could prove the running of the brandy and wine were Colin MacKenzie of Eaclaty and John Roy McLeod, tenant in Radishally both at Loch Broom [neither located]; Alexander McPherson, Robert Smith and Charles Nespair all of Gairloch; John Downie, late minister of Gairloch, now of Stornoway and James ? late tacksman of Easdale. In January 1773 the master was in command of a small sloop called the *Tartar* that followed the herring fishing upon the west coast and the previous summer carried a cargo or two of herring into Greenock.

The Flushing Cutters

In comparison with the local vessels bringing in cargoes of smuggled goods, the Flushing cutters tended to be heavily armed. On 29 October 1773 Duncan Aire wrote to the collector at Montrose 'the smuggling on this coast seems to be at present carried on in a new mode. The large lugger belonging to Flushing has been on the coast for this month past with a very large cargo of spirits in small casks and tea in wax bags. She bids defiance to all the yachts in the revenue of customs and excise. On the 19th inst we gave her chase without the Cape as she was to under easy sail. We could not come up with her so gave up the chase and put about and stood in. So soon as we put about she did the same and stood after us and came alongside of us with an English ensign flying, the tampions out of her guns and every man a lighted flare in his hand ready to engage. Her strength consists of six large carriage guns and twenty swivels. I was not on board the yacht myself but my mate, Mr Henderson, tells me he counted thirty-six men on deck, all stripped to the shirt. Mr Henderson, seeing the great advantage she had of him in sailing and strength, wisely declined engaging her without exchanging a single shot ... On Monday night last Captain Rutherford was off Johnshaven and saw her all that day off Montrose and judging very wisely that in the night she would make a push for Bervie Bay he sent his boat on shore [to Gourdon] double manned [with ten men on board]. But before the boat came, the lugger was in Bervie Bay and landed one boat load, which was escorted up to Bervie by the Flushingers and the gentlemen of Bervie, who had dressed out with Highland dress, upwards of a dozen of the weavers of Bervie, with sword and pistol in hand'. His letter concluded 'Now, sir, to what a deplorable condition is the revenue drove by a parcel of daring outlaws coming on the coast and by force of arms doing what they please'.

According to William Blews 'fifteen carts were employed in carrying them [the goods] from the beach and were delivered to Walter Sime, Alexander Thom and Robert Anderson, all merchants and smugglers in Bervie [see Chapter Four], who received the goods. Among the carts were two which belonged to Robert Napier ... and two of the carts belonged to Walter Sime'. Despite a postscript in the letter from Duncan Aire 'It is needless to send Mr Blews here to run a risk of being murdered by the Bervie gentry without military [protection]', the collector continued 'William Blews is to obtain the names of as many persons as he can for evidences.

'In a short space of time after the cargo was carried off the beach, a second boat belonging to the smuggler came ashore with another loading to the same place and the carts were attending to convey that away also. But William Blews and John Rodger ... with Mr Rutherford's men going among them before any part of this loading was landed the carts returned to the town empty and the smuggling boat returned to the ship with her cargo. Since which time the ship has not been seen on the coast nor any of her boats'.

In May 1778 David Garden, tidesurveyor, [see Chapter Ten] sent the collector at Montrose a letter 'giving an account how he was attacked by the crew of a Flushing cutter at the time she was smuggling in Bervie Bay and obliged them to leave the town, when there was a considerable quantity of goods therein, and of a second attack made by them upon William Brown and Robert Reid [two of Garden's boatmen - see also Chapter Ten], when they took their arms from them and cut Brown upon the head in a most unmerciful manner'. The collector requested a party of military [at least 12 men] to be stationed at Bervie to help the boat's crew and 'two pistols and two cutlasses to be sent hither in room of those taken from Brown and Reid'. On 2 July the collector supported William Brown's petition for assistance with his medical expenses 'as we believe him to be a poor man'.

There was information that a Flushing cutter had been off the coast of the Moray Firth in September 1780. She had run a quantity of tea and geneva around Auchmedan Bay [not located but apparently near Gardenstown] and that on the 16th she passed Fraserburgh, steering southward 'but as the wind since that time has blown hard from the south-east quarter it is probable this vessel is at present in the Moray Firth'.

Andrew Blair was watching the coast with his boatmen in October 1780 when 'he had unexpectedly fallen in with the Flushingers at Skateraw, where they attended some run goods ... they had used him ill and hurt him and wounded one boatman. They however got away from them and have got home. James Davidson the boatman is cut in the head. We ordered a surgeon to attend him and his wound appears not dangerous'. As most of the goods had been taken on board the Flushinger again 'it is probable he is still on some part of the coast'.

Fishing Boats: The Tales of four Crichtons
At the other end of the scale there were the constant small smuggles undertaken by the fishing busses.

The *Charming Katty*

In June 1773 the collector and several officers were obstructed while making the seizure of a boat with spirits, tea and other goods on board in Stornoway harbour. The boat and a large chest, supposed to contain prohibited goods, were carried off. 'The penalty which the crew of the boat are liable to pay is much more than all of them are worth therefore they would depone before us that they were set upon us at the time of making the seizure by **William** Crichton. We beg to know if such proof would not be ground enough for a prosecution against him, who certainly be the person that ought to be prosecuted for it is surely the boat belonged to him ... the goods were taken out of the *Charming Katty*, John McDonald master, the property of Crichton, which fitted out at Kirkwall for the summer buss fishing, as she arrived in this harbour the same night the seizure was made and several of her crew appeared about us during the time we were discharging the boat and were running to and fro and lurking behind stones, no doubt with a design to carry off the goods if an opportunity offered, which was the reason of our abandoning the boat in order to secure the goods that were lying on the shore'.

When the *Charming Katty* came into port from the fishing on 21 October the master 'declared solemnly in the custom house that from the time she had been cleared outwards for the fishing at Kirkwall to that day there was no kind of goods taken on board or discharged out of her except salt, herrings and other necessaries for the fishing ... we have no means of finding ground to contradict the same'. On 5 February 1774 a messenger with two men arrived from Ross-shire with a warrant to apprehend the four men who deforced the officers. 'Two of the men we suppose are before now at Leith viz John McLeod on board the *Charming Katty* of Stornoway, **David** Crichton master, and James McIverson on board the *William*, likewise of this, Donald Ross master. The other two arrived here on Monday last before break of day on board the *Barbara* of this place, John McGuire master, from Belfast, and although diligent search has been made for them ... they could not be found. We understand they have been put out of the way by **William** Crichton, and that they will not return until the 23rd of this month expires so that we have no prospect of catching hold of them. Therefore the messenger and the party intend to leave this by the first packet'.

There was a further, somewhat odd incident, possibly involving the *Charming Katty*. A letter was found in a vessel full of water by a servant in the comptroller's kitchen on Monday night, 22 January 1787. Next morning the comptroller contacted the collector, who was attending a roup of the materials of a Swedish vessel recently driven ashore. The letter claimed that the '*Katty*' had brought a cargo of geneva from Holland in November 1786.

According to their enquiries, the *Charming Katty* had fitted out on the bounty fishing at Stornoway in July 1786, returned with a full cargo of herrings in August, proceeded to Leith with them in September and arrived at Stornoway a few days before with a new cargo of herrings from Loch Broom. Alan Morrison cleared out as master to Leith, bought another vessel there, the *Janet* of Stornoway, and got her fitted out for the fishing bounty. Recently the *Janet* had returned to Stornoway with a large quantity of herrings, said by the letter to be mostly bought at sea. She was at liberty to do this as she had been at sea for almost four months but from the master's journal and the affidavit in the sufferance inwards it did not appear that any of her cargo had been bought rather than caught. Three sailors mentioned in the letter as being aboard the *Katty* on the voyage to Holland were listed on the back of the *Janet*'s licence. 'Whether they are really the men cleared out in the *Janet* is more than we can say as the master having taken and submitted the oath as required by law ... we find ourselves entirely at a loss to know whether the matters set forth in the letter are real or fictitious'.

The *Barbara* of Stornoway

On 21 February 1786 the *Barbara* of Stornoway, **Kenneth** Crichton master, was seized by Captain Cash of the *Prince Edward* revenue cutter in Stornoway harbour. She had fitted out on the bounty fishing early in the season and cleared inwards again. The owner afterwards appointed **Kenneth** Crichton as master and took out a coasting permit for barrels of salt and nets 'in order to prosecute the winter fishing in the course of which spirits were taken on board [at Loch Kessern - not located - by order of the master] for which she is now under seizure'. The Board ordered that the vessel should be delivered up and the master prosecuted for treble the value of the spirits seized.

The *Margaret* of Stornoway

Norman Crichton was the owner and master of the *Margaret* of Stornoway, which was seized by the *Prince Ernest Augustus* for running goods. Myler Morrison, one of the mariners, 'having lately returned to the port we examined him with regard to the means used and by whom to secret himself so that he could not be found to be subpoenaed at the time of the trial, when he freely declared that **Norman** Crichton, the owner, had directed him to withdraw to secrete himself and that during the time of his concealment that he, Crichton, would pay him monthly wages such as he had when actually employed on board the *Margaret* ... All the other hands belonging to the vessel who were intended to be evidences and absconded are absent'. In August 1790 **Norman** Crichton was ordered to the pay costs incurred by prosecution against him for withholding the ship's register.

The Story of HMS *Dauntless*

On 18 September 1810 HMS *Dauntless*, commanded by Captain Barber, arrived at Lerwick from a cruise in the North Sea. That afternoon one of the officers went to the collector to find out whether a parcel of rye meal, taken out of a vessel 'deserted by the enemy', could be landed and sold. 'The officer was answered by the collector that by law no prize goods could be landed in this kingdom until after condemnation but that if HMS *Dauntless* was encumbered by having those goods on board and that it was necessary for the good of His Majesty's service to have the goods landed ... [they would be] lodged in the king's warehouse'.

The next day Captain Barber went to see the collector with Charles Ogilvie, 'a respectable merchant in Lerwick' who was prepared to purchase some of the prize goods, if possible. He later listed these as 'eighty-six bags of rye meal, nineteen bags of flour, either sixteen or twenty sacks of foreign salt, some bales of canvas, 50 yards in each bale, some coils of cordage, some fishing lines, eighty hanks of hemp, two or three hawsers, two bags of tobacco, three anchors and two graplines, some bags of pease, some bags of unground rye, some bags of hops and some bags of manna'. The collector repeated what he had said before and Barber stated that he would carry the goods to Scotland or England in his ship.

'Had we suspected that a captain in His Majesty's service could possibly ... have acted as Captain Barber has done, we would have sent an officer (the only tidesman at the port) on board, however insufficient his efforts might have been to prevent the fraud which has been committed'.

On the nights of Friday 21st and Saturday 22nd September a quantity of rye meal and other prize goods was landed. This was 'carried out in the dead of night, when it happened to be extremely dark, and in such a way are many of the warehouses in Lerwick constructed that without rowing about the harbour all night in a boat smuggling may be carried on without the possibility of detection by the officers on shore'. However, sufficient information was provided to the custom house for it to be possible to reconstruct what had happened.

'Upon the 21st or 22nd September the brig *Don* of this port, 80 tons burthen, was late at night hauled alongside of the *Dauntless*, from which vessel a parcel of coals was put into the *Dauntless* and a great quantity of rye meal ... put out of the *Dauntless* into the *Don* and upon the same night landed out of the *Don* at Lerwick'. On the night of 22 September three large boats were used to bring more goods ashore. These belonged to merchants in Lerwick: James Greig, whose boat was manned by Mouat Brock, George Hughson and Thomas Nicholson; James Hay - manned by Peter Johnson, alias Turvelson, and John Hughson and Charles Ogilvy - manned by Robert Cheyne and Magnus Mouat.

'The boats carry about two and a half tons each and each boat carried two cargoes on shore ... Charles Ogilvie ... Andrew Grierson, of Quindale, and George Sutherland senior, butcher in Lerwick, will prove ... the purser's presenting a list of goods and offering them for sale. James Sutherland, merchant in Lerwick, will prove his having gone on board the ship *Dauntless* and seeing the anchors and cables, which were offered to him for 25 guineas, but which he declined to purchase. The anchors and cables were afterwards delivered to James Greig. The goods when landed were delivered to James Hay, James Greig [six bags containing 2 to 3 cwt of rye meal were found in his warehouse] and Gilbert Angus, merchants in Lerwick. A few days after the *Dauntless* sailed, James Hay opened a sale of rye meal ... Barclay Johnson and John Williamson assisted in landing and warehousing the goods. William Clark, shopkeeper to James Hay, and Robert Laurie, master of the brig *Don*, are persons well acquainted with the particulars of James Hay's concern. The persons who landed the goods are common labourers, very poor and dependent'.

'James Hay, the person principally concerned in promoting and carrying on the present fraud has long been the greatest smuggler in the country and has acquired a large fortune. The other two persons concerned are people of shorter standing but we believe equally disposed to take every advantage of the revenue which circumstances may put their way'.

The Story of the *Tartar* of Dublin

The *Tartar* of Dublin, Captain Nanse commander, arrived at the Birchen Isles in December 1779. On the 17th Nanse went to Stornoway in the ship's boat. He explained that his vessel held a British letter of marque and had been ordered from Madeira to Gothenburg. The master produced a British register 'yet it was suspected that he was following an illicit trade as it was improbable that a ship should come from Madeira to cruise to the northward'. He returned to his ship on the 19th.

Also on the 19th the *Resolution* of Dover, Mark Bailey commander, a privateer mounting twenty 24 pounder carronades and two 6 pounders with one hundred and eighty men on board came into port. The collector told Bailey about the *Tartar* and the next day he sailed to Birchen Isles. Once Captain Nanse, Mr Gordon, a passenger, and seven of their men were on board the cutter, Bailey fired 'a few guns' at the *Tartar* and took possession of her, bringing the prize to Stornoway. The *Tartar* had sailed from Dublin with salt and linen supposedly for New York but instead she had gone to Virginia where she took on board two hundred and sixty-one hogsheads of tobacco and some staves. The ship had been to North Faro where she should have unloaded the tobacco into small vessels sent from Ireland. Her papers included an American commission for the *Dolphin*, George Hunter master, carrying sixteen guns. According to the crew this was the name the *Tartar* had passed under in America and Hunter had gone over in her. Bailey sailed with

Nanse, Gordon, the ship's doctor and one other man and both vessels 'to some British port'.

When it was too late to take any action, the collector remembered that Bailey had been in Stornoway the previous April with another privateer, the cutter *Liberty* of Dover, carrying fourteen guns. Then he was suspected of carrying on an illicit trade and soon afterwards the vessel was taken on the coast of Galloway or Ayr by some of the revenue cruisers. The *Liberty* had been recently advertised for sale at Greenock.

The Story of the *Happy Return* of Lerwick

This calendar of events has been extracted from the Lerwick custom house letters:

<u>11 September 1795</u> a sloop seen from the high ground above Lerwick, standing from the northward and eastward towards the southern part of the Island

<u>12 September</u>, morning, the collector informed she had gone into Whalsay Bay. He set off after her with military support [a sergeant and four men]. 'But upon his arrival there found that the vessel had not stopped ... but, having taken a pilot on board, proceeded to the northward. By this time it blew so hard that the collector himself stopped at Whalsay but sent the men forward to Vidlin Voe, about seven miles, further in hopes of finding the vessel there. During the absence of the boat and crew the collector got particular notice of the place to which the vessel had gone, that she was the *Happy Return* of this port, Peter Leslie master, from Bergen in Norway and that there had been landed out of her some spirits and tea in Mid Yell Voe'.

<u>13 September</u>, morning, the boat returned from Vidlin Voe and was dispatched with James Ritchie, tidesman, with directions to bring the sloop down to Lerwick. 'They proceeded immediately and found the vessel under way coming out of Mid Yell Voe, an express having been sent by the people of Whalsay, who suspected the boat's errand, to give notice to the sloop. She was however secured and again brought to anchor'.

<u>15 September</u> brought down to Bressay Sound. Ritchie and the soldiers searched unsuccessfully for prohibited goods at Mid Yell.

<u>18 September</u>, Peter Leslie took a protest against customs. 'The account which he there gives of his conduct is certainly false and completely contradicted by his journal ... We judged it most prudent for the safety of the cargo to deliver it to Andrew Grierson, the owner ... the collector having no place to put it where it was not exposed to be stolen or injured by the weather. This vessel sailed upon her fraudulent voyage almost immediately after being registered

and, with a view no doubt to conceal what was intended, intimated at this office for Liverpool the very day the certificate of registry was granted, which was the 15th August ... the vessel is new and cost £300 to £400 this last summer.' As the collector, who discharged the vessel himself, found two boxes of tea on board, containing 30 lbs each. He seized her.

According to a petition from Grierson 'the master of the vessel instead of carrying her to Papa in Shetland, as he was directed, went or was drove to Norway, where he took in a cargo of deals etc with which he returned to Lerwick on the 15th September and next morning gave in the manifest of his cargo at the custom house for entry ... the master immediately owned to the collector that the tea was his property and taken on board without the knowledge of the owner etc.'

However, the collector believed that he could prove that the vessel was 'sent to Norway by the owner, that a part of the cargo of wood was the property of James Edmondson, merchant in Lerwick, and that Mr Grierson never meant to bring the vessel to Lerwick with the cargo on her bottom or to pay duty for it'. According to the master's journal, the vessel sailed from Bressay Sound on 22 August and two days later Leslie was at Bergen, where he delivered all his letters but could not get the ballast out because of 'great rain'. Next day the ballast was unloaded and he began to load his cargo. 'From leaving Bressay Sound till his arrival in Norway the journal takes no notice of his having been blown off the coast or of his intending to go to the Island of Papa in Shetland'. The journal continued: 7th September left Bergen and 9th sighted Sumburgh Head.

Although this was the last entry, the collector could prove that Leslie then went into a bay near Grierson's house and that on the 11th in the morning he passed by the Island of Bressay to the northward. Instead of coming into Bressay Sound he went to Whalsay Bay, twelve miles from Lerwick and took in a pilot to carry him to Mid Yell Voe, over thirty miles to the north of Lerwick, where he discharged some prohibited goods and had begun to unload the wood cargo when he was detected and the vessel brought down to Lerwick. 'The two casks of tea found on board and marked E would have been out of the vessel with the rest at Mid Yell Voe, if they had not been stowed away in the heart of the cargo, which is another argument that she was never meant to come into Lerwick, as the officers must have fallen in with the tea in the course of the discharge and, as to its being the property of the master, we are not inclined to believe it. The collector's information as to the prohibited goods landed at Mid Yell was that there were from thirty to forty ankers of brandy and some packages of tea ... the witnesses to prove the fact are John Henderson, the pilot taken in at Whalsay, who helped to discharge the goods, John Work and David Burgar, two of the crew, who run away from the vessel when she was taken, Mr William Spence of Mid Yell and Mrs Agnes Archibald his wife, into whose charge the goods were delivered'.

The tailpiece to this chapter describes an enquiry into an outbreak of distemper in short-horned cattle. The next chapter considers one particular branch of smuggling: the pretended voyage.

A STORY OF AN OUTBREAK OF DISTEMPER

On 19 March 1770 the collector at Aberdeen reported to the Board 'The provost of this place having upon the 17th current received intelligence from a gentleman at Banff that there was the appearance of the distemper among the horned cattle having broke out at Portsoy, there having been nine cattle belonging to James Robertson, merchant there, [see below] which had died suddenly, he immediately sent off an express to Banff to obtain certain intelligence touching this matter and which express brought him a letter from Mr Derom provost of Banff ... being all the information can be had hitherto upon this subject it first being said that the distemper has been brought from Holland in some packages with hay or straw smuggled. Having had no advice from any of the officers at Banff or Portsoy of any vessels from Holland arriving there or being upon that coast smuggling we are at a loss what to think of this. They had all received the strictest injunctions repeatedly to be attentive in preventing the infection being brought into the country, as directed by your Honours.

'The report of its being brought in the *Diligence*, as mentioned in Mr Derom's letter, has been enquired into and it appears that the vessel came last from Newcastle with a cargo of coals which was entered here the 13 ult and cocket dated 27 January last.

'There is all appearance of this being the distemper and as it's not at all improbable that it has been brought in with some packages, which have been smuggled into Portsoy we have dispatched an express to Mr Lawtie landwaiter and the officers at Portsoy to let no ships whatever sail out of that place until strictly examined that there be no straw or hay packages on board that the infection may be no farther communicated and also to concur with the gentlemen in that neighbourhood in exerting their utmost power to prevent the spreading of this infection'.

The same day the collector wrote to George Lawtie 'We are much surprised that we have had no sort of intelligence from you or any of the officers at Portsoy of the distemper said to be broke out among the horned cattle there. But as it seems certain that the infection has been brought in to the country among hay or some packages smuggled from Holland you will upon receipt of this proceed to Portsoy and with the assistance of the officers there

contd

A STORY OF AN OUTBREAK OF DISTEMPER contd

be at the utmost pains to search every vessel in the harbour and take care that neither hay or straw of any sort or any other sort of suspected packages be concealed in any vessel nor be allowed it be exported from thence that this distemper may not by any means be suffered to spread'.

On 22 March 1770 the comptroller at Aberdeen replied to a letter from the Board 'This day came into this harbour the ship *Jean & Bell* of this place, James Cruikshank, master from Portsoy and Peterhead. As the distemper was broke out before he left Portsoy, we immediately carried him before the provost and magistrates here ... and have stationed two tidesmen and two soldiers on board his vessel to prevent any of her cargo from being landed till we have your Honours orders there anent.

'PS The collector set out for Portsoy yesterday in consequence of an order from Mr Charles Jollier which he received by express'.

The comptroller received information from the collector at Portsoy on 28 March 1770 that 'there doesn't appear to be any more distemper'. This was reported to the Board.

In the meantime 'they, with the assistance of Mr Abernethy, boatman, had examined the hold, cabin, steerage and forecastle [of the *Jean & Bell*] in the strictest manner and found nothing on board but ballast and provisions We have ordered them to remain constantly on board ... we are also advised by the tidesmen at Fraserburgh that upon the 29th inst the *Farmer & Margaret* of Portsoy, Alexander Gray master, the *Sarah* of Portsoy, James Sangster master, from Alloa load with coals and the *Mary* of Portsoy, John Horn master, from the same place with coals arrived in that creek. We have ordered the tidesmen to remain on board these vessels and to permit nothing to be brought on shore from them. The *Mary* of Portsoy was in the creek of Fraserburgh the 26th of February last from whence she sailed to load the present cargo of coals. When in the harbour of Fraserburgh she had nothing on board but ballast. This vessel is also suspected to have been of those ships by which the infectious distemper was brought to Portsoy and as warrants will be applied for to us for unloading these cargoes we beg your Honours directions whether we shall grant the same'.

contd

A STORY OF AN OUTBREAK OF DISTEMPER contd

The collector was back at Aberdeen on 3 April 1770. 'I took to my assistance one of the trustiest officers and also Mr Lawtie, landwaiter, from Banff and ... incurred a necessary expense of £11 6s 3d on our journey and support at Portsoy'.

In May 1770 the *Christian* cutter of Aberdeen, John Gyan master, ran a cargo of spirits at Cove and Findhorn, which was seized by Captain Peter Leslie of the *Meredith*. The cargo of spirits was loaded at Dorf in Holland 'when the distemper among the horned cattle was then raging'. The sheriff of Kincardine took a precognition at Stonehaven on 7 September 1770. This produced 'clear proof' that the master paid several fishermen to run the goods. It also appeared from the depositions of Alexander Gyan and Alexander Allan younger that a yawl belonging to Alexander Allan senior, fisherman at Cove, was used. 'This man, Alexander Allan senior, was in court but being examined he swore he knew nothing of the matter and it appears from the depositions of some of the other evidences that he was not on board his yawl the night on which the smuggle happened'. [The Allans were also involved in a landing at Crawton in May 1771 - see Chapter Four]. Gyan was now master of the *Baskety* of Aberdeen and 'we suspect he is presently employed in the same illicit trade'.

In 1775 there was an enquiry into a permit presented by James Robertson & Co for four hogsheads of wine delivered from Portsoy to Inverness. 'No officers would pay regard to a dispatch obtained five days after the wines were stopped ... it behooved to be discovered and answered no other purpose but to cut off the credit of the merchant and expose his villainy'. The collector went to Portsoy and showed the permit to William Aven, tidewaiter. 'He said that he never saw the paper before, that the figures and date appeared evidently none of his but that the subscription was so like his own that he could perceive no difference but he was certain he had neither gauged nor shipped any wine in hogsheads for that company at any time in the month of May'. David Greig, Robertson's cooper, explained that the original permit had been for five hogsheads to be shipped on the *Diligence* of Banff to London. When instead four hogsheads were to go to Inverness he 'cut off from the top of the note one of the hogsheads and altered the date from 15 to 24 May'. But there was no sign of the five hogsheads in the customs records. 'Upon the whole of this matter I see the baseness of Robertson & Co's conduct so much that nothing they say can be depended upon'.

CHAPTER SIX: PRETENDED BOUND

'I thought proper to acquaint you that on the 9th October last was brought into this port by stress of weather a brigantine (square-stern, burthen about 60 tons, belonging to John Gordon late of Peterhead) called the *Mary* of Leith, James Brodie master, from Rotterdam with a very considerable cargo, upwards of six hundred ankers of liquors, on board, pretending to be bound for Douglas in the Isle of Man, and consigned to one David Forbes there. But by accounts and bills of lading found in the ceiling above the master's bed it appears that the cargo belongs to several merchants in Scotland in the neighbourhood of Banff (Alexander Davidson being supercargo) freighting paid to deliver the goods there, being exempt in the bills of lading from sea hazard and searchers. Enclosed [no] is an account of the marks and numbers on the packages of the goods and to whom consigned. This vessel in now taking on board her that which had been taken out on account of damage and salvage, and may be ready to sail in about a week's time. I thought proper to give you this early notice that proper directions may be given to look out for this vessel, as her cargo is unentrable package. In case she shall be met with, I have copies of the several accounts and bills of lading found on board her, which may be of service. There is on board this vessel a hole or concealment between the decks, near the mainmast, in which it may be proper to look in case the vessel should be met with ... As Scotch vessels are sometime put into this port a correspondence might be of service if agreeable to you I shall always give you notice of anything that may be necessary'. [Letter from the collector at Whitby to the collector at Aberdeen, dated 9 February 1758 - the Aberdeen letter-books for this date no longer exist]

One of the main excuses for being in the wrong place at the wrong time was that the vessel was in fact bound for a foreign port but had been forced on to the Scottish coast through stress of weather, shortage of supplies or for one of several other familiar reasons. The customs officers found these excuses highly suspect and would refer to the vessel as 'pretended bound'. On 25 March 1747 the collector at Aberdeen wrote to all the tidesmen at the creeks 'the *Marjorie & Anne* of Montrose, a square-sterned sloop about 45 tons burthen, William Napier master, from

Campvere pretending bound for Bergen in Norway with a cargo of spirits, wine, soap, tobacco, tobacco stalks and other prohibited and high duty goods, having deforced the officers at Montrose and sailed yesterday, therefore you are to give orders to the officers under your inspection that if the vessel comes in to any of the creeks whereof you have the inspection to detain her and acquaint us by express. Likewise to keep a very strict watch to prevent the running any part of her cargo upon the coast'.

This letter from the custom house at Montrose to the tidesmen at Arbroath, Usan, Milton of Mathers, Johnshaven and Gourdon dated 4 June 1772 explains why the collectors were suspicious: hogsheads of French wine were going both north and south. 'The *Charming Baby* of Peterhead, a square sterned brigantine about 40 tons burthen, William Brodie master, lies ready to sail from Aberdeen pretending to be bound for Bergen in Norway having on board ten hogsheads of French red wine. As also a small sloop, the *Happy Return* of Newburgh, cutter-rigged about 40 tons burthen, David Wood master, lies ready to sail from Newburgh pretending to be bound for Campvere, having on board eight hogsheads of red French wine'.

It was not always possible for the customs to prove their suspicions or to catch a vessel in the very act of running her cargo. When it was apparent that a smuggle might have taken place, the evidence needed included information about the weather that particular day and on the preceding few days to support or disprove any claim of 'distress', the state of the vessel and the amount of provisions on board together with proof that the vessel had hovered within two leagues of the shore and the names of the owners and crews of boats hired to run any part of the cargo.

It is not a coincidence that most of the examples given in this chapter come from the eastern outports [see Figure 7, which indicates some of the more common 'pretended bound' routes] but the Stornoway collector also identified similar problems - see the story of the *Daniel*, which is described below. In this cases the vessel pretended that she was bound from Ireland to Danzig. A standard excuse for heading towards the west coast was that the vessel was bound for the Isle of Man.

Stress of Weather

The commonest excuse given by a master for being off course was that he had been 'forced on to the coast by stress of weather'. In December 1748 the tidesmen at Stonehaven sent an express to the collector at Aberdeen informing him that the *Prince William*, James Stewart master, from Campvere had been put in there 'by stress of weather'. Eventually the master reported six hundred and twenty casks, big and small, forty matts, twenty boxes big and small, three chests quantity unknown for Bergen, explaining the delay because 'his ship was not safely moored and he was indisposed by reason of the stormy weather he had at sea, which he undertakes to prove'. He promised to give a hovering bond but on 13 July 1749 'he deforced the officers on board his ship and went to sea'.

The *John & Jean* of Sunderland, Andrew Baxter master, 200 tons burthen, was boarded by Mr Vitty in the Aberdeen Road on 6 September 1770. He had first seen her off Bervie and then she had sailed close to the coast to anchor a mile from Aberdeen harbour mouth. Her cocket, dated 18 August, was for fifty-six chalders of coals for Copenhagen. As the journey from Sunderland should only have taken forty-eight hours, she was brought into harbour and the coal was unloaded into lighters. Seven feet down Vitty found seven hundred ankers of geneva. The master alleged he was put upon the coast by contrary winds. But Vitty could prove the wind was at south and south-east for four days before he boarded the vessel.

Want of Provisions

On 1 November 1748 the *Prince Charles*, Alexander Stewart master, arrived at Portsoy from Rotterdam with flax for that port and wine etc for Bergen. The same day the master went to the custom house and made a report. On 18 November he entered into a hovering bond and the *Prince Charles* sailed 'upon her pretended voyage'. She was back in Portsoy on the 20th 'the weather being stormy' and John Rollo, the landwaiter, was ordered to take a look at the cargo, which had not changed. 'Since that time the weather has been very stormy and the vessel continued at Peterhead'. Then on 21 December Rollo reported that the master 'after having continued so long at Peterhead, where had she wanted provisions or anything else necessary for the pretended voyage

1. A list of some of the vessels 'pretended bound' between Rotterdam and Bergen, indicating where and when they appeared on the Scottish coast
Rotterdam to Bergen:
  Happy Isobel of Fraserburgh: Cromarty 1750
  Mary & Jean of Aberdeen: Peterhead 1747
  Katherine of North Berwick: Peterhead 1747
  Swallow of Rotterdam: Portsoy 1747
Bergen to Rotterdam:
  Pretty Peggie of Fraserburgh: Fraserburgh 1748

2. Some of the vessels 'pretended bound' for North Faro, indicating where and when they appeared on the Scottish coast
From Campvere:
  Ann of Portsoy: Arbroath 1778
From Bordeaux:
  Jean of Portsoy: Cromarty 1775
From Bergen:
  Meanwell of Spey: Spey 1780

Figure 7: Pretended Voyages: A Story of North Faro

On 16 January 1778 the brigantine *Ann* of Portsoy, John Simpson master, 50 tons burthen, from Campvere was put into the harbour of Arbroath 'by a violent gale of wind'. The master reported that 'he left Campvere upon the 13th inst. This we have great reason to believe is not fact but are rather of opinion that this vessel has been smuggling to the northward, as she is at present not half laden. We thought proper to give you [the collectors at neighbouring outports] this information and entreat you will endeavour to learn if she has been either smuggling or hovering on any part of the coast within the district of your port'.

At 11 o'clock on 17 January the master went to Montrose custom house where he reported that his cargo consisted of two hundred and fifty-eight ankers, three half ankers, ten matts tobacco, two dry casks, six bundles and five hogsheads consigned to George Rosenmeyer & Co, merchants in North Faro. When the collector and surveyor went to Arbroath early on 18 January, 'the master acknowledged to them that he had omitted out of his intimation sixty-seven ankers and three hampers belonging to himself and his men'. Mr Garden, his crew and the coastwaiter were ordered to make a strict rummage which 'they found could not be a done before tomorrow as the hatches had not yet been opened. Notwithstanding they found ten or twelve pieces of Indian silks concealed under the master's bed ... we were informed by William Blews, tidesman, that an attempt was made last night to carry some of the goods on shore and several ankers were brought to deck for that purpose'.

The Board instructed the collector to examine the master and sailors separately with respect to the place where the goods were shipped, the time when they sailed, the winds and weather during the voyage and the different courses kept throughout and to enquire of the sailors whether they were engaged by the master or for the run and in either case for what place they were understood to be bound. But 'the crew of the ship had left her immediately after she came into the harbour of Arbroath for fear of the Press and were gone to their respective places of abode before we had an opportunity of examining them'. The collector wrote to Portsoy, where Alexander Cook, commander of the revenue boat, was stationed. On 8 February Cook reported that 'the cargo belongs to Patrick Brown, James Imlach and Primrose Robertson, merchants, and Andrew Mitchell, baker in Portsoy, William Anderson and John Young, merchants in Cullen and Alexander Young and John James, merchants in Elgin'. The *Ann* was wrecked at Burghead on 15 February 1785, after running a cargo of spirits and tobacco.

she had sufficient time to be provided yet when the wind proved fair for this ship to proceed the master, pretending his provisions were at Fraserburgh, intimate by protest to Mr Rollo that he behooved to proceed to that place for same, which he accordingly did'.

On 2 February 1749 the Board sent orders that the *Prince Charles* should be seized. In the meantime a party of soldiers [a sergeant and twelve private men, two on duty during the daytime and four at night] had been kept on board - these remained until 4 March, when she was brought round to Aberdeen. The case was tried in the court of exchequer, where the ship and cargo were found not to be a seizure.

In August 1770 James Wilson, formerly on board a boat belonging to Duncan Aire's ship *Royal Charlotte* [see Chapter Ten], brought the *Janet* of Johnshaven (20-25 tons) 'with the sole purpose of smuggling'. She sailed from Johnshaven in ballast and went to Bergen, which port she left on 28 August bound for Campvere. Four days later she was in Johnshaven 'for provisions'. According to the surveyor there were 25 lbs beef, one pilote of oatmeal, 3 lbs weight candle, 6 lbs barley but no bread or water on board. The mainsail was torn from head to foot and the main boom was broken. The collector was suspicious. 'How the concerned of her could propose to make a freight by becoming a carrier from Bergen to Campvere with five hogsheads - three French red wine and two white - and a few deals to support the master and four other hands on board is beyond our comprehension'.

On 11 September the master told the surveyor that he would go to the custom house to report his cargo. But on 14 September the collector received an express from Alexander Simpson, the tidesmen stationed on board, that at one o'clock in the morning a mob had assembled, boarded the vessel, beat down the officers who were on watch and carried off two of the hogsheads, which were later found empty on the beach. Several of the deals were also missing. The military brought the remaining hogsheads of wine to Montrose by land carriage. The wine was still in the warehouse the following April. 'Two of these hogsheads being red are sour and unmerchantable, the other white is of poor quality'. They were put up for sale on 19 April 1771 'but nobody appeared to bid'. [See also Chapter Nine: The Tidesmen at Gourdon - James Philip]

Illness on Board

The tidesmen at Stonehaven sent an express to the collector at Aberdeen on 12 November 1750 stating that the *Three Brothers* of Aberdeen, Charles Leys master, from Campvere pretending bound to Aberdeen and Bergen had arrived at that creek. 'We ordered out two officers from this port to come round with the vessel and be very careful that no embezzlement happened'. She arrived on the 13th 'whereupon Mr Ogilvie, tidesurveyor, boarded her and gave strict charge to the officers on board'. The master did not report until 15 November because both he and his mate had been seized with a fit of ague 'which indeed seemed to be true by the master's appearance'. The report was of old iron, cordage and flax for Aberdeen and a number of small casks and bundles, quality unknown, for Bergen. But Thomson, general supervisor of excise at Aberdeen, and Thomson, supervisor at Montrose, had put a party of soldiers on board because they had heard the master had broken bulk. All the goods were seized.

On 29 May 1780 Alexander Cook, commander of the king's boat at Portsoy, boarded the *Meanwell* of Spey, Alexander Brand master, about six miles off Portknockie. She was from Bergen with wine, salt and wood and claimed to be bound for North Faro. She had gone into Spey in the night time to land a passenger on board, William Falconer merchant in Garmouth, who was suffering from 'sore eyes', and to take in provisions. Cook found two boxes of tea floating beside the vessel and so he took her into Portsoy. Cook gave 'a particular account of the provisions he found on board'. But he 'could perceive no such cause of complaint', when he looked at Falconer's eyes. There was no information that the *Meanwell* had been in two leagues of the shore or within the limits of a port before Cook boarded her. Nor was there evidence of any boats being hired for running the goods from her.

The cargo, which included wine in French and Portuguese hogsheads, belonged to Primrose Robertson, Patrick Brown and James Imlach, merchants in Portsoy; Jacob Anderson, merchant in Lochaber and John Hanna, William Falconer, James Allan, John Cumming and Edward Norman, merchants in Garmouth. Part also belonged to merchants in Forres but the master did not know their names. Imlach subsequently sent a petition to the Board about the seizure.

Wrong Time of Year

In November 1764 the *Daniel* of Stornoway, Daniel Morrison master, with 20 tons Irish salt, 19 cwt wrought iron, five hides, three hogsheads English porter, twelve barrels oatmeal and three pieces Irish linen from Ireland arrived at Birchen Isles and the master went to Stornoway to get her mast repaired.

'The circumstance of the vessel's burthen, which the people here acknowledge at the utmost to be no more than 40 tons, together with her being bound to Danzig at so unseasonable time of the year make it more than probable that she intended to run her cargo but that she had any such intention or run any part of it has not hitherto been in our power to fish out, the people here being so strongly attached to one another'.

Chased by a privateer

On 30 May 1760 the *Margaret & Marjory*, James Brebner master, from Campvere was brought into Fraserburgh from Banff by Mr Murray of the *Princess Ann* sloop with spirits, tobacco, tobacco stalks and tea on board. The next day James Watson, the mate, went to the custom house as the master was unable to go there himself. The vessel was bound for Bergen but having lost her bowsprit in a storm and been chased by a French privateer was obliged to steer for the coast of Scotland.

There were so many privateers and other foreign vessels around the coasts that this was a difficult story to disprove. On 9 January 1779 the *Elizabeth* of Aberdeen, James Martin master, between 40 and 50 tons burthen, from Campvere with about half a cargo of apples, linseed flax and wood hoops for Aberdeen was forced ashore on the sands to the east of Montrose by a Flushing cutter. The *Elizabeth* was off Johnshaven, when she fell in with the cutter. As the master explained this vessel 'gave him chase, she fired several shot at him and he not knowing but she might be an enemy's ship, stood close to the land till he struck upon the bar. The vessel stood off and on all night and at daylight next morning he discovered her to be a Flushing cutter with her boat astern'. When the *Elizabeth* was refloated and brought into Montrose, David Garden and his crew [see Chapter Ten] found on board sixteen stone bottles and ten dozen choppin bottles containing 66 gallons of geneva, one dozen choppin bottles of French red wine, one dozen choppin bottles white wine, one paper parcel containing 6 lbs nutmegs, one paper parcel containing 3½ lbs cinnamon and one paper parcel containing 3½ lbs camphor, which were seized.

Lack of papers

The *Betty* of Rosemarkie, Donald Edic master, cleared out from Prestonpans on 28 August 1749 with 872 bushels of salt for Hamburg. Three days later Mr Lobban, landwaiter, reported that she had arrived at Peterhead with the wind at the north-west, pretending bound for Drunton in Norway. The collector at Aberdeen forwarded to the Board 'the master's account [not transcribed] for his not having a cocket, which we look upon as nothing but evasion'. The *Prince William* sloop, Captain Read commander, was advised of the vessel.

Wrong direction

On 27 August 1765 Duncan Aire, commander of the *Royal Charlotte* excise yacht, boarded the *Elizabeth* of Down, William Watt master, off Troup Head. She was from Danzig with spruce beer, soap in firkins and starch, pretending to be bound for Lisbon. He stayed on board until the morning of the 28th, when finding her to steer a different course from that to Lisbon, he boarded her and the master then told him that he was to go to Bergen … upon which he [Duncan Aire] brought her into Fraserburgh. On the 31st the master went to the custom house with an intimation of his voyage and his affidavit together with that of one of his crew touching the voyage'. The vessel was allowed to proceed.

Double Report

Sometimes when vessels were 'caught' or came into a legal port they would make a double report, claiming that some of their cargo was for that port and the rest for overseas. The double report tended to make the collectors suspicious. In February 1747 the collector at Aberdeen wrote to John Rollo 'we expected before now you would have acquainted us whether the goods on board the *Swallow* of Rotterdam, George Bain master, pretending bound for Bergen … agreed in every article with the master's report and especially the quality of the goods … if there be the least difference you are to stop her and acquaint us. You will take care that you be present with the officers at Portsoy when the ship sails and be sure to acquaint the officers to the northward and southward'.

By a letter of the same date the collector wrote to the officers at Inverness 'The *Swallow* ... a square-sterned brigantine of about 60 tons ... lies now ready to sail from Portsoy with the following goods ... to wit five hogsheads, four half hogsheads, spirits or wine, three ankers of spirits, two firkins and four half firkins soap, fifteen bundles, five casks quality unknown. We have given orders to our officers at Portsoy to run an express along the coast immediately upon this ship's sailing to advise your officer at Portknockie and he to advise his neighbouring officer so that all your officers may be put on their guard, which we always do in such cases but we thought it our duty to acquaint you in case the master intends to run any part or whole of the cargo that you may give proper directions'.

On 10 April 1747 the *Magdalene* of Arbroath, Andrew Law master, came into Peterhead bay from Norway bound for Newburgh and on 12th in the forenoon she came into Newburgh, where she was boarded by Mr Lobban, landwaiter. The master reported that he had a cargo of wood for Newburgh, Peterhead or Stonehaven and no other place. As Lobban suspected that there were some prohibited or high duty goods on board the collector sent Captain Starks' mate and a party of soldiers to Newburgh. On their arrival the master then 'appeared to Mr Lobban and told him that he had also on board his ship some oil and brandy for the Isle of Man'. A complete list was made of the cargo. The master granted a hovering bond and on the 10th May she sailed from Newburgh. 'Upon the 17th [she] came into Fraserburgh having nothing on board but ballast and the master told that he had been at the Isle of Man and discharged his cargo there ... however we apprehend it is hardly possible to make such a quick voyage as the master pretends to have done'.

In July 1775 Henderson, mate of the *Royal Charlotte* excise sloop, Duncan Aire commander, boarded the *Dolphin* of Portsoy, Alexander Robb master, from Boulogne off Troup Head loaded with wine pretending bound for Bergen. The master said that he was first to call at Portsoy for orders so Henderson 'parted from her without putting any hands on board. That evening her cargo was run off Portsoy, except fourteen hogsheads of wine and twelve tierces of vinegar, which were reported, entered and discharged. The wine was run into a cellar belonging to James Robertson & Co, hard by the harbour at Portsoy. The collector went to Portsoy and discovered 'this cellar is just opposite to the harbour and the place the wine landed is hard by it at the back of the quay'. If the officers, John Barras and William Aven, tidesmen, had been on the quay they would have discovered the smuggling. But as the tide was out they were not there between midnight and three o'clock as 'they thought nothing could happen in that time'.

On 5 September 1775 the collector wrote to Barras and Aven 'Having laid before the Honourable Board the charge we lately gave you ... in relation to your neglect of duty in not watching the harbour of Portsoy upon the evening of the 19th and morning of the 20th July last ... They have been pleased to direct us severely to reprimand you, which we hereby do, for not attending you duty agreeable to your printed instructions, which are that when you are posted upon duty by night or day you are not to leave the same till duly discharged, which ought to have been observed by you. One of you who had the watch ought not to have left his post until relieved by the other in which case the fraud detected by the officers of excise would have been discovered by you. We further acquaint you that upon any future occasion if you shall be found negligent in the execution of your duty you will be dismissed. You are to take notice that its being low water will be no excuse for your not attending the harbour'.

The *Peggie* of Aberdeen, David Gray master, from St Martins bound for Aberdeen to get orders from his owners whether to unload there or proceed to Bergen was boarded by Alexander Ritchie, commanding a boat belonging to the *Princess Caroline* sloop, off the Cove on 13 May 1775. The ship came into harbour with the night tide and on 15 May came to the quay. When he delivered her to Andrew Rutherford, tidesurveyor, Ritchie stated that he had seen a sloop in the offing for three or four days, which he believed to be the *Peggie*, but he did not comment about the weather at that time.

The master made his report on 16 May including a parcel of salt, forty-four hogsheads of wine, nine casks, twelve boxes prunes, three casks almonds, a parcel of cork and hoops for Aberdeen and forty-two hogsheads and two half hogsheads of French wine for Bergen. Both lots of wine were taken ashore as the collector was suspicious because the master had not commented on the clear marks indicating ownership of the French wine. The owner, Thomas Bannerman, complained that 'the wines lodged will suffer by the heat of the sun as we have no vault to lodge [them in] and proposing to give us a vaulted cellar hard by the custom house, below ground, where he says they will be out of danger ... he will give us any security that nothing shall touch the wines and they will also be under the charge of the watch upon the custom house and secure locks put upon this vault'. This time the vessel was returned as a seizure and her hull was burned in July.

Sometimes the distress was genuine. On 13 June 1749 the collector received a letter from the tidesmen at Peterhead about the *Thomas* of Kincardine, William Nicol master, from Rotterdam, pretending bound for Bergen. On 14 June the mate went to the custom house and produced a certificate from Dr Gordon of Peterhead, attesting that the master was not able to travel. 'The mate could not condescend on the quality of the cargo and as the master nor mate made no proof of distress we ordered the tidewaiters to stop the vessel'. On 17 June William Nicol produced a protest taken by James Mullikins, his supercargo, saying she was 'put into Peterhead by reasons of a strong northerly wind'. The affidavits of Mullikins and Nicol and William Sim, master of the *Janey* of Alloa, and James Murray, his mate, confirmed that Nicol was in great distress at sea for want of provisions. He had been given two ankers water, three dozen biscuit and some coals by the *Janey*, which also had been put into Peterhead by a strong wind from the north.

The tailpiece tells the story of the pretended voyage of the *Margaret* of Arbroath, David Lamb master. In the next chapter the problems of hovering off the coast are emphasised by the number of smuggling vessels that were wrecked.

A STORY OF THE *MARGARET* OF ARBROATH

On 22 June 1790 David Fowler and his boat's crew (then at Stonehaven) 'accompanied by David Findlay, tidesman stationed at Stonehaven, went from hence by land as far to the southward as Braidon Bay in expectation that goods might be smuggled there that night, having previously learnt that the *Margaret* was expected on the coast. About two o'clock on the morning of the 23rd inst observing a boat come from sea and stand into Braidon bay they immediately went to Catterline (a fishing creek about half a mile to the northward) and procured a fishing boat on board which Fowler and four of his crew went in order to prevent the boat first mentioned from getting out to sea again. The other two boatmen and Findlay proceeded by land to Braidon shore to secure said boat on that side. Upon their coming up to the boat on the sea side they observed one man in her, who upon their approach quitted her and ran off but being met by the land party was by them brought back. Another man had been on board said boat but made his escape and has not since been seen. At the time of coming up with the boat there were two ankers geneva on board her and two more and a box containing manufactured tobacco (supposed about a hundred weight) lying on the beach. They made a seizure of the boat, geneva and tobacco. The man whom they had seen in the boat said she belonged to and had come from David Lamb's sloop, which he had left the night before at four or five o'clock about four leagues off the shore. Having sent off the boat and goods to Stonehaven under the charge of one of the boatmen and Findlay, they again went to Catterline and procured a large fishing boat in which they put to sea and proceeded in quest of the sloop *Margaret*. About eleven o'clock of the forenoon of the 23rd they got sight of the sloop, then about 10 leagues off shore standing to sea with her topsail set. When they had got within two miles of her she put about and stood towards them till they were within half a mile, when her head was again turned to sea and she was laid to. Upon boarding her they found only two persons on board viz the master and a seaman, name unknown. The master said he had come from Flushing and was bound to North Faro with one hundred and ninety-six ankers geneva, fifty ankers rum and five boxes manufactured tobacco. Upon being told that his boat had been seized with four ankers geneva and one box manufactured tobacco he said he had sent her ashore for provisions and that the goods had been put in her for ballast. They examined his provisions and found he had on board about half a hundred weight bread, half an anker of beef and one hogshead and an anker of water. The crew had consisted of the master and three mariners. The

contd

A STORY OF THE *MARGARET* OF ARBROATH contd

wind being southerly they carried the vessel into Stonehaven but being apprehensive of the smugglers in that neighbourhood they had judged it expedient to bring her here [Montrose], also the boat and goods seized. Beside the provisions aforementioned there were two or three pecks of oatmeal on board ... Finding the man who was on board the boat at the time of seizure to be no-wise partial to the master they have kept him in hopes of his being brought to divulge what he knows respecting the voyage.

'We have examined the man, who says his name is Alexander Ferguson, that he belongs to Aberdeen, that previous to this voyage he had been one voyage along with Lamb to Sunderland for a cargo of lime, part of which was discharged at Braidon and the remainder at Stonehaven. Lamb there engaged him to go with him another voyage but did not inform him of the destination. After they had put to sea he was informed that they were bound overseas. The crew outwards consisted of the master, four Flushing seamen who had belonged to a vessel that had been seized and himself. The crew on the present voyage from Flushing consisted of the master and two men, whose names were George and John but their surnames he never heard, and himself. George, he believes, is originally from Newburgh in Aberdeenshire but is married and resident at Flushing, as is John also. The master told him at Flushing that he was bound for North Faro. They left Flushing on Sunday the 13th inst. They arrived on this coast on Saturday the 19th inst when they saw land, which he supposes was the Todhead. They then lay to and stood off and on (although the wind blew strongly from the south) from the period of their arrival on the coast to the afternoon of Tuesday the 22nd inst, when between the hours of two and four in the afternoon he was ordered into the boat along with George. Four ankers geneva, one box tobacco, some bread and water were put into the boat. He received no orders respecting the destination of the boat, that having been entrusted to George. When the boat landed George ordered him to put ashore the goods on the beach while he went for people to carry them off. During George's absence the boat and goods were seized. He cannot say how near the vessel might have been to the land at the time they first saw it nor during the days on which they stood off and on nor at the time he quitted the vessel but insists that he is certain that she never at nor during any of those periods was within four leagues of the shore ...

'PS Ferguson says that the vessel had never been boarded by any boat since her leaving Flushing till he quitted her nor had any goods been put out of her other than those sent ashore with him'.

CHAPTER SEVEN: WRECK!

'I am sorry to acquaint your Grace that we have just received advice from London that a Swedish ship with a very large parcel of teas belonging to the merchants of Douglas was lost in the north-west Highlands in some part of Lord Cromarty's estate. Besides the loss of the duties to your Grace, I am afraid it will bear hard on some of the concerned for although the cargo may be insured yet it will be long before they recover their money and at least will be attended with great loss'. [Letter from Governor Lindesay, Castletown, Isle of Man, to the Duke of Atholl dated 18 March 1745]

The custom house letter-books for the northern shores include frequent references to wrecks. One of the problems facing the smuggling vessels was that they had to hover off the coast, sometimes in bad weather, so that the chances of being wrecked were greater than if they had headed directly for a port. This chapter describes some of the instances when it became obvious that the wrecked vessel was, in fact, a smuggler.

The *Friendship* of Portsoy and the *Jean* of Findhorn

The *Friendship* of Portsoy, James Gray master, was one of two vessels attempting to smuggle tea from Gothenburg that were wrecked in November 1780. On Friday night, 3 November John Kilman, master of a boat at Sandend, and his crew took five boatloads of tea ashore from the *Friendship*. At three o'clock the next morning William Aven, tidesman at Portsoy, 'hearing a noise in town' got out of bed and went into the street. 'Meeting a woman whose name he does not know, he asked her what all the stir was about. She told him the *Buck of Garden*, meaning the *Friendship*, was put ashore near Sandend ... as he had a son, mariner on board, he proceeded directly to Sandend, being anxious about his safety. Before he got to the place where the ship lay on the sands, being about four o'clock in the morning, the master, another sailor and his son had got ashore and he met them opposite to the vessel. At this time no goods had come ashore that he saw nor did any come until about half an hour afterwards, when the ship went all to pieces and the packages with the teas were passed ashore by the sea and scattered all over the beach ... he employed four country people and four fishers to collect the packages and by seven o'clock they were all collected ...

'Being interrogate why he did not call upon his brother officer and upon Mr Cook and his boatmen, when he had intelligence of this vessel being ashore, as it appears to us impossible for he himself to secure the revenue and prevent embezzlements, he said he was so much taken up with the danger he apprehended his son would be in that he thought of nothing else. When he was arrived near the ship, as soon as he could find anyone to engage to go for these officers, he employed three or four at different times to go. He was told by one of these people that they heard of these officers on their way to the place of the strand.

'Mr Cook says that about seven o'clock in the morning one of his boatmen came and informed him that John Barras had been just told that the *Friendship* was ashore near Sandend upon which he himself and the boatmen and John Barras set out as fast as they possibly could, John Barras calling on his way to William Aven at his house to go with them [but Aven was on the shore already]. Upon their coming to the sands, where the ship was stranded, they found many of the goods scattered along the beach on the sands. The precise quantity he cannot say but they think about one half of them, which they assisted to collect and secure. John Barras went off directly for the military from Banff'.

The collector was clearly displeased with Aven, 'it appearing to us that it could not be in his power to do this [secure the cargo] considering that the smugglers and country people, who are generally in their interest, would do everything they could to carry off the goods'. Despite this Aven had seized forty-three boxes and twenty-seven casks of tea while the other officers seized a further twenty-eight boxes, forty-four casks and a canister. These contained 382 lbs fine tea, 843 lbs coarse tea and 3½ lbs green tea, all sound, and 4,953 lbs fine tea and 2,352 lbs coarse tea totally damaged.

'There has been no proof offered to us by the master of the vessel or otherways of any duress bringing her on this coast or to the nature and intention of the voyage. We are informed that the vessel went all to pieces and everything belonging to her lost'. Aven was instructed to encourage his son to keep better company in the future.

On 7 November 1780 the collector received a letter from George Lawtie, landwaiter, informing him that the *Jean* of Findhorn [alias the *Marjory*], Alexander Lyle master, was put ashore at the Bar of Banff. He replied immediately 'Mr Garden, tidesurveyor, set out from this last night and will have been with you before this reaches you. You are in conjunction with him to use every means in your power to save the cargo and lodge it in a secure place and give the strictest attention to prevent any embezzlement'. Garden reported on 8 November that the *Jean's* cargo was properly secured 'and guarded by the officers of the revenue and military'. They had managed to salvage seventy-one boxes and forty-three casks of tea and two sets of china.

According to a report from the collector to the Board dated 7 December 1780, the *Jean* 'was twice within the limits [of the port] and actually unload a small part of her cargo before being taken with the storm in which she ran ashore'. Alexander Fraser, merchant in Forres, had applied to the Board for the delivery of the vessel [reckoned to be about 40 tons burthen] to her owners, upon their granting bond for her appraised value. As a result Robert Nicol and Neil McCallum, two of the boatmen, had appraised her at £52 sterling. The collector recommended to the Board that this bond should be accepted as it would avoid the cost of getting the vessel off the Bar. In the meantime Lyle, the master, had presented an intimation of distress.

There was a further complication over the claim of John Fordyce, tidewaiter at Portknockie, 'pretending to have had an interest in the saving and securing the teas saved'. Robert Henry, tidewaiter at Down, had presented a petition to James Duff, one of the justices of the peace, 'praying that a precognition might be taken before him in relation to the circumstances of saving and securing the cargo'. From this precognition it appeared that Robert Henry and Thomas Miln, tidesmen at Down, and James McNure, excise officer at Down, were the first revenue officers at the wreck. 'Robert Henry sent off Thomas Miln and afterwards James McNure to Banff for a party of military to their assistance, which they

Figure 8: The *Happy Isobel* of Fraserburgh

The *Happy Isobel*, Joseph Simpson master, was bound from Rotterdam to Aberdeen and Bergen. But ...

2 November 1750 she went past Fraserburgh up the Moray Firth with the wind to the south. This was the first time she was observed upon the coast.

7 November officers were put on board at Cromarty because of some tobacco not mentioned in her manifest. When the tidesurveyor, Mr Dingwall, went on shore, the mate put to sea with Thomas Forbes, tidesman, still aboard.

8 November she passed Fraserburgh to the south, the wind west-south-west.

10 November she came to anchor in Peterhead Bay. Alexander Law, merchant in Fraserburgh, went on board and ordered her to sail to Bergen. Thomas Forbes 'endeavoured to put a stop to [this] but being afraid as he could get no assistance from the shore was obliged to come ashore in the pilot boat [he arrived at Aberdeen on 13 November]. She sailed southward with the wind north-west.

12 - 15 November anchored near Slains. On the 15th, when the wind came to the south, she set sail back to Fraserburgh Bay, where she anchored and one of the hands went ashore. In the afternoon she went to the south, the wind then north-west. That night she anchored in Peterhead Bay.

16 November she sailed away.

18 November she returned to Fraserburgh Bay.

19 November came to anchor off Fraserburgh but the wind increasing she was obliged to make sail. About two o'clock she was put ashore on the rocks, the wind at north-west.

20 November the tidesmen at Fraserburgh were instructed secure any salvaged goods under joint custody with the admiral substitute [provost of Aberdeen].

23 November George Reid, the mate, as the master was unable to travel, came to the custom house with a list of the goods 'demanding liberty to export the cargo in another vessel'. He wanted to have access to the goods 'so as they might be cared for and dried. We refused to take his report ... But wrote Mr Lobban to give liberty with the consent of the admiral to allow the damaged goods to be taken care of and dried ... and when done to secure all again'.

6 December the admiral substitute demanded access to the goods and liberty to expose them for sale for exportation. The collector referred this to the Board.

27 December according to the magistrates, the goods from the *Happy Isobel* could not be brought round until the salvage was paid 'whereupon we intimate to them that they must be answerable for any damages or embezzlements that may happen from this delay'.

very soon obtained. Robert Henry assisted in saving and getting ashore the master and crew and also the master's chest, in which he thought there might be some papers in relation to the nature of the voyage and he therefore secured the chest in a house at some little distance from the place where the vessel lay and immediately returned back to the ship. It appears from the proof taken that John Fordyce behaved in a most insolent manner to Mr Lawtie, his superior officer, and the other officers, by giving them abusive language and that he appeared also to be too often hurt with liquor'.

As late as 4 January 1785 the collector transmitted a statement of the proportion of the seizure money owing to McNure. This totalled £59 8s 6½d, including £2 9s expenses. From this had to be deducted £16 18s 2½d [his proportion of the solicitor's account - £112 13s 7½d] and £16 3s 10d [his proportion of the expense of defending against the claim of John Fordyce]. This left £26 6s 6d. But 'We acquainted your Honours in our letter of the 24th ult that arrestments were laid on at the instance of McNure's creditors in the collector's hands and a process ... is depending here anent before the magistrates'.

The *Dispatch* of Aberdeen

At about nine o'clock on the morning of 28 January 1772 the sloop *Dispatch* of Aberdeen, Peter Moor master, was driven on to the Bing (beach) of Bervie. James Philip, the tidesman at Gourdon [see Chapter Nine], sent an express to the collector, stating that he had been on board the vessel at ten that morning and she was bound for Aberdeen in ballast from London. As he did not enclose any 'document or other voucher' proving that she really was from London, the collector was suspicious. 'We had reason to think that she was really from foreign parts and that she had been smuggling along the coast'. The collector also 'desired' Philip to seize the sloop but as he explained to the Board subsequently 'this was only meant that he should detain her till we had received further information concerning her. But from that we never intended that she should be his property as a seizure, as we knew we could not trust him'.

The following day, about five o'clock in the evening, the collector received a second express from Philip 'giving an account that he had wrote his former letter in a hurry upon what the master had told him upon his first going aboard the vessel. But that afterwards he was informed that there had been tobacco stalks taken out of her after she came ashore upon the beach. Immediately upon this intelligence the comptroller, surveyor and Mr Arbuthnott, landwaiter, set out for Bervie with a party of the military. Having patrolled the streets and beach all that night they began a search in the town for what part of the cargo might still have been there. Next morning they fell in with and seized one hundred and ninety-one matts of tobacco stalks in two houses of the town and having continued their search all that day they found nothing else but some sails and rigging belonging to the vessel, which they collected together and deposited in the excise warehouse at Bervie.

'It is remarkable that this vessel no sooner came ashore than the crew set immediately to the unrigging of her and cut the shrouds ... the surveyor judged it his duty from the information he had received upon the spot that both tobacco stems and spirits had been smuggled out of her, even after she struck upon the bing [beach] of Bervie, and that she had come from Dunkirk, which place she left on the 19th January last, to seize her with her rigging, float boat and furniture. To this he was the rather excited from the appearance of the master and several smugglers both from Aberdeen and even from Dundee, who have advertised her to be sold by public roup on Wednesday next at ten o'clock, and the running of continued expresses to Aberdeen and other parts of the coast upon this subject ...

'The surveyor is informed that with very small reparation she might be made to swim and brought about hither, unless an easterly storm of wind comes in which will infallibly destroy her. The crew of this vessel went to Aberdeen the next morning after she struck and nobody belonging to her has appeared, except the master, who seems to be an audacious desperate fellow'.

When the collector and other officers attended the auction, 'a protest was first taken against them for detention of the vessel and immediately afterwards she was exposed to sale and nominally purchased by one Fladden, a merchant in Aberdeen, for £64, who we find was one of her former owners ... as the charges of so many soldiers as we were obliged to employ in guarding and protecting the rigging and furniture was like to become very considerable, we caused the same to be carried from the excise warehouse ... and gave the charge of her to William Blews, leaving with him four soldiers, sending the other two home, with directions to Blews to employ proper hands to rig and bring her about hither, if it was practical, the then next tide, as it was the top of the stream. But if it so happened that she did not float, Blews has along with him another trusty officer, because we did not think it proper to employ James Philip'.

The vessel was 'detained in that place some days after she was appraised by storms of north-east winds, which would not permit her to come to sea'. In order to get her off the beach, 'it was found necessary to lay out the anchor for assisting wind the vessel ... and as no time was to be lost in bringing the sloop hither they came away without it and when she came into the harbour the mariners who were employed in that service were desired by us to use their utmost endeavours to regain the anchor but we heard no more of that matter till the 27 April, when having understood that it was found and in possession of a man in Bervie [Joseph Kydd, merchant] we wrote to James Philip and directed him to go and seize the same and bring it hither, which he did'.

The *Dispatch* was set up for sale at £135, the appraised value, on 20 March. 'Nobody offered upon her' but later Charles Thomson, writer in Montrose, proposed a payment of 90 guineas, on behalf of someone else. The shipbuilder who appraised her now admitted 'she suffered some damage on Bervie beach after he saw her'. On 8 April she was sold to Charles Thomson for £120 10s. In May Thomson sent a petition to the Board demanding that he should be given her anchor, as part of the sale price. 'As to the allegation of Mr Thomson being told ... that the purchaser of the vessel would have a title to it we have made enquiry into the truth of it, as Mr Thomson says he was told so by Charles Reid, clerk here. But he absolutely denies he ever said so'.

The case of the *Dispatch* occupied the collector's correspondence for some time to come. As late as 1777 Philip was still claiming that he seized her the 'first day she was on the beach'. But the collector could produce detailed proof that this was not so. As Alexander and James Gowan and Robert Watt [the collector's three main witnesses] had been on the beach since seven o'clock in the morning, the master asked them to look after the wreck. 'When he [James Philip] thought proper to appear in the road from his own house at midday the smugglers no sooner spied him than they went directly to meet him, and after going all in a body to the town of Bervie without his coming to the ship, which was only 200 yards from them, when they no doubt settled all matters among them'. The collector later claimed 'There was not one of the letters which James Philip sent to this office anent this sloop but what was shown and approved of by Walter Sime ... under whose pay it is asserted Philip is when Sime has any smuggle to do'. For 'many ships have unloaded their cargoes consisting of prohibited and high duty goods within half a mile of his own house and within the bounds of his district, where there is a water miln for the manufactory of tobacco, the property of Robert Napier and Walter Sime, who not only smuggle for themselves but as agents for all the smugglers in the country'.

At 'about one after noon' Philip arrived on the beach and was helped on board the *Dispatch* by the Gowans and Watt, 'who it is remarkable all join in swearing that although they were close by Philips they neither saw nor heard him make a seizure of the vessel. James Philip's carelessness about this seizure, which he pretends he made, in not giving any directions about taking care of her but leaving that to the master ... is a circumstance which must be convincing that he did not look upon her as his seizure or if that acted very unbecomingly as an officer and indeed he never gave himself any trouble about her nor was at any expense upon the occasion but left that entirely to the surveyor'. On 29 January Philip asked Robert Mearns, a sailor with Captain John Read, 'to go down and seize the sloop for him'. As a result 'he went down to the sloop and having no chalk in his pocket he made a cross on her stern with a bit of stone, when if she had been seized before ... there would have been no necessity of this commission to Mearns'. When the master, Moor, was told that the surveyor had seized the vessel, he fell 'into a passion ... swearing that as she was seized first by James Philip she should be his seizure'. Philip's lack of concern continued. 'During the time that Blews and Simpson were on board the sloop while on the beach of Bervie, which was from the 5th to the 22nd February last ... Philips never once offered these officers the smallest assistance and indeed never appeared but in the company of Moor, the master, and one Gordon and another Fladden, all concerns of the ship and reputed to be three of the most desperate smugglers in the north of Scotland'.

Despite all this, in March Philip arranged for proof to be taken in the presence of Provost Christie in Bervie that he had seized the *Dispatch*. 'We beg leave to observe that the application as well as the interlocutor and the witnesses depositions are all of the handwriting of James Strachan, a bankrupt smuggler in Bervie, who since the failing of his circumstances has commenced a writer and messenger in that place, and is the known agent and doer of all the smugglers on the coast and their friend and abettor, among whom we must beg leave to reckon the unfaithful officers of the revenue. We do verily believe that the pretensions of James Philip to the *Dispatch* sloop is prompted and stimulated by him with the assistance of the concerns of the sloop, by whom Strachan was taken into their service the day she came ashore and he it was that acted as notary judge and clerk in the pretended sale of her'.

'In Philip's first letter also to us he says he saw the tracks of some carts that had carried up the men's bedding chests and some sails, which must be false in fact for your Honours will be pleased to observe that [the witnesses] ... all swear that these particulars were lying upon the beach, when Philips came on board ... without any notice being taken of them by him'. The collector concluded 'His suffering the sails and rigging to be carried off plainly indicated that it was not the emolument of the crown he was anxious for nor the support of his own character as an honest officer but alone his own private gain which appears to have been stipulated'. When the comptroller and surveyor asked Philip about the guns and sails 'he seemed very much inclined not to enter into conversation about it, after telling them that he had lodged them in the excise warehouse, which upon enquiry into they found was an absolute falsehood for that Clark the warehouse keeper actually declared to the comptroller and surveyor that he had never seen them, which angered the comptroller and surveyor so much that they ordered him directly to find them ... and at length he confessed that he [had] got them in a corn yard, where he had seized fourteen matts tobacco stems that he had found there the day before, which tobacco stems the comptroller, surveyor and landwaiter from the best intelligence they could discover understood that they were thrown in his way as a blind to cover his fraudulent practices'. The remaining rigging and ropes were found by the comptroller, surveyor and landwaiter in cellars belonging to Robert Napier and Walter Sime while three pieces of sail were in an old house, the property of Lord Arbuthnott.

The *Rover* of Galway

The *Rover* of Galway, a common carvel built sloop of about 23 tons burthen, Edmund Bodkin master, was stranded on the sands of Carrick, twenty-six miles from Stornoway, on Sunday 13 January 1805.

The original cargo had been three hundred and sixty-eight bales of leaf tobacco, totalling 44,160 lbs, one hogshead of port wine, thirty-five small bags of brandy and geneva, four bales of roll tobacco and one keg of sugar cleared out from Guernsey for Bergen. But the collector suspected that the cargo had been destined for the west coast of Ireland 'from whence there is little doubt of her being drove by stress of weather after landing part of the cargo, though the master gives out that he hove what was wanting of it overboard to lighten the vessel. It was undoubted that they were in great distress for want of provisions and intentionally ran the vessel on shore to save their lives, being almost exhausted to the last pitch. The goods were discharged and scattered over the country for and on behalf of the master and by agents employed by him with the promise of being rewarded in proportion to what they may save from the search of the revenue officers ... The master sold the vessel and materials to some seamen who were fishing near where he ran on shore but which sale was conditioned by the purchasers to be non-effective in case of seizure by revenue officers'.

The custom house had no knowledge of the wreck until Saturday 19th, when the comptroller 'received private information' about what had happened and set out with 'a sufficient party'. By the time he arrived at Carrick the next day, the cargo was completely discharged and dispersed over 'a great extent of very rugged country'. He seized the vessel and what remained of her materials and forty-eight bales of tobacco at Carrick 'in the custody of servants inhabiting that village, injured by salt water'. This was brought to Stornoway on a local fishing vessel. 'What escaped the pillage of the country people of her sails and rigging was

113

given to honest persons in charge of whom it could be properly secured. Two men were given charge of the hull'. The comptroller returned to port on the 24th. In March 1805 the *Helen* of Stornoway, James Boyle master, took 17 cwt 20 lbs sound leaf tobacco and 41 cwt 14 lbs wet or damaged leaf tobacco to Greenock.

The collector justified the expense of making and protecting the seizure. 'We are aware that the expenses, particularly the articles for Malcolm MacLeod and John Morrison, tenants in Carrick, will be considered extravagant but it was impossible to get the business therein stated effected on easier terms from the open and exposed nature of the place where the vessel lay and the obstinate disposition of the country people to tear down and carry away under silence of night every portable article. The sails were so dirty by mud and slime that it was judged advisable to wash them to prevent their rotting which, with drying and airing them frequently, makes the articles for them exceed what might be thought reasonable'.

The master entered two protests to the Board, claiming it had been impossible to protect his cargo. However, 'intelligence of such an event [the stranding of the vessel] could have been received at Stornoway ten or twelve hours thereafter and the assistance of civil magistrates and revenue officers immediately procured, who would effectively check every kind of pillage and deprecation'. Instead the event was 'industriously concealed'. 'That Bodkin was in a feeble state when he landed out of the vessel on the evening of the 13th was not denied. But he could speak and in a language (Irish) to be understood by every peasant in the country ... the most ignorant peasant boy could inform him that there were justices of the peace at Stornoway as also officers of customs and excise and that the minister of the parish of Uig, who is besides a justice of the peace, was within two miles distance of the place where he ran the vessel aground. Had he directed any intimation to be made to either of the above classes of persons ... he would have had a specious argument should any officer under such circumstances attempt to make seizure of it [the cargo].

'It seems Mr Bodkin was able to appear next day after running on shore before Mr Munro, minister ... with whom he entered protest against wind and weather, and stating the distress he and his crew experienced previous to that event ... had he sought his [Munro's] assistance, he had sufficient influence to keep the country people in due subjection. Bodkin after remaining at Uig and thereabouts for some weeks recruiting his health and making the best sales he could of his cargo came to Stornoway, where he resided for more than eight days ... After acting in such a manner and quitting the country with a considerable sum in his pocket, the proceeds of a part of the cargo clandestinely sold by him, it is truly astonishing how he could think of addressing your Honours for the liberation of the vessel and seized part of the cargo so justly forfeited'.

In July 1805 the Board wrote to the collector at Inverness because Bodkin reckoned that he had left the register with Donald McDonald of that town, magistrate. The collector was instructed to call on McDonald for the register to transmit to the Board, as the vessel had gone into condemnation. Despite the request from her purchaser, Mr Chapman, 'factor of this country' that the wreck should be repaired and used as a packet boat to replace the current one which was 'far from being in a sufficient condition so that the conveyance of mails and passengers are precarious and hazardous' the hull was completely broken up. This took five days and cost £2 15s 'in personal charges and boat hire crossing and recrossing arms of the sea that lay in their way'.

The inaccessibility of the various islands in the Outer Hebrides is emphasised by the story of the *John* of Calmar, wrecked at Scalpa in December 1809. It was impossible for those left to watch the wreck 'for the benefit of the concerned' to save anything 'as it was in such a perishing state as not to be worth the trouble and expense that would attend the salvaging. Besides the wreck was on an uninhabited island where there was no place of security for any goods that might be salved and subject to the nocturnal depredations of many boats and men from the adjacent coast, who perpetually hovered about the wreck for the sake of pillage. The persons who purchased the hull were determined to clear the hold with all possible dispatch. It must then be evident that we had no other choice for the safety of the revenue than to order the goods to be completely destroyed. After Mr Reid of the cutter had landed the officers here he returned again to Scalpa to see this service effected and we have heard that in the short interval between his leaving Scalpa with the officers and his return the persons that had been left in charge were not able to prevent some depredation being made. Captain Reid on his return took immediate measures for rendering any further attempts fruitless by effectually destroying what remained'.

The problems of silence/non-co-operation from the 'country people' is illustrated in the story of the *Marion*, Donald McDonald master, which was stranded on North Uist in November 1772. As the collector reported to the Board, the local inhabitants: Donald McDonald, factor to Lord McDonald and tacksman of Baleshare; Donald McDonald, tacksman of Balranald; Neil McLean, merchant in Lochmaddy; Angus McDonald, charge keeper at Paible; Lauchlan McLean, tacksman of Haysher [not located]; Peter Nicholson, merchant, Allan McLaurin, minister and Mr Kimmankind of Berneray must have known that a small sloop took several cargoes of wood from the wreck to John Montgomery, merchant in Newry, Ireland.

The tailpiece tells the story of the wreck of the *Anna*. Having concentrated on the smuggling story from the viewpoint of the smugglers, the next three chapters consider the revenue officers and others who attempted, in theory, to stem the flow of smuggled goods on to the northern shores.

A STORY OF THE *ANNA*, GEORGE MITCHELL MASTER

On 3 February 1800 John Sim, collector's clerk, and William Corbet, junior excise officer, seized the sloop *Anna*, George Mitchell master and registered in Prussia, on her way from Alderney to Bergen but stranded on the beach north of the Don mouth, five miles from Aberdeen. With the help of the military, the whole cargo was landed, carried 'without the high water mark' and lodged jointly in the cellars of the excise and the king's warehouse at Aberdeen. The seizure included: twenty-five boxes manufactured tobacco, twenty ankers brandy and five hundred and ninety-nine ankers geneva. Subsequently the *Anna* was got off the sands and brought round to Aberdeen.

George Mitchell was present when between two and three o'clock in the morning Alexander Christie, a spirits dealer in Aberdeen, first informed Sim that the vessel was ashore. But he did not say that he was the master 'nor did he make any intimation of distress to him at the time nor afterwards'. 'The winds and weather at the time the vessel came ashore and for some days preceding were not such as to afford any pretence that she was forced in by stress of weather'. This the assistant tidesurveyor, James Medcalf, 'from his keeping a journal of the weather' and John Miller, commander of one of the *Princess Royal*'s boats 'who is supposed does in the like manner' should be able to prove. The logbook was demanded immediately on boarding 'but Mitchell affirmed it had been lost by being in the boat with him when he first came on shore to give notice of the situation of the vessel. We have reason to think that the story as to the loss of it is not true and that if Christie were questioned on oath he must acknowledge that it was not lost'.

The master and mate stated that the vessel was leaky but the collector reckoned that she came ashore due to some mistake and not leakiness. The leak was not noticed while the cargo was being discharged, as the vessel was 'deep sunk in the sand. But John Reid, servant to John Gill shipbuilder in Aberdeen (whom we have examined) says he was sent by his master to repair said leak and that there were two leaks, one of them within her ... keel and another pretty far up but occasioned by the starting of bullards[?] of planks. But whether this happened from the vessel's thumping on shore or before he could not ascertain. People of experience are, however, of opinion that if the bullard of a plank had been started, the vessel must very soon have gone down at sea'.

'It is a pity the master and mate were not examined about the cause of

contd.

the disorder in the hold and of the tallies on the side of the hatchway, both of which were observed by George Limmers, landwaiter, and James Medcalf ... but the number of tallies was not ascertained by either. Mr Limmers' cause for seeing the water up to the middle of the third tier of ankers before the discharge began was that he observed two tier of these had been removed or were wanting on the side to which the ship keeled, immediately upon opening the hatches, which enabled him to see how high the water reached and he is clearly of opinion that a vessel could not have made an overseas voyage with the cargo in that situation, as the ankers that were stowed higher on the other side must have naturally been displaced and fallen down by the rolling of the ship'.

The owners of the cargo, mainly one Henry Farmer, threatened to take Sim to court, which resulted in an enquiry.

Henry Sharpy of Arbroath was believed to be a partner of and local agent for a merchant house abroad [supposed to be in Flushing - see Chapter Five], who sent great quantities of contraband goods to Scotland. Andrew Mitchell, farmer at Whiteness, parish of Slains, whose farm was situated hard by the Ward of Cruden, where a number of contraband cargoes had been run 'these last few years' was another witness and 'is most likely concerned in this cargo and of course must know that ... [it] was actually intended to have been landed on this coast'. It was believed that Alexander Christie was expecting to distribute the cargo because Mitchell went to him when he first arrived and 'resided in Christie's house during the time he remained in Aberdeen, after the vessel and cargo were secured'. Luckily Christie was 'a man of more honour than the generality of those of his profession' and he provided most of the information. On 3 December Christie said to Sim that 'he was ... disappointed with him [Sim] at the claims not being withdrawn because Sharpy, not doubting that he would get the other part of the cargo compromised with the customs, as it had been done with the excise, had absolutely sold it to him, Christie, deliverable in Britain, which he could insist on whether the goods were condemned or not. But that he was in daily expectation of hearing the claim was withdrawn. There were no witnesses at this communing'.

At the last minute Farmer et al dropped their claim to the vessel and its cargo.

CHAPTER EIGHT: ALL THE KING'S MEN?

'On the 30th we received the enclosed letter from the tidesmen at Fraserburgh, advising us that upon the 28th ult one John Chalmers, officer of excise, came in to that place with seventeen matts on horses and upon their knowing it to be tobacco they went and demanded access to seize and bring it to the warehouse here. But Chalmers ordered the soldiers whom he had with him to keep them off and not allow them to come near it and told them that no man should seize it but Mr Stewart, who has a deputation from your Honours, who was at that time twenty-four miles distant. Upon which they got a notary public and protested against Chalmers ... and demanded access to the tobacco under form of instrument, which Chalmers likeways refused and ordered the soldiers not to allow the notary public or tidesmen to come near it and took Paul White, one of the tidesmen, by the collar and dragged him off. The tidesmen wrote to Mr Rollo, then at Peterhead, but as he was at that time much indisposed he could not go there. We are humbly of opinion the tidesmen have better title to the seizure than Mr Stewart and that John Chalmers has committed a daring insult on your officers by refusing them access to seize run goods, when he had no commission but a title to stop them. By Chalmers deforcing the tidesmen the horse on which the tobacco was carried got off. Mr Stewart upon the 30th brought the tobacco to this warehouse, where it is lodged weighing 2,012 lbs and this day demanded to return the seizure, and offered us a return attested by John Cumming collector of the excise to be sent your Honours which we refused until we had your Honours directions'. [Letter from the collector at Aberdeen to the Board, dated 1 August 1749]

In the context of this chapter 'all the king's men' include the customs officers on land, the excise and the military.

The Customs

The problems facing the customs officers were immense from the sheer size of the areas to be covered by one outport, to staff shortages, to the hostility of the local people, to the rivalry not only between the officers of customs and excise but also between those at the same port or creek over the right to return a seizure.

The majority of Class 1 letters were written by the collector and it is often possible from the style to identify those from a particular individual. The collector's role was far from easy as he was at the interface between his staff and the general public and his staff and the Board. The tailpiece to this chapter is the story of a collector at Aberdeen while a Montrose collector features in the tailpiece to Chapter Four.

In January 1786 the Board received a complaint from Mr MacKenzie of Stornoway about the behaviour of John Reid, collector there 'representing 'that you had publicly declared at leaving Stornoway to go to Edinburgh that you would do all in your power to ruin Stornoway; that on a certain time when you had spent the public money and had a considerable defalcation in your books, when the inspector was going round, you waited on some of the merchants and extorted money from them to make up your balance under threats of informing against them for smuggling if not complied with; that another fact is recent and is the clearing out busses without taking bonds; that by this ingenuous manner if the vessel smuggles or carries on any trade during her fishing time and escapes detection all is well and the bond is then signed and dated as if duly taken but should the vessel be caught infringing the laws it is immediately pleaded that she is not on the bounty, having given no bond'. We hereby give you these matters in charge for your answer which you are to lay before us for our consideration'.

The reply, dated 31 January, does not exist but on 6 April the Board wrote to Reid 'your having stated in answer to that article [not taking bonds for the herring busses] that at times when stamp paper could not be had bonds were taken for such vessels upon unstamped paper but renewed upon stamp paper when it could be got, we direct you to take notice that nothing can exceed the irregularity in taking such bonds upon unstamped paper and therefore we will not admit of any apology in future. There appearing to be a difference between you and Mr Humberston MacKenzie of a private nature we recommend you to behave with decency and civility to him, which is by no means inconsistent with your duty'.

Reid continued as collector at Stornoway. In 1805 he is listed as having been the comptroller at Stornoway from June 1765 to September

1775, when he became collector. He was now fifty-nine years old with twelve children.

The comptroller was frequently co-signatory with the collector on all letters to the Board etc, although on 7 June 1771 Robert Hunter, collector at Montrose, wrote to the Board 'I am apprehensive that if the comptroller knew the above particulars he might come to divulge the same, to prevent which I have signed this letter alone', The next letter about the *Peggie* of Johnshaven, dated 22 June, was signed by both the collector and the comptroller [see Chapter Four]. But when John Duncan, writer and postmaster in Stonehaven, sent a confidential letter to the collector in July this also was kept from the comptroller [see the excise section below].

Other staff included the (land)surveyor, tidesurveyor in charge of the king's boat and crew [see Chapter Ten] but also active on land, the riding officer, the landwaiters, often covering large areas and the tidewaiters/tidesmen at the creeks. Because of the length of time covered by this book and the frequent staff changes, no attempt has been made to produce comprehensive staff lists. However, the style of information available is indicated in Figure 9. This includes stories about landwaiters - their wide-ranging duties can be seen from the frequent references to these post holders throughout the book. Stories relating to various other categories of staff have been extracted to illustrate the first section of this chapter. This is followed by comments on the other assistance given to the customs officers, in particular from the excise.

Riding Officers

There were few riding officers appointed in Scotland, compared with England. Their main task was literally to ride along the coast. The collector at Aberdeen reported in May 1800 that according to his journals, Mr McEachran 'when not otherwise necessarily engaged on duty or confined by disposition ... has been sufficiently active as a riding officer for preventing smuggling. Although he has not for the last twelve months made any very considerable seizures, yet we have reason to think that his exertions have been of material service to the revenue by checking smuggling on that part of the coast'. In November it was noted that McEachran had paid out 40s in horse hire and travelling.

In Obedience to Your Honour's Orders of the 7.th Aug.d 1744, underwritten a List of the Officers at this Port, their Names, Ages, Family, Capacity & where and how long employed in each Station

Names	Station	Age	Fam:	Where and how long employed
James Gellie	Landsr.d	53	7	Widower, employed here since 1720, being Tidesr.d &c
Theo.s Ogilvie	Tidesr.d	26	3	married, employed here 4 Years
Rob.t Kinner	Landwaiter	35	6	married, employed here & at Air since Oct.r 1738
John Rollo	D.o	37	2	Widower, employed here & at Anst.r since 1743
George Lobban	D.o	40	1	married, employed here near 9 Years
William Pantoun	Tidewaiter	53	1	married, employed here since 1723
James Forbes	D.o	30	2	Widower, employed here since March 1747
James M.cGuffock	D.o	55	1	married, employed here since 1725
William Masson	D.o	39	6	married, employed here since 1740
Alex.r Grieg	D.o	50	5	married employed here since 1740
John Carnegie	D.o	65	7	D.o
Rob.t McGilligan	D.o	47	3	married, employed as Salt Watchman from 1734 to 1740 at Alloa & since here
Rob.d Ramsay	D.o	49	5	married employ'd here near 19 Years
James Pantoun	D.o	50	2	widower, employed here near 7 Years
James Smith	D.o	43	3	married employ'd here 13 Years
Alex.r Morison	D.o	43	3	employ'd here & at P.t Glasgow 8 Years
W.m Brown	D.o	39	3	married, employed here 7 Years
Patrick White	D.o	51	3	married, employed here 20 Years
George Mearns	D.o	52	2	married employed here & at Kirkaldy 15 Years
Alex.r Keith	D.o	65	6	married employed here 18 Years
James Mercer	D.o	70	9	married, employed here 3 Years
John Craig	D.o	42	11	married, employed here since April 1747
George Sutherland	D.o	30	7	D.o
Adam Baxter	Cooper	49	3	married, employed here 5 Years
James Knew.s	Boatman	49	7	married, employ'd here since 1730, 19 Years
Roderick Forbes	D.o	43	5	married employ'd here since 1730
William Freeman	D.o	62	4	married employ'd here since 1722
And.r Millar	D.o	48	3	married employ'd here since 1738

We are &c. J.O.
A.M.

Figure 9: The Aberdeen Staff List 31 July 1747: Landwaiters

On 25 February 1765 the collector at Aberdeen wrote to George Lawtie, landwaiter at Banff. 'Enclosed we send you additional instructions for all the tidesmen under your inspection viz at Cullen, Portsoy, Banff, Down, Gardenstown and Auchmedan, Rosehearty and Fraserburgh, which instructions you are to deliver them out of your own hand and see them insert in their journals. You are to exert yourself to cause all these officers execute them to the utmost of their power and oversee them as much as you can in the execution thereof ... You will also inform all these officers that as the government have it at heart to quash the detestable practice of smuggling that if they do not exert themselves in their respective limits to prevent and detect the running of goods and execute every point of their duty faithfully, honestly and diligently they will not hold their offices'.

One of the main problems facing the landwaiters was that of exhaustion. In 1747 George Lobban 'did remonstrate to your Honours ... he did not think himself safe in that place [Banff] and thereupon obtained orders from you for his remaining at Peterhead'. John Rollo 'had undergone the same fatigue which Mr Lobban complains of for the space of five years, though he does not at all appear to be so fit for fatigue as Mr Lobban [see quote at the head of this chapter]. Mr Lobban has sometimes complained of colds and other ailments but we never could learn he was reduced to any low pass. Both from our own observations and from the accounts of the landsurveyor Mr Rollo gives far better attendance to his duty and is better qualified for it than Mr Lobban'.

On 22 August 1760 John Burrow, tidesman at Banff, seized a hogshead of wine and 'conveyed the same to the house of Mr Lawtie ... (there being no military in the town) as the safest place he could lodge it in until he could get it brought to the warehouse here. Some days after Mrs Aurn, wife of William Aurn merchant in Banff, whose property it would appear the wine was, came to Mrs Lawtie when Mr Lawtie was at Portsoy upon duty and told her she ought to allow the wine to be taken away and Mrs Lawtie, who with her family had been insulted in the grossest manner upon account of her husband's doing his duty upon a former occasion in the prosecution of Aurn for deforcing the officers, was so much frightened that she said she could not hinder them to do as they pleased and upon that Mrs Aurn it seems employed some persons to draw off the wine and carry it away. Mr Lawtie ... upon hearing what had happened made so much noise about it they thought proper in the night time to lay down the wine in a hogshead at the cellar door, which is now brought in here sound and good'.

Tidesmen

The tidesmen were the backbone of the customs operation against smuggling. Placed along the coast at widely spaced intervals, they were either deforced for their attempts to guard the revenue or accused of 'collusion with the smugglers'. The story of the tidesmen at Gourdon between 1768 and 1785 is told in the next chapter. Here are details of the tidesmen at Inverness, the problems of family connections and attempts on the part of local landowners to intervene.

Inverness Tidesmen 1783 and 1790

In September 1783 Andrew Simpson, tidesman at Elgin, in formed the collector at Inverness that 'James Hutcheon, extraordinary tidesman at Spey ... has had improper connection with dealers and has been acting in collusion with smugglers, by whom he is said to be frequently bribed'. At the same time George Henderson, tidesurveyor at Cromarty, proposed 'the removal of Hutcheon, as also of George Brodie, tidesman at Garmouth, and Alexander McAulay, tidesman at Lossiemouth, from their present stations there being reason to suspect improper connection with the people of business'. The comptroller went to Garmouth to investigate these allegations - his expenses totalled £3 9s 8d. The Board 'dismissed the compliant for want of proofs'.

By May 1784 Hutcheon, who was suspended, and Brodie were under scrutiny again 'relative to a fraud committed by the smuggling of some goods out of the *Betsey* or *Chappiestane* in April' at Garmouth. Henderson was still concerned about Alexander McAulay and the Board concluded 'there being reason to suspect that Hutcheon, Brodie and McAulay may be improperly connected with people of business at their respective stations we direct that they be removed to such part of the district as you shall think proper and their places are to be supplied by those of the most trusty tidesmen from your port. The suspension of Hutcheon being hereby taken off you are to return to him his deputation without loss of salary'.

In April 1790 there was a dispute between David Anderson and Peter Bremner, tidesmen at Lossiemouth. A parallel complaint about George Brodie, now at Buckie, and David Ross at Portknockie led to a major reshuffling of posts:

David Anderson at Lossie to be stationed at Buckie, 'a place which has of late become remarkable for smuggling';
Peter Bremner at Lossie to be stationed at Garmouth;
George Brodie at Buckie to be stationed at Inverness;
David Ross at Portknockie to be stationed at Dornoch;
William Melvill at Cromarty to succeed David Anderson at Lossie;
Alexander Leggat at Garmouth to succeed Peter Bremner at Lossie;
James Hutcheon, extraordinary tidesman at Inverness to succeed David Ross at Portknockie and
Alexander McAulay at Dornoch to succeed William Melvill at Cromarty.

However, David Anderson sent a petition to the Board, 'remonstrating against his being removed to Buckie ... and throwing out certain insinuations against his superiors ... if Anderson does not remove immediately and if he shall in future throw out any improper reflections against his superiors he will be assuredly dismissed the service'. William Melvill was also unhappy about his new posting 'having applied to the Board submitting that the exchange may be deferred till Whitsunday next on account of the loss he will sustain in house rent and the difficulty of procuring a proper house at Lossiemouth ... he must pay immediate obedience to the order ... and that neither he nor the other tidesmen ... may be put to expense or inconvenience, the tidesmen are removed to occupy the houses possessed by each other at the respective stations'.

Family Connections

The collector at Aberdeen reported in 1765 that Robert McGilligan [see Figure 9] 'was removed several years ago from Gardenstown by your Honours orders upon his inactivity and connections there and there being no creek where there is less trust than at Newburgh was stationed there, as there is hardly one ship in a twelvemonth at that creek from foreign parts. Since he came there he has made no seizures but as to his connivance we have not had any proof of this otherwise it would have been laid before your Honours. The want of military aid is always an excuse made by officers, where there is no military, in not being able to make seizures and indeed it is a strong one, as it is hardly possible to make one seizure without them, let the running be never so great. Robert McGilligan has a son, who set up as merchant at Newburgh and as we are informed is concerned with smugglers, for which reason we are humbly of opinion that Robert McGilligan should be removed from thence'. There were several other references to Robert McGilligan junior [see Chapter Four and Appendix II].

In May 1788 the Board wrote to the collector at Inverness about John Fordyce, tidesman at Lossiemouth, 'out of whose house a cask of geneva was seized, the property of his daughter who deals in uncustomed and prohibited goods, and we acquaint you that it being improper that Fordyce would remain at a creek where his daughter is a dealer in spirits we have resolved to remove him from his present station'.

Outside intervention

In 1770 the Earl of Errol proposed placing John Davidson as an extraordinary tidewaiter at Collieston. The collector believed that an officer 'under the patronage and assistance of his Lordship would be a very material service done the revenue, it being a place where smuggling is often carried on and the boats from thence much employed by the smugglers'.

According to the six monthly report, 'John Davidson has prevented the boats in that and the neighbouring creek of Old Castle [Slains] from being employed in the smuggling trade ... and the countenance the Earl of Errol gives in preventing his fishing boats from smuggling ... and takes every opportunity to punish the fishers when he has account of their being involved, it is our humble opinion makes it of much more importance to the revenue to have a man under him stationed at Collieston and whom he can depend upon to execute his scheme of preventing the fishers from thereabouts from aiding the smugglers than the salary of such an officer. We are also informed that although Davidson has not fallen in with any smuggled goods since he went to Collieston, owing to there being few or no goods run about that place, yet he is active and attentive'. However, the problems at Collieston did continue [see Chapters One and Eleven].

The Excise: Three Tales of William Cock

William Cock, officer of excise, and Benjamin Smith, tidesman, at Stonehaven 1765

In August 1765 William Cock, excise officer, and Benjamin Smith, tidesman, both stationed at Stonehaven, seized eighteen ankers of brandy.

They were deforced during the seizure - Cock was wounded in the cheek by a pistol shot and Benjamin Smith was 'much bruised'.

'The goods would have been rescued from them without the aid of the country people near the place where the seizure was made'. As a result five people, all from the parish of Fetteresso in Kincardineshire, were paid a reward of £5, which was distributed as follows:

William Duthie, tenant in Brunthole of Arduthie £2
John Duthie, his son £1
Robert Edwards in Miln of Cowie £1
Peter Robertson and Alexander Knowles, Edwards' servants, 10s each.

'It appears that George Watson merchant in Montrose was the person who attacked Benjamin Smith but that they do not as yet know the person who fired at and wounded Mr Cock, though that may probably appear upon examination [by the sheriff of Kincardine] of the carters and others ... who possibly know him. We humbly submit it to your Honours whether a justiciary warrant upon the affidavits of these officers may be procured for apprehending and incarcerating George Watson ... and whether it may not be proper to cause examine before the sheriff of Kincardine the persons mentioned in the officers' letter in order to discover the unknown person who fired at Mr Cock that if he be discovered he may also be prosecuted'.

On 3 September the sheriff substitute went to Stonehaven 'to take the precognition ... [which] was accordingly done in the fullest and most distinct manner and every method used to bring out the whole facts. Every person the officers or the collector could think of was called and examined to discover the unknown person that fired at and wounded Mr Cock. But notwithstanding all our endeavours no discovery was made of him. The collector then ordered Mr Cock to proceed to Brechin and with the aid of the collector of excise, with whom he was to meet there, to make particular enquiry about him, as one of the people examined in the precognition says that the carter he had hired to take away the spirits resided there, though he knew not his name. But it appears by Mr Cock's letter to the collector this day ... that he has made no discovery. We shall continue to cause make all the enquiry possible in our power and if we discover the man's name endeavour to fix a proof that he was the person who wounded Mr Cock.'

Eventually the man was identified as Charles Edwards, who lived at Burn of Meallie, shire of Forfar. As the collector explained to the Board on 7 October, the problem was that the sheriff of Kincardine could not question him while the sheriff of Forfar could not 'oblige the necessary witnesses who live in Kincardineshire to appear to confront Edwards, were he apprehended by a warrant from the sheriff of the county where he resides'. As a result on 23 November Cock took James Thomson, servant at Miln of Stonehaven, and John Youngson of Miln of Forest, both of whom had been formerly precognised at Stonehaven and who saw Edwards, 'the one before and the other after the riot'. They were examined by the sheriff. But 'although John Youngson was positive that he [Edwards] was the man who came to his house immediately after the riot and narrated to him the circumstances thereof yet James Thomson did not know him to be the same person he saw the day before the riot at Stonehaven'.

William Cock and Alexander Anderson, excise officers, Aberdeen 1770

When Mr Vitty, tidesurveyor, received information about a smuggle to the south of Aberdeen in February 1770 he 'went over with some of the boatmen to Fishtown of Torry to make a search but found nothing. Next morning [he] ordered two of the boatmen over again in order to search such places as they had not searched before and to endeavour to procure information. Accordingly John Bothwell, one of the boatmen, went over and passed in the ferry boat along with William Cock and Alexander Anderson, officers of excise, whom it seems also went over to search. John Brodie, another of the boatmen, came over in about a quarter of an hour thereafter. Bothwell and Brodie say that how soon they landed upon the south side of the river Dee they proceeded to search such houses as they thought most suspicious in the lower town of Ferrie and that the officers of excise went to search the town of Benagask and the neighbourhood, a little to the south of the town of Torry. In about an hour after they came to Torry they received information that a hogshead of spirits was concealed in a dunghill about 300 yards north from Upper Torry and having procured a gripe they went to said dunghill and having turned off the earth found and seized a hogshead of geneva, part of the chime of which was visible. There were no marks of feet on the dunghill. At this time the officers of excise were searching upper Torry and upon observing Bothwell going to the dunghill with a gripe Alexander Anderson ... run towards them and called out for them to stop for that he had been there before and knew there was a hogshead there. But by this time it was uncovered and seized by Bothwell. A dispute having arose betwixt our boatmen and the officers of excise in relation to the seizure of this hogshead Alexander Anderson ... went over to Aberdeen and brought from thence a party of the military and placed three of them upon the dunghill, where the hogshead of spirits was still lying, and proceeded on their search of upper Torry with the rest of the party. Soon after this Bothwell received information that another hogshead of spirits was concealed in the same dunghill upon which the three soldiers were at this time placed. On his coming again to the dunghill to search for the hogshead, one of the soldiers told him that he had discovered it and this second hogshead is not pretended to have been seen by any of the excise officers previous to this.

'We have examined several of the people in Torry, none of whom saw the excise officers at the dunghill before the boatmen were there. Nor can the excise officers point out any person who saw them there. But a farmer of the name of Spark says that previous to the boatmen having been there Alexander Anderson told him that there was some spirits concealed in the dunghill, pointing to it, and desired his carts to convey them away. At the same time he told him that he had discovered some hogsheads at a place called Benagask but which was not true, he having found none there. Upon our asking him why he said so to Spark he said there were some empty casks there.

'Upon the other hand William Cock and Alexander Anderson ... say that they and also a constable who was along with them are ready to make oath that they discovered the hogshead in dispute at the dunghill about an hour before the boatmen went there. But acknowledge they put no mark of seizure upon it and left it to proceed on their search without any person with it but still keeping the dunghill in sight. Mr Vitty and the boatmen say that had they had the smallest reason to believe that the excise officers had seized this hogshead they would not have interfered. But not finding any person that saw them there nor any mark upon the cask and no person near it they could never imagine that they had been there and it appears strange that as the eyes of many people would be on the procedure of the different officers that the excise officers can find no person who saw them near the dunghill'.

William Cock and Benjamin Smith, Stonehaven, 1771

In July 1771 the collector at Montrose received a highly confidential letter from Duncan, the writer and postmaster at Stonehaven. 'Sir, It was in an overly way that I heard some of the merchants complaining of Mr Cock's bringing cargoes of coals and selling them out here in small parcels. George Walker, merchant here, who deals in coals, was one of them saying it was hard that gaugers who had settled salaries from the government and while in the service of the revenue should deal so deep as he did and break the merchants' trade. John Lawson ... knows everything. Only he will say that the last cargo of coals was offered to George Walker first but Mr Cock was preferred [because he offered as much or a little more for the cargo]. George Bisset, the next material witness, is gone on a voyage and is from home so he will not be got at this time. George Walker, merchant in Stonehaven, may be called next. Peter Cushnie, merchant and late shoremaster ... then Robert Fidders, who handed out of the ship the last cargo in absence of George Bisset, next the brewers and then the merchants and others in the list. I think Benjamin Smith should be examined how many cargoes Cock sold out. I believe there will be no proof against Benjamin Smith, though it was the common report that the last cargo of coals belonged to him and Cock in company. Mr Cock it seems has signified that he is to deal no more in the coal trade so that the merchants are now very bad and not so forward as formerly and I believe nothing will be got out of them but upon oath ... If one be examined it will be no more a secret what you are about. I do not want to be seen or suspected in the least. For that reason I have not ventured to speak to any about the affair but only to one or two. and that at the greatest distance in an overly way. If I can be of any service to you it shall not be wanting but the facts are true whether they come out on proof or not and a great deal more though it cannot be proved'.

The preliminary enquiry showed that during the last two or three years, whenever the *Peggie* of Johnshaven had run cargoes of geneva on the coast she would then go to Newcastle, Sunderland or the Firth of

Forth to load coals. William Cock abused his position as excise officer at Stonehaven by retailing the coals so that he 'disappointed the merchants who had coals selling in Stonehaven for getting any custom or change till William Cock's coals were all sold off, as he got all the brewers maltsters and victuallers in his division to buy from him rather than from the merchants'. The coals were advertised by handbill and sold to more than one hundred and eighty people. 'By this means the smuggling sloop was from time to time licenced again into fair trade, when this officer, who it must be presumed knew that she had been smuggling, ought rather to have seized her than taken her into his service'. One of the most remarkable aspects of the whole case was for the townspeople to 'see the officers of the revenue come up from Arbroath and Montrose to seize her and did actually so when in the service of William Cock, unloading a cargo of coals at Stonehaven the very first voyage after she had brought home a smuggling cargo'. Another charge was that 'Mr Cock keeps a warehouse or cellar below his kitchen and keeps and sells out to sundries loaf sugars, candles, dressed leather and bond leather and other merchant goods'.

'The collector set out from this for Stonehaven on the 16th inst ... and having called upon John Lawson coal weigher in Stonehaven he did declare voluntarily before him ... Robert Fidders workman in Stonehaven being called next he declared what is contained in his declaration. The collector then sent for several others on the list but they either refused to come or would not give any declaration at all before him, which obliged him to apply to Mr McDonald sheriff substitute who lives three miles from thence, by whom William Gilmore shoemaker in Stonehaven was solemnly sworn and interrogate ... then Mrs Lawson was called and dismissed as she declared she knew nothing of the matter, [as did] James Officer, shoemaker, Alexander Duncan, merchant in Stonehaven. Agnes Erskine, relict of Alexander Cushnie innkeeper there, deponed that within these last two years past she was solicited by Mr Cock to buy coals from him, which she did more than once both Scotch and English and paid Mr Cock for the same and that she once bought a large loaf of sugar from him but knows nothing of his dealing in any other articles of merchandise. As George Walker and Peter Cushnie merchants, who were said to be material evidences, in regard they could not be found on the 16th instructions were left with Robert Burness writer in Stonehaven to have them examined on 27th before the sheriff, which was done accordingly'.

The rest of the evidences were not examined. George Scolla, brewer in Stonehaven, 'was a known friend of Cock's and Smith's'. John Colvin, merchant, William Park, merchant, Elspit Thompson, relict of John Duncan brewer, William Middleton, baker, John Smith, manufacturer and Lieutenant William Meldrum of the navy, all from Stonehaven 'could not be found and as it was agreed that they could only say as to Mr Cock's selling coals, which was a fact already established, they were past from rather than to incur an additional charge by a second day'. 'Not one of the evidences could say, at least would not, as to the concern that Benjamin Smith had in his trade.

'Your Honours will please observe that John Lawson and Robert Fidders who both declare, the first as to three several cargoes of coals out of the *Peggie* of Johnshaven and Fidders two cargoes of coals out of the sloop; the rest of the evidences condescend not upon the name of the sloop, except George Walker and Peter Cushnie the last of whom depones to three or four cargoes and one or two Scots coal which he thinks were all on board the *Bervie* sloop but one which was out of a vessel called the *Gourdon* sloop, which it is well known was in the illicit trade and in the employment of Robert Napier and Walter Sime merchants in Bervie who were the proprietors of the *Bervie* sloop before she was seized.

'This is all we could make out upon the subject of the information though at the same time we must beg leave to observe that from the frauds which are said to be committed in that place and its neighbourhood it would appear that these two officers, William Cock and Benjamin Smith, must either be extremely negligent in point of duty or must connive with the smugglers because we never do hear of any seizures made by them or any fraud detected'.

The Military
The collectors frequently made applications to the Board for assistance from the military. In February 1730 Aberdeen requested support at Banff 'As we have frequent intelligence of the barefaced

practice of the smugglers residing near to these places, which neither we nor our officers were they ever so willing are able to prevent without military assistance and as we have at present certain accounts that several ships from the bay of Biscay load with wines and brandies and others from Holland with the goods usually smuggled from these parts are daily expected thereabouts all whose cargoes will certainly be entirely run if not prevented by the above mentioned'. The case for military at Banff was strengthened the following May when it was reported 'no less than four or five vessels have run their cargoes in these parts this season'.

In June 1735 officers of customs and three soldiers were imprisoned at Inverness 'in relation to the deceased Hugh Fraser, merchant there, who was killed by one of the soldiers when out in the boat to protect the king's officers. The collector was to intervene so that McAdam would be 'liberated from the stocks or irons, so that he may only remain in prison in an open and free manner till he is tried by due course of law, and the surveyor general and collector are in the meantime to furnish him with comfortable subsistence and to acquaint the commander of the troops that the Board will protect him'. McAdam, and the other officers, received a royal pardon.

On 27 December 1778 David Garden and his crew seized fourteen boxes of fine bohea tea. A military party including a sergeant, corporal and six private men of the 83rd Glasgow regiment escorted the seizure to the king's warehouse. Accompanied by the soldiers, they continued the search, finding another three boxes of tea. The seizure totalled 1,411 lbs and was sold for £423 11s. By December 1779 nothing had been paid to the soldiers, who were now in Guernsey. It was agreed that the allowance should be to the sergeant 9s 6d, corporal 5s 6d and six privates at 2s 10d each amounting to £1 12s 'a reward adequate to their service, the same being agreeable to the rate to be observed for rewarding the military for their attendance day and night on a large seizure and their subsistence for one day in town'.

Other references to military support have been made throughout the book. The next chapter considers in detail the customs staff stationed at one locality - the tidesmen at Gourdon.

A STORY OF AN ABERDEEN COLLECTOR

On Wednesday night, 27 June 1744 'we received intelligence that there were several vessels from Holland smuggling upon the coast upon which we posted all our officers at the seaside and at different avenues to the town by land with orders to call upon us in case they saw occasion. Accordingly betwixt three and four of the morning Mr Fraser, tidewaiter, sent and called the collector telling that he was already in possession of some goods but was at a loss how to manage as he apprehended there might be some attempts made to rescue them. Upon which the collector got immediately out of bed and went to where he was, which was about a mile distant from this town, and in his road thither he espied eight or nine horses, which he immediately caused pursue. Thereupon the carriers threw down the goods and rode off with the horses and the collector immediately seized them and got horses and carried them to where the goods in James Fraser's possession were lying and then conveyed the whole to the king's warehouse ...

'The *Vernon* of this place, John Ferguson master, and the *Providence*, David Thomson master, came both into this harbour yesterday. We had repeated informations that there were no less than another three vessels, two of them belonging to this port and the third freighted from Holland for this place, busy smuggling upon the coast and that a great quantity of goods were coming into town by different roads last night. Upon which we caused the officers refresh themselves with sleep and at night called them up and the collector carried James Fraser and William Panton, tidewaiters, and William Freeman and James Forbes, boatmen, along with him and went towards the northward, having first obtained warrants for searching and assistance from Mr Middleton of Seaton. Having appointed Mr Skinner, landwaiter, with some assistants to guard a pass called the Denburn, upon the collector's passing by the place ... he sent William Panton and James Forbes to go and see what Mr Skinner was adoing and to meet him at a place he appointed, being but a small distance. Soon after their parting they met two horses, one laden with two ankers and the other with two matts, which they attempted to seize but were immediately attacked by a mob of people disguised in women's clothes and some of them with swords and other weapons and their faces blacked. Upon which they called out violently for assistance. When James Fraser and William Freeman, who were nearer them by a considerable distance than the collector, run to them and found the mob mauling them, and were immediately attacked

contd

A STORY OF AN ABERDEEN COLLECTOR contd

themselves with great fury. The collector hearing two or three shots fired and hearing a clashing of arms run up as fast as he could since till then considering the late vigorous resolutions entered into here and elsewhere [the individual burghs making resolutions against smuggling] he had not the least apprehension of a mob, especially as he had not met with the least appearance of resistance the former night. But before he came up the fury was ended and the mob had dispersed only that at a distance he saw several persons in women's apparel. Upon finding the mob had risen, the collector immediately carried back all the officers to guard the king's warehouse, as he apprehended that the mob being once on foot might attack it and indeed we still have the greatest apprehensions of their making that attempt, since we have no soldiers to support us and even our persons are not safe in going about our duty.

This morning we are informed that there was a young man, a merchant's son in this place called George Copland, unhappily killed in this fray and a merchant wounded, called Walter Fleming, and the magistrates having taken a precognition of this affair have committed James Fraser and William Freeman prisoners in our tolbooth. But as this melancholy affair happened merely in their own defence and in the execution of their duty and assisting their fellow officers and that they were both miserable beat by persons in disguise it's humbly hoped your Honours will be pleased to stand by them and procure their liberation or admitting them to bail. We are likewise credibly informed just now that there is a strong combination to procure a warrant for apprehending the collector and the greatest spite of malice against us both for attempting to do our duty so that if your Honours do not support us soon by military assistance we can not but apprehend the most fatal consequences. It is not possible just now to get the extract of the precognition as it is not quite finished but shall send it by post. Meantime we thought it our duty to lay this affair before your Honours without loss of time'.

The next letter was dated Monday, 2 July 1744. The magistrates were still working on the precognitions. 'They have left no stone unturned to procure a warrant for committing the collector to prison and have been very industrious for procuring evidences for that effect. But both the magistrates and justices of the peace have hitherto refused to grant them. There never was more fire among a set of people than these have shown who prosecute this affair and a set of people who find it both their interest and inclination are very

contd

135

A STORY OF AN ABERDEEN COLLECTOR contd

ready supporting them. And as to running of goods they do not only employ the night but likewise in broad day they carry them in the streets in contempt of all law and our officers dare not venture considering the present spirit to interrupt them so that we are at the greatest loss how to behave'.

On Wednesday 4 July the comptroller reported 'The collector was yesternight apprehended by a warrant from James Petrie, sheriff substitute of this county, and put into gaol notwithstanding the precognition was not taken before him and the magistrates and whole justices that were applied to having absolutely refused to grant such a warrant ... [They had applied, unsuccessfully, for bail] We have been obliged to send this by John Delgatie, one of our tidesmen, because we could not get any express we could trust to'.

The next report was dated Monday, 9 July 1744. 'Last night our express returned with the Lord Advocate's opinion etc for the collector's liberation and this morning the sheriff was required to set him at liberty, which he complied with. We did likewise this day apply by petition to the magistrates for setting Fraser and Freeman at liberty, to which they delayed till tomorrow till they had given out our petition to Mr Copland's friends to see and answer. We would have protested against them immediately but as the law seems to allow them twenty-four hours we delayed till tomorrow'.

On Tuesday, 'we renewed our application ... But the magistrates still demurred upon pretence of their sufficiency ... last night our provost, Mr Aberdein, arrived here and ... he acquainted us that he had directions from the Lord Advocate to take a further precognition, which he intended to do tomorrow morning ... In the meantime with our request till he should see how the matter came out upon being thoroughly sifted'.

On Saturday they reported 'Our magistrates have this afternoon admitted our two officers to bail. What we now want is to know whether your Honours will be pleased to order a further enquiry in this affair and in what manner. We can certainly find no evidences other than our own officers and those that were in the mob and we are informed those already called were of that number'.

CHAPTER NINE: THE TIDESMEN AT GOURDON

'We have received your Honours order of the 30th ult with respect to the seizure of the sloop *Dispatch* and directing us to acquaint **James Philip**, tidesman at Gourdon, to repair to Montrose at Whitsunday next to be stationed there and to send another tidesman to Gourdon in his room, such as we shall think fittest for that station. In obedience to which we instantly made the required notification to **James Philip** and having attentively considered the last part of said order respecting a successor at Gourdon we humbly beg leave to refer your Honours to the characters of the officers of this port in our list for last year whereby it appears that all of the tidesmen are suspected of being in the interest of the merchants. But as there is a necessity for employing such as we have we are of opinion that **John Rodger**, now at the port, from his knowledge of the coast and the nature of the trade carried on there as well as the inhabitants in that part of the country but more especially from the assurances and engagements he has made to us of being sincerely and heartily in the interest of the Crown and that he will exert himself to the utmost in preventing or detecting illicit trade in his division may have a trial of that charge. If his conduct, over which we shall have a watchful eye, shall be inconsistent with his profession we shall notify the same to your Honours that he may be dealt with according to his demerit and of this we shall give him fair warning that he may be on his guard to prevent such complaints'. [Letter from the collector at Montrose to the Board, dated 27 April 1772]. [See also Chapter Seven for the wreck of the *Dispatch* and the tailpiece to this chapter for John Rodger]

Between 1768 and 1785 a series of tidesmen was appointed to Gourdon, 'about little more than a quarter of a mile from Bervie, which we understood was then the grand scene of action and the general rendezvous of the smugglers'. Their district stretched from Gapple, the boundary with the Aberdeen collection to the north, to Johnshaven. Each one in turn became 'in the interest of the merchants' to the extent that they were either dismissed or transferred to another part of the Montrose collection. This problem was partly a result of the very nature of the area 'as there is more smuggling for ordinary on that part of the coast than in all the precinct besides' and there was only one tidesman against the 'whole country'. It was also partly a result of the strong character of the smugglers based at Bervie - Walter Sime and Robert Napier [see Chapter Four]. As the collector wrote in 1770, since Philip's transfer to Gourdon 'the merchants there used such prevailing arguments with him as were too strong for his virtue and honesty and ... [there was] convincing proof ... of his being led astray from an honest attachment to the trust committed to his charge and thereby connected with the enemies to his country, to truth and to the laws'.

James Philip (1768 to 1772)

Appointed as an extraordinary tidesman at Johnshaven on 24 December 1764, at a salary of £18 per annum, James Philip 'supported his character very well and was obnoxious to the smugglers'. On the Board's orders he was moved to Gourdon in 1768. The next year 'in the exercise of his duty when making a seizure [Philip] lost his left eye in a scuffle by Thomas Morris baker in Johnshaven, who was prosecute ... but for want of evidence was acquit, the actual beating his eye out not being proved. His other eye having been tender ever since [he] has desired us [26 June 1770] to apply ... for leave to be absent from his duty for the space of three weeks in order to take advice for having his eye restored to its former strength'.

In May 1770 Philip seized ten ankers containing 86 gallons geneva in the houses of Ann Greig and Janet Watson at the Townhead of Bervie. Despite the Board's instruction 'to commence prosecutions against the women' the justices did not meet again until August when the collector attended and 'observed such a behaviour in him as left him no room to doubt that Philip was not the officer he took him for when at Johnshaven. He was called as an evidence in the cause and being objected to by the procurator for the defendants he declared that he did not know but that he might be entitled to a share of the penalties prosecuted for, upon which he was cast out as an evidence and so the women were acquitted'.

The case of the *Janet* of Johnshaven

The surveyor made a complaint against Philip in October 1770 'for getting drunk when on duty on board the sloop *Janet*, James Wilson master [see Chapter Ten and Appendix II], from Norway, then lying in the harbour of Johnshaven and for deserting his duty when on board that vessel'. The collector examined upon oath Alexander Simpson, tidesman at Johnshaven, John Rodger and William Blews, who was a mariner on board the *Princess Caroline* sloop and 'occasionally in Johnshaven'.

Having considered their proof, the collector 'gave the matter in charge to James Philip ... and received his answers thereto in writing ... which principally contains a few frivolous and trifling objections to the testimonies of the three evidences admitted against him with a denial of the whole, joining with the smugglers in the outcry against Blews by a letter to us dated the 23rd October. He desires fourteen days to bring in his exculpatory witnesses but not inclining they should appear before us he applied to Thomas Christie [provost of Bervie] ... by petition craving that they should be examined before him, which the said provost having found reasonable agreed to'.

Philip's evidences were 'all of one class of people, the smugglers'. They included: John Leighton, 'designed brewer of Johnshaven but a common mariner on the *Janet*'; James Strachan, 'designed writer in Bervie, yet well known to be a smuggler and aider of the smugglers'; Andrew Law, 'who had been dismissed as a mariner on the *Princess Caroline* revenue cutter, known to be connected with the Bervie smugglers'; David Croll, 'merchant in Johnshaven and a bankrupt smuggler'; James Innes, 'merchant in Johnshaven, a noted smuggler' whose 'care of Philip' was demonstrated by the fact that he went 'ashore for a great coat for him' and John Buchan, a tidesman at Temple of Kinneff, who belonged to the port of Aberdeen, so that the collector did not know him, except that, like Philip, he was 'in the interest of the smugglers on that part of the coast'.

The collector concluded in his report, dated 5 November 1770, 'Without taking notice of the extraordinary step of Philip having his witnesses examined by a country magistrate, which plainly indicates his terror of their not being sustained as unexceptionable by us, considering their trade and employments, your Honours upon considering their testimonies and the warmth and keenness they express therein of their friend Philip being acquit from the accusation laid against him will see what degree of credit is due to them against the concurring evidences of

Figure 10: The Tidesmen at Gourdon: The Creeks to the Northward

The picture actually shows the coast to the north of Todhead, the boundary with the Aberdeen district. The tidesmen stationed at Gourdon were frequently out along the coast to the north and this gives the impression of the inaccessibility of many of the coves used by the smugglers.

In May 1769 the collector at Montrose went to Whirtleberry, ten miles to the north, to make an enquiry into some information sent to the Board in an anonymous letter signed Solomon. There he took the declarations of Robert Watt, skipper of a fishing boat at Shield Hill and his crew, Andrew James, John Watts and William Jamie 'with respect to a fraud having been committed by Mr Blews, second mate and commander of a row boat belonging to captain John Read'. According to the information Blews seized two boats and then returned one, together with two hogsheads of geneva, to the smugglers. Considering all the other information about Blews in this book, it is not surprising that the accusation was not proved.

Robert Dickie was an extraordinary officer of customs at Milton of Mathers. In November 1772 he was directed to keep a journal of his proceedings. When this was transmitted to the Board at the end of six months, it included accusations of neglect and refusing to correspond with him. Apparently this referred to John Rodger 'for not informing him of a fraud that was committed to the northward till it was over and then too late, in the month of October last'. According to Rodger 'having some suspicion of a smuggle that day, from what he understood going through Bervie, he went to the Gapple, the northmost creek in his division, four miles from his residence and from thence to Catterline and called upon David Findlay tidesman there, what is in the district of Aberdeen. Having met him they together searched ... without success. When he returned home that night he wrote a letter to Alexander Simpson, tidesman at Johnshaven, giving him the above account because Simpson's house is a mile nearer than Dickie's. Both Alexander Simpson and Robert Dickie came to him at Gourdon but then, as observed before, it was too late. In Rodger's letter of the 3rd October he says that one or two boats with tea had come in that morning to Gapple, Catterline and/or Braidon Bay. But [he] could not learn where they came from or into whose possession the goods were delivered. Robert Dickie was much to blame for not making his complaint recently and for postponing it to the time he gave in his journal and we have recommended it to him if he has any such accusation again to make it directly when it happens all which is humbly submitted to your Honours consideration.' Dickie was discontinued.

the witnesses on the other side, whose testimonies we humbly apprehend are not in the least invalidated by what Philip has alleged'. Philip remained in post at Gourdon. [see Chapter Four for further details of the *Janet*]

The story of the wreck of the *Dispatch*, Peter Moor master, is told in Chapter Seven. On 30 March 1772 the Board ordered that Philip 'repair to Montrose at Whitsunday next there to be stationed as extraordinary tidesman ... in which order their Honours have been pleased to judge that your conduct respecting the sloop *Dispatch* lately seized at Bervie has been such as to forfeit any merit you had in giving the first imperfect account of the arrival of the sloop and therefore adjudged the moiety of the seizure to belong to your superior officers.' Philip was moved to Ulysseshaven, Buddon and finally Montrose. On 3 June 1777 John Keith, the surveyor, wrote to the collector and comptroller 'the insolence of James Philip, extraordinary tidesman at this port, is so great that I cannot forbear making you acquainted therewith in order that you may state the same to the Honourable Board' and 'Philip's conduct has for some years frequently borne every mark of insanity or intoxication, as is well known to all in this office.'

John Rodger

Originally appointed on 9 June 1755, John Rodger replaced Philip at Gourdon at Whitsunday 1772. By September he was in trouble over salmon shipped in the name of Lord Arbuthnott, part of which was not included in the sufferance as 'you was from home'. This seemed to set the scene for his subsequent behaviour. A problem with Robert Dickie is described in Figure 10. On 12 July 1773 the collector wrote to Rodger that he had received information about two smuggles of tea, asking him to report 'where you was then and you are to inform us what measures you took to prevent or detect the same and also you are to intimate to us the names of the vessels and masters of them'. He was dismissed on 17 August 1774. Details of Rodger's subsequent claims to seizures are given in the tailpiece to this chapter.

Thomas Mills

On 18 February 1775, the collector reported to the Board that Thomas Mills, who lately came from Fort William, where he had been a tidesman, was 'a stout and vigorous young man' so that he was appointed to Gourdon. On 16 May 1776 he was deforced and the collector and surveyor went to Gourdon to investigate what had happened.

When the *Peggie*, Alexander Paton master, arrived from Kirkcaldy, Mills was given a warrant for discharging 23 tons 2 cwt of coals. 'When the quantity in the warrant was out, he stopped work till money should be deposited with him for the duties of the remaining quantity and thereon received 5 shillings upon which he allowed them to proceed till he found that they had landed upwards of 5 tons, when he again insisted on more money being deposited for the excessive quantity already landed and what remained to be landed. Upon which one George Morris, baker in Johnshaven, who managed the discharge (the owner of the vessel being in prison at Montrose for debt), swore that he would proceed in spite of Thomas Mills and the custom house and accordingly caused put more coals ashore, which Mills threw back on board the vessel and which Morris and his associates forcibly relanded and proceeded to weigh and send off. Upon which Mills, unaided by any, judged it prudent to take himself away, at same time hearing Morris declare that it was a pity he had not made a Philips of him ... who in the execution of his duty had an eye knocked out by a brother of said Morris. Thomas Mills is uncertain the quantity there landed when he was obliged to quit the shore but judges it not to have been considerable'.

George Morris took out a petition against Mills. When the collector and surveyor went to Gourdon to enquire into the matter they were told 'by neutral persons' that Mills 'is usually ill-treated by the skippers and others concerned in these coal barques ... In order to supply the defect of his not being present at the discharge of that part of the cargo from which he was driven by the threats and menaces of the petitioner and the mob then on the beach he made enquiry who had received the coals ... and he showed us a note of their names'. £9 9s was still due. Morris refused to pay this, saying that he had only acted as agent for David Law, who was currently at sea as master of the *Peggie*.

On 25 January 1777 Mills seized five ankers and one ullage anker of brandy and a cart drawn by a single horse, the property of James Will, carter in Bervie. 'He declares that the seizure was made about eleven o'clock at night, pitch dark, and that there was a crowd of people about him, who threatened to carry off the seizure altogether if he would not part with the cart and horse. During the time he was securing the spirits in the house of Mr Thomas Christie, provost of Bervie, which was with difficulty effected, the mob carried off the horse and cart'. These were subsequently reseized, condemned by the justices, appraised and sold on 3 February 1777.

Nine days later the collector wrote to the Board that Mills 'appearing to be a stout and vigorous young man and able to undergo a good deal of fatigue was appointed to the station for Gourdon, where smuggling then was and still is carried on in a higher degree that in any station or division of this port or on this coast. We must acknowledge that we had great expectations of his success both in detection of frauds and in preventing their being committed within his division. But in this we have been greatly disappointed for except a trifle of six ankers of spirits on the 25th January last he has not made the seizure of a single article of any kind of goods whatever since he has been on that station, although sent many informations. We have good reason to suspect that large quantities of prohibited and high duty goods have been fraudulently run and smuggled within 200 yards of his dwelling house, many of which frauds he has been unlikely silent upon and kept concealed and since he has given us trifling and cursory intimations of after the fraud has been over. If we had been certain of convicting Thomas Mills of his collusion by a legal proof we should have laid it before your Honours before this time. But no such thing can be had here from the obstinate attachment of those people who would be proper evidences to the smugglers. Our suspicion of this officer's confederacy with the illicit merchants we have certified to your Honours annually since he was removed to Gourdon.

'Such then being the conduct of this man, the truth of which we are satisfied with in our own minds, we beg leave to move your Honours that he may be ordered to change stations with William Buchanan at Buddon at the term of Whitsunday next. As Thomas Mills has shown some degree of attention to the discharge of his coal duty he may be of some use at that creek ... Buddon is a place not now used by the smugglers but is a creek where many vessels are unloaded with coals coastwise from the Firth of Forth ...

'We are much concerned for the presumed infidelity of Thomas Mills because we were at all imaginable pains to put him on his guard at going there against being corrupted. We set forth the many advantages that would accrue to himself and his family by sticking fast to integrity and being diligent in the faithful discharge of his trust and laid before him the fatal consequences of a contrary conduct. We have often expostulated with him to this purpose both by word and write and remonstrate against his supposed viscous and unfaithful conduct'.

As if the tidesman knew that the writing was on the wall, on 4 March 1777 the collector transmitted return of seizure No 177 by John Sharp and Thomas Mills for one cask of tea and three ankers geneva.

On 18 March the Board instructed that Thomas Mills should be accused of negligence. The proof had to be taken in the presence of a justice of the peace 'whose authority we found absolutely necessary to compel the witnesses to appear in case of their being refractory, as they commonly are upon the like occasions'. There were six witnesses:

Andrew Lamie stated that since Mills was stationed at Gourdon he has been informed there has been frequent smuggling at the Bing of Bervie 'once a fortnight or twice a month ... in the month of October or November 1775 he knows that James Freeman, Thomas Mills and others were in company in his house and that all the company except Thomas Mills and another were the worse of drink ... he has heard Thomas Mills declare that he would not seize or choose to seize a single anker of spirits, if it was kept out of his way ... his [Lamie's] sister-in-law, who passed Thomas Mills' house before he came to it, left some coarse sugar and thread to the value of 16s and that he had heard Thomas Mills' wife did sell some coarse sugar but never heard that she sold any tea and that there was no tea sold at her sister-in-law's roup'. There were objections against this testimony and Lamie himself implied malice and resentment against Mills in the execution of his duty.

The second witness for the Customs was Alexander Gowan, ship master in Gourdon [see Chapters Seven and Ten] 'against whose testimony such a proof has been brought by the depositions of James Strachan, writer in Bervie, and James Christie of Maplepool as must render everything he says against Thomas Mills greatly suspected and that the evidence Alexander Gowan has given has proceeded from ill-will and resentment, owing to his having posted him on his coals. We were sorry to see Gowan's conduct at his examination so very forward and incautious and unguarded against Mills'.

James Strachan deponed that he never heard Thomas Mills say that before he would seize an anker of spirits from Mr Sime or others he would loose his commission.

Robert Gowan deponed that on the night the fray happened in Andrew Lamie's house he saw James Freeman throw a jug of ale at Thomas Mills.

James Freeman deponed that he never knew nor heard that Thomas Mills's wife kept a shop or retailed any goods and that he never gave information of smuggled goods to Thomas Mills at any time

'Thus we have gone through the testimonies of the witnesses on both sides and we must acknowledge in consideration of the weight of the objections against the two first witnesses that the facts stated in the charge are not made ... nothing appears from the proof but that Mills had got the ill-will and resentment of the people in and about Gourdon for his attention to his duty with discharge of coals and as a good coal officer at Gourdon'.

On 26 February 1777 the Board restored Thomas Mills to his office, without loss of pay. But 'we are still humbly of opinion that it will be more eligible and more to the advantage of the revenue that he be stationed at Buddon against Whitsunday next, as little else but coals duty is to do there ... The expense Thomas Mills has been put to in making his defence amounts to £1 14s 6d'.

William Buchanan and John Sharp

In February 1777 the collector wrote to the Board 'William Buchanan is an active man and seems to be keen and zealous when employed against the smugglers. Seeing so many of our officers have been corrupted by the illicit traders of Bervie and Gourdon which hath been alwise considered as one station and one officer only appointed for it we beg leave also to propose that another officer be stationed there, which as the two places are but about a short mile's distance from one another they might be useful not only in aiding but be check on one another's procedure they might when necessary be mostly together when they go their rounds on the out look and be otherwise mutually assisting each other, which will be very necessary especially when they have no military to support them in the exercise of their duty. Should your Honours be pleased to approve of this arrangement we presume to name John Sharp at Milton to be the other officer to be stationed at Bervie, who is a stout young man and who prevented the smuggling in that quarter in that time he was stationed there before Thomas Mills was sent to that division [between August 1774 and February 1775]'.

In August 1773 John Sharp was appointed as an extraordinary officer at Milton of Mathers. According to the November report 'nothing improper in his conduct since he came to this district has reached our ears'. The favourable reports continued and on 15 July 1774 the collector wrote 'we do beg leave to observe that this officer is on all occasions diligent and active in the prevention part of his duty and in particular in assisting Alexander Simpson, tidesman at Johnshaven, the officer next to his station on this coast. In the part of his duty respecting the duty of coals coastwise we found upon his coming here he was defective in his writing and arithmetic, wherefore we recommended to him to make himself as perfect as possible. Accordingly he put himself to a writing school in the neighbourhood of his residence at Milton, where he is also taught counting, and every day since is improving himself in both these most necessary branches of education and will we hope and expect turn out to be accurate as he is greatly mended in each of them.'

By April 1775 he had not made a seizure because 'as far as anyone knows there have been no frauds in his area'. In January 1776 the collector reported he was 'honest and keeps free to the best of our knowledge from improper intimacies or connections with smugglers and gives attention to his business, according to the best of our information'.

On 21 February 1780 the collector at Montrose wrote to Messrs Buchanan and Sharp at Gourdon. 'We are directed by the Honourable Board to give you the strictest injunctions to be more exact in your journals, which from the examination made by the collector appear to be inaccurate, and your are not to fail on any pretence to give notice when any suspicion of a smuggle arises whether from the appearance of vessel on the coast or otherwise and in case any smuggle may have happened without you having any previous knowledge of it you are to send the earliest notice thereof to us notifying the same in your journals'.

Inevitably no information was sent to the custom house. On 20 May 1780 the collector reported that William Buchanan was ill and wanted to leave Gourdon. The Board agreed and suggested that he should be brought to the main port, where he could be under more direct supervision. However, 'none of the tidesmen stationed at Montrose appear to us proper for the Gourdon duty owing to age, bodily infirmity or having been formerly judged by your Honours as improper persons to be employed at Gourdon. Neither do we know of any tidesman within the precinct to whom some of these objections may not be made except David Hill, lately appointed, and William Blews stationed at Arbroath. The inexperience of Hill renders him rather ineligible. We would therefore humbly propose to your Honours that William Blews might be ordered to Gourdon and William Buchanan be stationed at Arbroath where he will be equally capable of the duty as at Montrose'.

In November Buchanan was still at Gourdon and the collector reported 'we have examined Doctor Hunter, who has attended him, and he declares that it would be improper if not impossible to remove Buchanan at this season, as the man is in great distress from a strangury with which he is sorely affected.' William Blews should have been posted to Gourdon at this stage, but he was too ill himself. Eventually Buchanan was replaced by George Swan.

Between 1782 and 1784 Swan and Sharp only seized fourteen ankers of spirits, thirteen of which they had received an information about and so could not avoid seizing.

On 5 January 1785 the collector stated 'We have some suspicions as to the fidelity of John Sharp and will endeavour to discover whether they are well grounded or not'. This related to a smuggle at Bervie on 19 November 1784. The Board replied on 10 January, requesting an immediate report on Sharp's character and conduct 'that they may from thence judge of the propriety of ordering you to be further continued or not. We again repeat to you in the strongest manner the injunction the collector gave you when at Montrose to discover all that you know of any frauds which have been committed in your neighbourhood (many of which have happened of late), whether you have in any way been accessory yourself or not, as the most probable means of procuring your further continuance as we must of necessity communicate to the Board all the circumstances of the affair of the 19th November last. So far as we know you and George Swan have not confessed, which must necessarily occasion the greatest suspicion of your honesty in the Board and may probably produce effects which we would not wish. Therefore out of tenderness to you we give you this further warning and desire your answer on or before Saturday next, on which day we are obliged to write an answer to the Board. After this repeated admonition to discover what you know of the fraud committed on the 19th November last or any others, whatever may happen you will have yourself only to blame.

'If you make any discovery of any frauds so as the revenue may be benefited, even although they shall have been committed with your own knowledge and consent, we shall recommend you to the mercy of the Board.'

But events caught up as on 13 January 1785 the Board sent a letter to the collector 'covering a copy of an information touching the conduct of the tidesmen at Gourdon in conniving at frauds committed by the running smuggled goods in that neighbourhood and directing us to make due enquiry into the facts set forth and to report the result thereof with our observations for your consideration ... Upon the 20th November last at noon we received a letter from George Swan, tidesman, and John Sharp, extraordinary tidesman, both stationed at Gourdon near Bervie of which the following is a copy viz

'This morning we went to Bervie and understand there had been a smuggle this last night we have gone to the country in search of the goods and is informed that they are gone the way of Brechin'.

'Immediately on receiving this letter we communicated its contents to Mr Garden ... and directed him and his crew to proceed up into the country and try to intercept the goods which had been smuggled on their way southward whither it was likely they would be carried. He accordingly proceeded as directed but met with no goods transporting, although he remained out forty-eight hours. However, in the course of his journey he heard that on the evening of the 19th November the officers at Gourdon had been in possession of a cart or carts laden with smuggled goods and that they had been deforced and the cart or carts carried off. This was all he could learn, which having communicated to us we (although we doubted the truth of the story, the tidesmen having taken no notice of so remarkable an affair in their letter to us. On the contrary they had said that they had only received notice on the morning of the 20th that a smuggle had happened the night before) set an enquiry on foot which we have continued ever since and are informed that the deforcement did happen as reported but have never been able to learn what persons actually committed the deforcement upon the officers'.

When the tidesmen were examined at Montrose by the collector, Swan acknowledged that between nine and ten o'clock on the evening of 19th November he and Sharp 'fell in with three or four loaded carts coming from the beach' near Bervie. They laid hold of one with approximately twelve ankers on it. 'But the carts being escorted by a number of people on foot and on horseback' it was rescued and they were detained by four men they did not know. After being kept in the fields for some time, they were given the option of staying there or going to a public house in Bervie. They went to the pub, where they drank porter with the four men until six o'clock in the morning. They were only released because they agreed not to tell the collector, although the men did not see what they wrote to him in their letter.

Both Swan and Sharp said that they did not know the identity of the four men. Asked if the landlord knew them, they said that he denied any knowledge of the men. The collector was convinced that they had connived in the deforcement or they would not have concealed 'an act of such violence from their superiors' and further that the landlord would not have allowed his pub to be used that way. Swan and Sharp would say nothing more about the incident and 'neither threats nor promises will move them'.

On 15 December 1784 a letter was sent to David Garden from 'a friend in the country'. As Garden was in Leith, the letter was opened by the collector's clerk, who had been authorised by Garden to open his letters in his absence. It mentioned a smuggle at the beach of Bervie on the evening of 13 December and that the goods were lodged among the caves and rocks near Bervie. The collector sent out a party to search for them but nothing was found. The same day Swan and Sharp also wrote to the collector:

'We went to Bervie yesterday's forenoon and saw a boat lying on the beach and several tracks of carts. We have reason to think that they had brought ashore goods with her. We sent a man immediately express to the office with this intelligence and we continued all day and night upon the outlook and called for the express in the morning. He was not arrived nor is not yet. It is reported that he was stopped by some of the gang or boat's crew which is lying in Bervie. We expect your advice in course what we shall do as to the boat etc.'

The collector never received the first express. On receipt of the 'second' letter he instructed the tidesmen that if there was proof that goods had been run out of the boat then they were to ascertain her tonnage and then burn her. He received no reply. The collector's clerk, who was in the area on 17 December, was told that the boat had been taken from the beach and anchored in the bay before they heard from the collector.

James Hadden, merchant in Montrose, was said to have been principal in and present at both smuggles and to have gone to the public house to entertain the tidesmen after the deforcement. On 22 January 1785 Swan and Sharp were told that they had been dismissed. William Blews was sent to replace them.

William Blews
William Blews was appointed as an extraordinary tidesman at Arbroath on 6 December 1770. At that stage he was 29 years old. According to the collector's report to the Board in December 1773 he was 'honest, diligent capable and active. He was at first employed only for three months and since continued by particular orders at the expiration of each period till lately that your Honours have been pleased to continue him for six months from the 10 October last'.

On 24 January 1785 Blews arrived at Gourdon. He stayed there until 31 May 1785 'when finding himself unable to perform in the fatiguing duty of this station by reason of sickness (occasioned by a hurt he received some years ago in the execution of his duty, the consequences of which recur upon him) he obtained leave to go home to his family for the recovery of his health'. He returned to Gourdon on 3

July. On 7 September he was told that David Fetters had been appointed to succeed him at Arbroath. He had been at great expense living one hundred and ninety-five days from home and the cost of bringing his family to Gourdon. The collector commented 'The petitioner has always supported the character of an uncorrupted officer, which induced him to employ him on the service above mentioned'.

On 13 December 1790 William Blews and Thomas Bouchart, tidesmen at Gourdon, were obstructed and abused by a party of Flushingers and merchants in attempting to seize twelve carts laden with goods which had been landed at the beach of Bervie from a smuggling lugger lying in the bay. James Christie junior and John Rae were the carters yet they could not say who had employed them. 'And from the depravity of morals of those people who are constantly employed by the smugglers there is no certainty that upon examination they would not deny their having been there'.

As Blews was an 'extraordinary tidesman' and so not on the establishment, it is difficult to track his subsequent career but he appears to have remained in post until at least 1805. At last the smugglers in the Gourdon district had met their match.

The tailpiece is based on the collector's reply to the complaint made by John Rodger, after he was dismissed, that he had been denied his rightful share of various seizures he had made while stationed at Gourdon. This reply includes more detail than is normally available about the actual process of searching for and seizing goods. The next chapter considers the revenue at sea.

A STORY OF JOHN RODGER'S NON SEIZURES

After he had been dismissed in 1775, John Rodger claimed that he had been involved in several seizures but had received no payment. There follows a somewhat shortened version of the collector's detailed explanation of what he thought was the truth.

1. Sixteen matts of tobacco stems in the haughs of Bervie, 13 April 1773 and seventeen ankers of gin in a smithy at Bervie, 14 April 1773

'On the morning of 13th April the collector received intelligence that in the night preceding there happened a large quantity of prohibited goods to be landed out of many boats at the Bing ... and what was still more astonishing the collector was at same time told that John Rodger, the tidesman, had left Gourdon on that same night the smuggle happened and come into Montrose and was in Montrose all night. The instant the collector was told of this fraud he communicated the same to Charles Reid and desired him to take what officers he thought proper for his assistance and proceed to rummage the country about Bervie but required him to have no correspondence with Rodger. About ten o'the clock Mr Rodger thought proper to appear at this office but not one word of the fraud the night before. Mr Rodger went off in a few minutes ... and having understood out of doors that several of the officers were gone to the eastward he followed them with a quick pace to be present at any seizure that might be seized, to give him a handle for a claim. This is all the collector or any of us knows of this transaction.

'After obtaining warrants from the provost, the officers divided themselves into two parties to make the proposed search and rummage with the greater accuracy and expedition. Accordingly Charles Reid and Alexander Arbuthnott took one part of the town of Bervie. The other party consisted of Mr Kennedy comptroller, Robert Dickie and John Smith, then both extraordinary tidesmen at the port, and were followed by John Rodger, though not desired nor employed by them. John Smith is not now in the country so that we are deprived of his evidence and Robert Dickie lying under some imputation of having gone too far when examined in the court of exchequer and as we know that he bore a grudge against John Rodger we did not examine him. So that Mr Kennedy and Mr Rodger, the other two who say they were in the smithy and both claim the mint of having discovered the seventeen ankers and their testimony being diametrically opposite to one and they we judged it altogether unnecessary to take down the same in writing because from it no

contd

153

A STORY OF JOHN RODGER'S NON SEIZURES contd

person could judge who was the seizer or who made the discovery, Mr Kennedy averring he it was that discovered them below the bellows and Mr Rodger declaring it was him.

'So that it will remain with your Honours to consider whether Rodger by his deserting and leaving the creek he had the charge of when the great fraud was committed and coming into Montrose eight miles distant, where he was all that night, merits any part of the seizure of the tobacco stems got in the haughs of Bervie on the 13th or even any share of the seventeen ankers gin got in the smithy the day afterwards, even admitting he was in the smithy when they were seized. For we humbly beg leave to observe that his being excluded from any part or share of the same was a just punishment for his abandoning his station at the period when smuggling was going on, which circumstance carries along with it a strong presumption that he was in the knowledge of it and nobody that is acquainted with Mr Rodger, his art, his management, his intelligence and superior cunning to most men, will ever imagine that he would leave his charge at so critical a juncture without his being satisfied and paid for the risk he run thereby of losing his place.

'After communing with Mr Rodger upon this subject, when endeavouring to make up these differences now under your Honours' consideration, he strongly denied that he was in the knowledge of the above fraud that night it happened ... Besides what is above set forth in relation to the seventeen ankers got in the smithy it appears by the declaration of Charles Reid that the real officers concerned in that seizure allowed Mr Rodger 15s as a gratuity for his trouble and paid him by Mr Reid on the 28 December 1773, with which Mr Reid declares he, Rodger, was satisfied nor did Rodger claim any more till after he was dismissed the service ... it is surprising with what face Mr Rodger can demand payment a second time.

2. Thirteen ankers gin seized in the mill of Garvock

'Mr Reid declares that he received a particular information upon the mill of Garvock, where Messrs Bisset and Arbuthnott and he got nine ankers ... he rewarded his information with 30s. He declares that next day Messrs Bisset and Arbuthnott, together with the supervisor and another officer of excise, on a further search through the country found four ankers gin ... Mr Reid and Mr Arbuthnott declare Rodger was not present at making these two seizures nor do they believe that he knew where they were ... The first night

contd

A STORY OF JOHN RODGER'S NON SEIZURES contd

after Messrs Reid, Bisset and Arbuthnott had seized the nine ankers ... it was late before they returned to Bervie so that no more could be done that night and being fatigued they went to get some rest and placed Rodger to guard the Lodging, a house so called in Bervie, till next morning that they could obtain a warrant to search it. However a little time after the officers had gone to bed Mr Rodger brought into them two ankers gin, which he says in his petition were seized by himself coming from the old Lodging of Bervie ... Rodger was placed at the Lodging to prevent goods from being removed in the night time ... Is it to be supposed that the smugglers would have attempted such a thing when they knew there were so many officers in town if they had not been certain the guard was in their interest? Surely not. Had Rodger done his duty that night a considerable quantity of goods would have been found there in the morning.

3. Ten ankers geneva seized in the Thieves Hole, Bervie and four ankers in provost Christie's house

According to Charles Reid, 'Mr Rodger saying it was his information is an arrant falsehood but if Mr Rodger had such an information why did he not execute it before Mr Reid and Blews appeared? But this seems to be apiece with his other averments respecting his informations. In those cases as well as in others Mr Rodger did obtrude himself upon Mr Reid and his assistants without being employed or desired. It is therefore submitted to your Honours if he merits anything, especially when your Honours will be pleased to consider that all the time Rodger was officer at Gourdon he never made a seizure by himself ... nor did he ever communicate a single information to any officer or officers, although we sincerely do believe he had it often in his power to do it. But it is supposed that Mr Rodger was gratified for his taciturnity and his negligence by the smugglers'.

4. Twenty-six ankers geneva seized at Craig David

'William Blews ... is by far the most vigilant and active officer in his sphere within this precinct, as well as most successful in making seizures, who being stationed at Arbroath has settled a correspondence with friends he has about Bervie, Gourdon and all along the coast, who informs him of a vessel expected or that may be arrived upon the smuggling trade. When he receives such information ... he comes directly and acquaints the collector of it and asks leave to go on the prosecution of them. It was on one of these expeditions that Blews was in the beginning of February 1774 at Gourdon being out on the

contd

A STORY OF JOHN RODGER'S NON SEIZURES contd

watch in the night time, sometimes by himself sometimes with the crews of row boats. The night preceding the day of seizure Blews was out but was unsuccessful but early in the morning he received information that a smuggle had been to the eastward upon which he went to John Rodger's house and awaked him out of his bed upon which Rodger looked out at a window in his shirt and having been desired to put on his clothes Blews communicated his intelligence and desired Rodger to go along with him, when they having agreed to go to Craig David the seizure was made. This is the history of this transaction from Blews, which we have no reason to discredit'.

'If the collector had admitted Mr Rodger to have returned the twenty-six ankers got and seized by William Blews, as Blews could not come to town with them himself because the collector had by express ordered Blews to serve subpoenas in the trial against David Law at some distance and directed Rodger to bring them hither he would have looked upon himself as justly reprehensible for such a piece of injustice done to Blews ... Blews has frequently offered Rodger two guineas for his trouble'.

'We beg to leave to observe that notwithstanding the merit that Mr Rodger claims in his petition he never made a single seizure by himself nor communicated a single information whereby a seizure was made all the time he was stationed at Gourdon except one of eight ankers gin, which had been given him in the most shameless manner by Mr Sime, a notorious smuggler in Bervie, upon Rodger's showing Sime a letter he had received from the collector threatening to lay him before your Honours for negligence and collusion and this Mr Rodger imagined would mitigate the collector's resentment against him ...

'It is our joint opinion that this officer was paid a certain sum of money by the smugglers in and about Bervie for his forbearance and for not giving them any trouble when they were about this illicit trade, as well as for his collusion in not advising his superiors in this office when frauds were committing or recently committed ... However what may be in this we shall not say but one thing is certain that since this officer's dismission he is now come to Montrose where he is turned merchant and as we are informed has set up and fitted a well-filled shop of such merchandise as he thinks most fit for the market and we can scarcely imagine that any man with a wife and children could save so much money out of £18 per annum as would furnish such a shop as he has'.

CHAPTER TEN: THE REVENUE AT SEA

'Yesterday morning some ill-disposed villains have carried away the custom house boat across the ferry, and with saws and axes have cut her in two by the middle, left the one half on the beach, and disposed of the other to the waves. The execution of this is owing no doubt to common people, but the contrivance to greater heads, and that it has been premeditated appears by the tools they had provided themselves with to perform it. 'Tis hard to tell where this will end. The warehouse has been twice broken open, the boat destroyed, the expresses from the outports stopped and the letters taken away, a person under suspicion of being an informer dragged across the Firth and his ears cut out, and hints every day given to myself to take care of my life; in short no part of the face of the earth is peopled by such abandoned villains as this country'. [Letter from the collector at Inverness to the Board, dated 18 May 1733]

Despite the fact that it would seem essential for each outport to have at least one boat, this was not the case. In 1747 John Rollo, landwaiter at Banff, complained 'much of a great deal of smuggling in the Moray Firth, which is not in his power to prevent. But if your Honours would be pleased to order a boat to be stationed at Banff or Portsoy he apprehends she would be of great service to the revenue and prevent in a great measure so many frauds as are committed in that Firth'. In the absence of a boat belonging to the customs, the tidesurveyor would have to hire one. In December 1748 the collector at Aberdeen explained the tidesurveyor's expenses of £2 15s 'charged for the boat employed by him during the time there was no custom house boat ... the boat was at the same time employed for the service of the revenue in boarding of ships to and from foreign parts and carrying the tidesmen on board of them'.

In May 1766 the collector at Stornoway reported that 'we have been in use since our arrival at this port to hire boats and men to board vessels that have been put into the harbour here by contrary winds, which frequently happens, some trading coastwise and a great many to and from foreign parts with full cargoes on board. We have not found the least difficulty in providing either till of late that we could not in more than two or three instances furnish ourselves with a boat and hands immediately on the arrival of vessels. When this was the case we observed boats go off, board the vessels and then row away along the coast so as to be out of our power before we could be provided with a boat and crew, which makes it more than probable that prohibited or high duty goods are frequently run on shore without our being able to put a stop to such a practice. This we are more apt to believe is the case as we now understand it has been the custom of the merchants in this place for several years past to furnish themselves with several kinds of foreign goods out of these vessels, duty free, which has made them very averse to pay duty for several small quantities they have entered with us since our arrival. This we thought proper to lay before your Honours in order that you may know that without a boat and boatmen being appointed at this port the merchants have it in their power to carry on a smuggling trade without our being able to prevent them, they having such prevalence over the common people as to put a stop to our being supplied with men and a boat to enable us to prosecute any information we may receive of their fraudulent dealings.

'Being thus situated we have not the least doubt of your Honours ordering a boat and crew for the port and therefore as there will be an occasion for his going a considerable distance from hence to creeks on the coast and to the neighbouring islands where vessels put into frequently and run goods ... we would humbly propose that your Honours would order a stout boat, the coast here being very rough, such a one as would take six men to work her properly, though four only might be established which would serve for boarding vessels in the harbour and assist in attending on board vessels to and from foreign parts and when there would be occasion to go from the port two extraordinary men might be employed.

'As most of the common people here could not be trusted on account of their being so much subjected to the better sort we are of the opinion that of the four established men three should be from other countries and one of this island, it being necessary to have one on board who knows the coast to serve as a pilot. For that end we beg leave to recommend to your Honours one Alexander McAulay, whom by the character we have of him we look upon to be a proper person for the purpose. He has been bred a sailor, served in His Majesty's navy several years, understands navigation and is thoroughly acquainted in the coast of this and all the islands hereabouts.

'We are likewise of opinion that to make the boat more useful firearms and cutlasses would be necessary. Upon the whole we humbly think that without a boat and crew the business of the revenue at this port cannot be carried on to that degree of perfection which it ought to be'.

On 9 June 1766 the Board directed the collector 'to state to us from the best intelligence and information which you can procure the value of foreign articles which may be smuggled into the island and what part thereof may be for the use and consumption of the inhabitants'. The reply was sent on 5 July. 'According to the best intelligence and information which we have been able to procure ... brandy and rum with some quantities of tea are the principal foreign commodities that are run into this island, a great part of which is consumed by the inhabitants and the remainder furnished by them to the people of the neighbouring islands and continent. With regard to the value of these articles we cannot possibly ascertain it, though we are of opinion it is considerable, as we understand that these commodities, particularly brandy, are used by the common people, having been credibly informed that no less than £700 was paid last year by the tenants upon one estate on the mainland for that liquor, which makes us conclude that the value of the whole consumption on the continent and islands must be considerable'.

The case for the king's boat had been made but there is no clear evidence of one being established at Stornoway. Instead the majority of seizures were brought into that port by revenue cruisers [see Figure x]. The following sections highlight some of the stories relating to the king's boats at outports on the mainland. Peterhead is described first because of the collector's comments on the role of a king's boat.

Peterhead

William Abernethy 'resumed' command of the king's boat at Peterhead on 9 June 1769. However, despite 'strong promises of vigilance' he had made no seizures by the end of the year and had not submitted his journal monthly, as agreed. The Board instructed that 'the collector is to investigate and report on how the boat has been used and reasons for lack of success. He is also to suggest how matters are to be improved'.

The collector's reply is quoted in detail. 'It appears to us that the success of preventive officers depends upon various circumstances and that the following qualifications and conduct are necessary to procure success viz: that the commander of a preventive boat have it at heart to do his duty; that he have a great deal of activity, be hardy and able to undergo a great deal of fatigue; that his cruise be not a narrow circle but that he be at different places where there is probability of running as well by night as by day and constantly on the watch and to these must also be added a certain capacity of procuring intelligence without which there may be no success though every other means be used and there is also a good deal of chance in making seizures though being thus in the way of them will more or less succeed.

'The collector therefore in the enquiry he was to make had these things in his eye. First he has no reason to doubt but Mr Abernethy is very willing to make seizures and from everything he could gather believes he has expended more than his salary in support of the boatmen and himself in quest of them so that he has lost money since he took command of the boat.

'As to the second qualification Mr Abernethy appears to be valetudinary, complains of his health and says that he has not found it to answer his expectations since he took the command of the boat himself so that he wishes your Honours would indulge him as formerly with some able assistants.

'The cruise which he and his crew consider as their charge and their hankering to be always at home at night, as they cannot bear the expense of living from it, is such a bar to success that the ablest commander and crew in the kingdom would have little chance except he supplied the defect by having the earliest and best intelligence from every corner and even that would not perfectly answer and Mr Abernethy's success has not pointed out his having had such intelligence.

'The practice followed by the crew of this boat is to keep an outlook at Peterhead and to send daily to the Stirling Hill in its neighbourhood to look out there for ships upon the coast. If none appear they consider the boat's going to sea as of no use and this accounts for her not being so often at sea. But Mr Abernethy says they always go when the weather permits and they see any ships to board. It appears by his journal for the month of December last that the weather was so stormy there was no going to sea except on the 13th when on an information he sent the yawl to Collieston with part of their crew and remained at Peterhead with part of the crew to watch a ship on the coast and the yawl returned on the 18th'.

Another problem was that 'there is almost constantly one or other of the excise yachts either in Peterhead or cruising off the headlands near it and when they are in the harbour their boats are sent to the adjacent creeks, where they lie. Indeed the station off Peterhead is a judicious one as ships coming on that part of the coast commonly make these headlands. In the course of things the smugglers, knowing how things are, well avoid except they are drove by necessity coming near Peterhead, and what is smuggled will generally be attempted in the night time towards Collieston about ten miles from Peterhead to the southward and Newburgh about three miles further and to the northward. If they do go into the Moray Firth they will attempt it about Cairnbulg and the little creeks thereabouts, eight or ten miles to the northward of Peterhead. This being the case the boat stationed at Peterhead should according to the discretion and judgement of the commander by no means keep a close residence at Peterhead but should be at Collieston and the other creeks to the southward of Peterhead and at the creeks to the northward and even in the Moray Firth, as discretion and intelligence may direct him. It is mere accident can give anything otherwise in the way of the boat in the present situation at Peterhead'.

Andrew Blair, who had been acting tidesurveyor at Aberdeen, was appointed assistant tidesurveyor at Peterhead. He was ordered to keep a journal and from these 'it appears to us that Mr Blair has been very active and diligent during this period [June to December 1770], although he has not been successful of making seizures. 'Upon the 22nd day of June last Mr Blair fell in with five horses in the sands of Belhelvie, about five miles to the northward of Aberdeen, which he suspected were loaded with prohibited goods. The drivers, suspecting Mr Blair, drove their horses from the sands into the links, upon which Mr Blair, having alighted from his horse to examine the goods and to seize the same if he found them to be prohibited goods, was laid hold of by two of the drivers, thrown to the ground and his hands and legs bound with ropes in which situation he remained from eleven o'clock at night until seven next morning. We ordered Mr Blair to be at the utmost pains in order to discover the persons concerned in this deforcement but he had not yet been able to find them'.

Aberdeen

Theo Ogilvie, was appointed the tidesurveyor at Aberdeen in 1747 [see Figure 9]. The collector reported that he 'is a young man and a very diligent officer. There are four established and two extraordinary boatmen. William Freeman and James Knows are the two oldest of these. Freeman has all along served with great honesty and has had from all his surveyors the character of carefulness and fidelity and his present surveyor commends him very much ... he is wore a little in the service but is still very willing to serve and able to go to sea. Knows has also served honestly and has suffered much in the service, the smugglers having several years ago knocked him down and beat him severely for his opposing their running a cargo from a ship where he was stationed, from which he has never thoroughly recovered, but he is willing enough to do duty and goes to sea. Roderick Forbes and Andrew Miller are the other two established boatmen, who are capable to row in the boat and go to sea. George Dun and Alexander Luper are the two extraordinary boatmen employed by order from your Honours since the 18 May 1747. These are sturdy men, good sailors and very fit to serve in the boat'.

In June 1749 Ogilvie was deforced of a seizure. 'He was in possession of a boat load with spirits and battery run from a sloop hovering off Cruden but he was attacked by George Dunbar, merchant in Elton, and a number of countrymen whom Dunbar had employed to carry off the goods, who forced him out of the boat and carried off the cargo ... George Dunbar ought to be prosecute as Mr Ogilvie can prove by several witnesses that he deforced him and threatened to murder him'. By August Ogilvie 'has laid himself out to get information how many and who were the accomplices of George Dunbar ... he can only condescend upon a few and that they had no firearms but only staves and stones. However, he says they had hands on him and threatened to throw him into the sea'.

Portsoy

In August 1780 the collector at Aberdeen reported 'touching the boat stationed at Portsoy under the command of <u>Alexander Cook,</u> it has been of singular service to the revenue as he has since the month of 1777 seized goods to the amount of in value of £1372 18s and none of which there is any probability could have been seized had not this boat been stationed where she is. Besides this service he has prevented much running of goods and occasioned the payment of duties, which otherwise would not have been paid but would have been run. We cannot therefore but be of opinion that this boat is of much service to the revenue nor do we think that in so wide a place as the Moray Firth one of the cutters stationed always in that Firth would answer perfectly without a boat stationed in or about Portsoy'.

Cromarty

From 1783 onwards <u>George Henderson</u> was tidesurveyor in charge of the king's boat at Cromarty. 'In consequence of the liberty given him by our order of the 12th of February 1783 he had cruised with the king's boat and crew during the different periods ... when he had advice of something being expected on the coast, and prays an allowance to the boatmen during those periods. We agree to your paying the boatmen at the rate of 9d per diem each for the respective periods ... making in all thirty-one days'.

In November 1790 the boatmen at Cromarty applied to the Board for reimbursement of the expense of a yawl 'which they, in conjunction with the tidesurveyor, have purchased to be employed in the service of the revenue ... as the boat has been purchased contrary to the express order of the Board of the 26th May last, no allowance whatever will be made on that account nor for repairs which she may at any time want. The tidesurveyor is accordingly, when any furnishings shall be made for the large boat, to make oath that no part thereof was applied to the use of the small boat and you are to inform the tidesurveyor and boatmen that they are not again to presume to trouble the Board upon this head'. The Board had second thoughts. In 1805 the old sails from the king's boat could be used to make a sail for the small yawl.

On 26 March 1800 George Henderson with his crew and an excise officer were 'deforced and grossly abused in the execution of their duty by Simon and Alexander Fraser, farmers at Cullanauld [not located] in the county of Ross, and sundry others at their instigation, and two ankers of whisky, which they had seized from the Frasers, had been forcibly rescued from them and destroyed'.

Montrose

The collector reported in May 1773 'we have been long of opinion that if a boat in the service of the customs under the command of an honest vigilant and active officer with a proper crew was stationed on this coast ... might turn out to be greatly for the advantage of the revenue in preventing or detecting the many frauds that are committed along that shore ... Sometimes boats both in the service of the customs and excise visit the creeks of this port that is at Arbroath, Johnshaven and Gourdon but the time they remain is but very short and when a vessel is on this coast the concerns take care to manage their matters so that she never appears within sight till the boats have taken their departure by wearying them out of their patience and no sooner are they gone than the first opportunity is taken to smuggle their cargoes which is immediately carried up the country ... The revenue upon arrival of ships in the river is put to considerable expense for boats hired in the harbour to cart the surveyor and the tidesmen on board of them and we are indifferently served by such, as often boats for that purpose can be found when sailors are out of the way and besides it is always against their inclination to perform this employment, more especially when they are to carry officers on board of vessels from foreign parts because they imagine there may be some things that may be wanted to be got ashore in a clandestine way. This boat when in the river may perform this service.

David Garden

'Upon the 6th ult [December 1777] Mr Garden, commander of the revenue boat stationed at Ferryden, received information that there had been a considerable smuggle to the northward. He, with five of his crew, immediately proceeded thither and left Peter Carey, another of the crew, to look after the boat. As there was reason to suspect smuggled goods would be brought by land into Montrose, he likewise ordered Carey to take the party of military here to his assistance and interrupt any goods that might be brought to town. Upon the 7th Carey received information that goods were to be brought in that night. He accordingly took part of the military with him and stationed them at a windmill about a quarter of a mile from the town. About eleven that night a chaise came from the northward, belonging to William Driver, vintner in Montrose, which the party attempted to stop but, being only three in number, the rest being at a considerable distance with Carey, they could not accomplish. A short time thereafter another chaise belonging to Driver came out of town and went to the northward. This last mentioned chaise had not been gone more than a quarter of an hour when it returned to town and, as William Driver was suspected to be in the practice of bringing prohibited goods to town in his chaises and this chaise returning so soon, Carey judged goods would be therein and therefore when the chaise came up he called to the driver to stop, which he refusing to comply with the party surrounded the chaise and the chaise driver and one of the horses was wounded by a bayonet of the soldiers.

'The procurator fiscal next day commenced a prosecution before the magistrates against Peter Carey for a riot, as did William Driver for damages, and they having examined sundry evidences by way of precognition found Peter Carey liable in the sum of £7 for a riot and breach of the peace and to be imprisoned until payment be made and postponed the consideration of the damages to Driver until the horse's recovery. Against the above sentence William Boullie, prosecutor for Carey, protested and appealed for redress to the ensuing circuit court of justiciary. What in our humble judgment makes this sentence of the magistrates unjust is that the horse was stabbed by the soldiers without any orders from Peter Carey and which is never so much as alleged by the pursuers or any of the evidences and as we have reason to believe that a similar sentence will pass against Carey for damages to Driver'.

The Revenue Cruisers
The presence of revenue cruisers on the coast had an impact on the smugglers as can be seen in this letter from John Steuart to Alexander

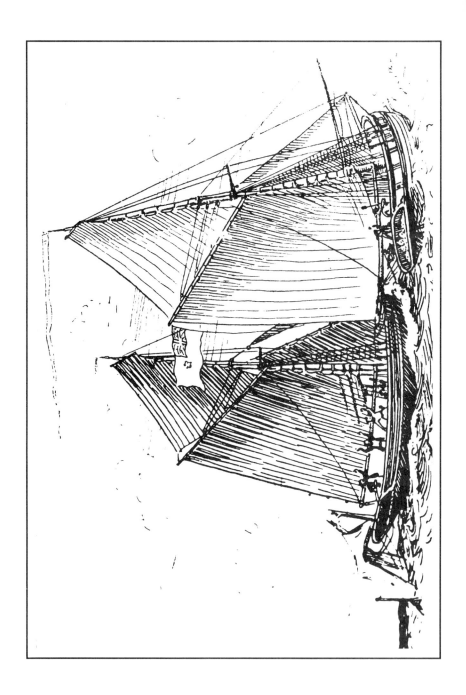

Figure 11: Stornoway seizures 1764 to 1810

<u>1764</u>: *Daniel* of Stornoway, David Morrison master, by the *Alarm* cutter, Captain Gordon

<u>1771</u>: *Cabersea* of Stornoway, John Robinson master, by the *Prince Ernest Augustus* cutter

<u>1774</u>: *Friendship* [with tobacco on board], by the Larne revenue cruiser, Joseph Mortimer commander and John Wardlaw mate

<u>1775</u>: *Margaret* of Stornoway, Murdoch McLeod master, by the *Royal George* excise yacht, John Ogilvie master

<u>1783</u>: *Martha* [owner Archibald Murray, Ballashammon, Ireland] by *Prince William Henry* cutter, Captain James Hamilton

<u>1785</u>: *Unity* of Stornoway, Donald McKay master; *Jean* of Peterhead, William Burnie master; *Margaret & Elizabeth* of Stromness, Robert Cruikshank master; *Peggie* of Portree, James McDonald master; *Batchelors* of Fraserburgh and a Dutch galliott in Stornoway harbour all by the *Prince Ernest Augustus*, Captain William Scott

<u>1786</u>: *Barbara* of Stornoway, Kenneth Crichton master, by the *Prince Edward*, Captain Alexander Cook and *Mary* of Mull by the *Prince Ernest Augustus*

<u>1787</u>: *Peggy*, Donald McKay master (see also the *Unity* in 1785), by the *Prince Ernest Augustus*, Sir John Reid

<u>1790</u>: *Margaret* of Stornoway, Norman Crichton master, by the *Prince Edward*, Captain Alexander Cook

<u>1805</u>: *Adventure* of Guernsey, by the *Prince Ernest Augustus*, Daniel Reid master and *Jean & Mary*, Angus Newton master, by the *Osnaburgh* cutter, Captain Hardie

<u>1806</u>: *Peggie* of Stornoway, Murdoch MacLean master, by the *Melville Castle* excise cutter, Henry Duncan Beatson and *Robert & Christian* of Fort William, Donald McDonald master, by the *Prince Ernest Augustus*, Daniel Reid

<u>1809</u>: *Marquis of Grahame*, Donald McCaskill acting master, by the *Prince Ernest Augustus*, Robert Clarke second mate

<u>1810</u>: *Two Brothers* of Stornoway, John Macaulay master, by the *Prince Ernest Augustus*, Daniel Reid

Note: The crew of the *Prince Ernest Augustus* in 1799 included David Reid commander, George Doug boatswain, Robert Clark gunner, John Reid carpenter, Roderick Mackenzie 1st mariner, Roderick Mackenzie 2nd mariner, John Munro, James MacDonald, William McNair, Murdo McJon, Hugh Murray, John Mackenzie, Normand McLeod, Alexander MacKenzie and Hector Lees.

Andrew in Rotterdam dated 9 July 1725. 'There will be now an effectual stop put to trade to this Firth from you, for this morning arrived two small cruisers from England in our road to attend all ships from you in this Firth hereafter, which I believe in the event will be good for this country'.

One of the main tasks of the cruisers was in escorting seizures. In April 1747 the collector at Aberdeen shipped on board the *Princess Caroline*, Arthur Starks commander, all the goods under seizure in the warehouse 'except thirteen hogsheads red French wine and twenty-six matts tobacco stalks, which the vessel could not contain ... we would have sent the red wine and chose rather to have kept some of the other goods unshipped but the vessel could not stow it, alone, without spoiling it as it behoved to have been close stowed to the fire place they keep in the hold and therefore we thought proper to send the white wine and the other goods.

'Upon our shipping the wine Alexander Bannerman, merchant in this place, appeared as agent for William Herdman, merchant in Stonehaven, and took a protest against us for shipping the wine, declaring it was claimed in the exchequer and we have told the seizure makers of this to put them on their guard, who have acquainted us they shall have proof ready'.

As always, there were clashes between the customs and excise over seizures. On 27 June 1774 Alexander Ritchie, commander of a row boat belonging to the *Princess Caroline* sloop, under Captain Laurence Brown, seized 481 gallons of geneva in small casks and other goods found in an open boat from Gourdon, David Craigie master, at sea about a mile from Portlethen. Having freighted a Johnshaven boat for the purpose, together with one of his men he returned the goods to Montrose, sending the Gourdon boat with the rest of his crew 'in search of the vessel out of which the goods had been unloaded'. The Gourdon boat was to be seized on her return from this search.

But on 29 June Ritchie reported to the custom house that when the boat returned to Gourdon, James Wilson, commander of a boat belonging to the *Royal Charlotte* excise yacht [see Chapter Nine and Appendix II], seized her and brought her into Montrose with only one of Ritchie's men on board, who was guarding an anker of geneva and 13 lbs of tea, found in the boat after she had gone back to sea. The collector intervened and 'Wilson and his crew immediately resigned her to Ritchie, who brought the furniture to the warehouse. The collector would not have allowed Ritchie to return the boat as a seizure 'if he had not been witness to Mr Reid, inspector of the outports, on the 25th June giving it in positive charge to Wilson to scuttle this very boat to prevent her being used in smuggling, which was not done, and his being convinced in his own mind that this boat was collusively left by Wilson to the former proprietors to be used as they thought proper and that she might by such collusive practices be condemned and sold to them again for a trifle'. Mr Strang, the collector of excise, contacted the collector requiring the boat, the anker of geneva and the 13lbs of tea to be delivered to him as Wilson's seizure.

'The acting comptroller avers that Alexander Ritchie accounts for this [the geneva and the tea being in the boat when she returned from 'seeking the vessel'] that in the hurry of unloading the Gourdon boat into the boat that was freighted there were left under the fishing lines that were then in the boat, which they did not take time to turn over, the anker and the 13 lbs tea which were descended upon on going in search of the sloop by Ritchie's crew and brought in with them again when Wilson and his crew took violent possession of her'.

The collector received the following letter, dated Gourdon, 19 August 1774:

I, James Wilson, commander of the Royal Charlotte detached boat, has made an enquiry about the boat that I seized that now lies at Montrose. The three masters of the seized boat declares that Ritchie knowed that the anker and tea was in the boat and likewise that same morning put ashore at Gourdon one anker and one matt of tobacco that was distributed among them. All this the three masters of the seized boat declares to be the truth and is willing to make oath to the same and signs this.

Andrew Watt   David Lawie   David Craigie (his mark)

The collector was instructed to undertaken an enquiry into this allegation and submit to the Board 'a report thereon and his own observations and opinion as to the character of the sundry persons to be examined and particularly of Ritchie and of James Wiison and of the three skippers'. Realising the problems he faced over persuading any witnesses to speak to him, the collector 'judged it his duty to apply to a judge with authority to compel such persons as were refractory to appear before him for the purpose of examination. [He] therefore assumed the liberty of calling Mr James McDonald, sheriff substitute of Kincardineshire, from Stonehaven, who upon every occasion the collector has employed him in has behaved with all manner of propriety in matters relating to the revenue or the officers employed therein'.

The witnesses included Andrew Watt, David Lawie and David Craigie, Ritchie himself and three of his crew, Andrew Soutter, who had been in charge in Ritchie's absence, William Young and Henry McGregor. Wilson was allowed to attend to hear the evidences. All three of the skippers showed 'rancour' and 'ill-will' against Ritchie because they claimed he had not paid them £10 for the use of their boat. Andrew Watt 'in consequence of this enmity says everything that he could against Mr Ritchie in order to fire the crime alleged against him that the fear of being contradicted and being sent to jail [for contempt] would allow him'. Yet even the skippers agreed that this had been on the condition that he brought them 'another cargo'. It was also clear that Ritchie had not been involved in Soutter and the others giving the owners of the Gourdon boat some tobacco 'the bulk of a matt' and the anker of gin, which had also been in the bottom of the boat. According to David Craigie, 'he and his crew laid their hands on the tobacco and the anker and with the assistance of Soutter's men and himself looking on they took them ashore and [he] promised to give them the other anker and the tea when they went to Johnshaven. But declares all this was in absence of Ritchie'. And 'from the acknowledgment of Soutter and Young in their depositions it appears that they with the other three of Ritchie's men did suffer the cask of geneva and the tobacco to be carried away by the crew of the seized boat'.

Ritchie explained how the goods had been 'left in the seized boat after the cargo was put aboard of the other boat ... When he was going into Gapple with the seizure he observed Captain Ogilvy's yacht at sea and Ritchie, being afraid that Captain Ogilvy might make a seizure of the smuggling vessel and the rest of her cargo before he, Ritchie, could get his seizure disposed of and go to the vessel, he hurried the goods out of the seized boat into a Johnshaven boat and considering the hurry and confusion of this operation it is no great wonder that these small parcels of goods might be overlooked, unobserved by Mr Ritchie who the collector is convinced and it does not otherwise appear that he knew of their being left in the seized boat'.

'As to the character of Alexander Ritchie, we do believe him to be a trusty officer and capable and never once heard of anything being laid to his charge that could affect him or his reputation as an officer of the revenue and neither did we hear anything as to neglect against any of his crew till this time. As to James Wilson we have heard of many particulars being laid to his charge: embezzlements of seized goods and returning of boats got by him ... as ought to have been seized for conveying of prohibited and high duty goods. But by his management it is believed when the persons came to be enquired at by us they minced and explained matters so that our efforts to ferret these things proved abortive. But [we] cannot pass over the trust and confidence that at present subsist betwixt Mr Wilson and the skippers, who have signed and laid this complaint against Alexander Ritchie ... As to the three skippers ... we are convinced that they are as the most of such are upon this coast a set of people who by the force of money and the consideration of their own interest are capable of being inclined to give their oaths which way ever they are desired or instructed or in any manner they think most conducive to their own interest, being well known to be the most unprincipled people on any cause by whosoever and therefore no faith can be laid on what they say, even upon oath ... the skippers insisted to be paid 5s each for that day's attendance, which Mr McDonald refused to allow them as they were not taken form their own homes'.

Figure 11 lists the vessels and boats seized by revenue cruisers either based at Stornoway or cruising nearby between 1764 and 1810. On 17 July 1786 the Board directed the collector 'to stop any seizure that may be due to Mr William Scott, commander of the *Prince Ernest Augustus* cutter, deceased till his accounts shall be passed'. A week later they reported that Scott was to be succeeded by Sir John Reid bart of the Royal Navy. The collector was to give him 'every information and assistance in your power for His Majesty's service'. When Sir John took over the command of the *Prince Edward* he was replaced by Daniel Reid.

Apart from the vessels listed, the crew of the *Prince Ernest Augustus* also seized goods. These included on 27 April 1785 one hundred and ninety-three whole, three half ankers rum; sixty-nine whole, five half ankers brandy; one hundred and sixty-two whole, fifteen half ankers geneva; four boxes, four small casks and five small parcels black tea and in September: five barrels and seven ankers containing 15 bushels small salt in an open boat, John McAlpine master, and two large copper rattles or cauldrons, for which there was no clearance; three barrels and six ankers containing 9 bushels small salt off Point of Sleat and an open boat, Donald McLachlane master and five barrels and one anker containing 13 bushells small salt and an open boat, Norman McLeod tacksman at Glenelg master, but leaky. The boats were 'set at liberty' but the salt was returned as a seizure.

The next and final chapter looks at developments in smuggling after the eighteenth century.

A STORY OF DAVID GARDEN'S BOATMEN

'Understanding that a boat in the service of the customs is fitting out here as also that Alexander Gowan, shipmaster in Gourdon, is to be one of the sailors for said boat, from a regard to the revenue service I can't help acquainting your Honours that Gowan is a very improper man for said service, as he was formerly one of David Law's sailors in the like service when he often aided and assisted the smugglers, even personally, for which it consists with my knowledge he was well rewarded'.

Signed: A Well Wisher, 25 June 1777

Inevitably the collector was asked to comment and he replied to the Board on 10 July 1777. 'It is true that Gowan was a sailor in the boat commanded by David Law and that he continued one of her crew till she was put out of the service but was never suspended or convicted of any fraud whatsoever nor did we ever hear or learn that any censure was put upon him for any failure of his duty or in the commission of any fraud while he was in the service. On the other hand it consists with our knowledge that Alexander Gowan has been often and on many occasions useful to the revenue since he was in the service and has often given such intelligence as was of great use in the detection of frauds and it is our humble opinion that this 'Well Wisher' to the revenue is no other than some of the smugglers about Bervie, who are apprehensive that Gowan from his connections will be able to receive good intelligence of all their transactions and communicate them to his superiors accordingly'.

Alexander Gowan's evidence respecting the wreck of the *Dispatch* was described in Chapter Seven. In December 1773 William Blews, when he delivered a letter to James Kennedy the comptroller, stated that 'he expected a smuggle to happen in a few nights, that had been put off by bad weather'. It was agreed that Kennedy and Blews should 'take care of the north' while Alexander Arbuthnott, accompanied by Peter Grant, excise officer, would 'look after' Johnshaven, Seagreens, Milton and Houghhaven The three customs officers would share any seizure. Blews 'had the fortune to fall in with a seizure of fifteen casks, containing 1,071 lbs sound and 13 lbs damaged common bohea tea, four ankers, containing 34 gallons geneva and one matt containing 44 lbs leaf tobacco. He refuses that ever such a communing of that

contd

A STORY OF MR GARDEN'S BOATMEN contd

above mentioned happened betwixt us, consequently he pretended that he is not obliged to communicate the benefit of any part of the seizure-makers share to us, thereby endeavouring to defraud us of our just right' [signed James Kennedy and Alexander Arbuthnott]. The collector undertook an enquiry in February 1774. Alexander Gowan, shipmaster in Gourdon, was one of the witnesses and he, with Andrew Lamie, also a shipmaster, 'afford great reason to suspect that no such bargain ever was made'. Blews was allowed to return the seizure, the collector adding 'William Blews during the course of this winter has often applied to us for leave to go to Bervie to go out against the smugglers, both before 24th December last and since, which must have put him to an extraordinary expense, being so far from his family at Arbroath and having had parties of the military patrolling with him in the night time. It would considerably increase his expenses as he was unsuccessful till he was fortunate as to fall in with the tea in dispute'.

Gowan resigned on 12 August 1777.

David Garden replaced him with David Reid, who was 'thirty-two years of age, five feet seven inches high of a fair complexion and wears his own hair'.

He resigned on 25 March 1778 and was replaced by John Watt, 'who is every way properly qualified for the service ... he is thirty years of age'.

On 6 March 1779 William Brown 'absented himself from his duty' and 'has since bought a vessel at Aberdeen'.

He was replaced by Robert Reid 'a stout young man of twenty-four years of age'.

He left the service on 5 January 1780 and was replaced by John Stephen 'a stout young man of twenty-eight years of age, a thorough bred seaman and every other way properly qualified for a boatman'.

CHAPTER ELEVEN: AND THEN ...

'**Boat route claim denied**: A Belgian skipper accused of smuggling cannabis denied yesterday that he had taken a yacht up the west coast of Ireland to avoid the risk of being caught drug running'. [*Aberdeen Press & Journal* 1 February 1994]

Most of the material in this book comes from eighteenth century records. Yet, as can be seen from Figure 12, the smuggling has continued. This chapter attempts to encourage others to study the custom house records.

A Survey of Smuggling
In September 1807 the Board directed the outports 'to procure the best possible information respecting the smuggling trade carried on upon the coast of our own and neighbouring ports and to transmit a state of the same to your Honours together with our opinion of the most effectual means of suppressing the same'.

The collector at Stornoway wrote 'In obedience thereto we beg leave to state ... that the smuggling trade carried on upon the coast of the ports of Stornoway, Isle Martin, Fort William and Tobermory, being the extent to which our information connects, is principally confined to and carried on by three or four cutters or luggers of and from Guernsey, who generally visit the most remote lochs and creeks of the above mentioned ports once and sometimes twice a year. The articles of which their lading chiefly consist are rum, brandy, geneva and wine in small casks, each of the contents of 9 gallons, and unmanufactured tobacco in matts or bales, weighing 120 lbs each. These goods are disposed of in small quantities to the gentlemen, tacksmen, tavern keepers, small tenants and fishermen inhabiting the coast and adjacent country of the different lochs and creeks at which they call, landed in small open boats from the shore, manned by the natives, and immediately dispersed over a large tract of country,

Figure 12: Wreck 1993 Style

The *Ambrosia*, a 75 foot yacht built in 1943, with about 4.6 tonnes of Moroccan cannabis resin [estimated street value £23.5m] on board, concealed in a concrete covered hold, was wrecked at St Fergus in early October 1993. This led to the largest drug seizure on the east coast of Scotland. The story, as revealed in the Aberdeen High Court in January and February 1994, has several familiar aspects:

- the skipper was employed to take the yacht from Portugal to Oslo. Setting out from Vilamoura in Portugal he probably called at Fhir in Morocco before heading north. Instead of taking the direct route through the English Channel, he sailed up the west coast of Ireland 'to avoid the risk of being caught'

- there was a 'supercargo' on board who 'took all decisions'. He had been present on two previous voyages from Italy to Holland via Spain and Morocco and from Holland to Portugal

- in the North Sea, about sixty-five miles east of Peterhead, the yacht was caught in a Force 11 gale with 20 metre high waves. She began taking in water. The skipper sent out a Mayday signal and the three men on board were taken by an RAF Sea King helicopter based at Lossiemouth to Aberdeen Infirmary. Vagueness about the yacht's destination alerted one of the rescuers, who contacted the coastguard suggesting that they should inform customs. Having been interviewed by the police, all three men went to Aberdeen

- large packets of cannabis resin, 2 feet long and wrapped in hessian sacking, were washed up on Scotstown beach, confirming the possibility of a smuggling connection

- the skipper returned to Aberdeen to arrange the salvage of the yacht - he was followed from the airport to Boddam and an undercover customs officer was on the 'diving team' to be employed by him

- bad weather prevented the salvage operations for a couple of days. Then, under 1.5 inches of concrete and 1 inch of wood, a large storage area 14 feet 6 inches long was found - it was half full, containing 120 blocks of cannabis

- after a ten day trial, the skipper was found not guilty of being concerned in supplying the cannabis resin on the *Ambrosia* or of 'contravening Customs & Excise regulations'.

being for the most part carried on men's shoulders. The quantities so landed in the course of the last twelve months on the coasts of the above specified ports may amount to betwixt 1,200 and 1,500 gallons of spirits and wine and from 1 to 2 tons of tobacco.

'We are much of opinion that on the coast of our own port and probably on the coasts of the other ports mentioned the pernicious trade might be greatly suppressed if the different landed proprietors were to give their hearty concurrence by not only discouraging their factors, tacksmen, small tenants and fishermen but by threatening them with their severest displeasure in every instance where they could be detected in purchasing contraband from to anywise aiding or assisting a smuggling vessel or any person having concern therewith. In case this measure may be resorted to we subjoin a list of the proprietors who have property in the district of this port and it is very probable that the numerous volunteer forces along the coast might be found, under proper regulations, very serviceable in checking this illicit trade'.

The list of landed proprietors included the Right Honourable Lord Seaforth, the Right Honourable Lord MacDonald, Mr Hume of Harris, Mr MacDonald of Clanranald, Mr MacDonald of Boisdale and Mr MacNeill of Barra.

The collector also commented on the distribution of seizure money. 'A further remuneration to the seizing officers might have a very good effect on the officers at this port, [who are] exclusive of ourselves ... the tidesurveyor and two tidewaiters, whom we consider at present as fit and able for the execution of their respective duties. Yet neither they nor we can prevent the clandestine running of goods in the remote creeks and bays of our district, as it is very possible for a smuggling vessel to be for a month and upwards on the coast without our knowledge, the communication by land being almost inaccessible and by sea very uncertain'. What was happening elsewhere?

The Coastguard

The following information comes from Atton and Holland's *The King's Customs*.

The Parliamentary Committee report on the revenue of Scotland in 1823 commented unfavourably on the prevention system. Mr Arrow, the inspecting commander of coastguard in the Aberdeen district, produced a statement describing his successes since the coastguard was established in 1819. The local fishermen helped the smugglers but 'if the Scottish fishers and coast peasantry had the daring, or, more properly speaking, the want of feeling, that the smugglers on most parts of the English coast have, the weak patrols of the present force would not be effective. So long as the above orders of society continue their present habits, the wish to appear at kirk with a clean character, so long will the present force of the coastguard be effective'.

He emphasised the difference between the level of smuggling before and after 1819. While the coast was protected by the revenue cruisers, there was 'a regular passage of smuggled spirits, tea and tobacco from Flushing into Aberdeen'. There were two smuggling companies at Collieston, each with two vessels. 'One syndicate failed in 1802, but the other (directed by two notorious fellows named Mitchell and Christie) held on till 1817, and then 'broke'. But business began afresh in 1818 under the directorship of one James Dickie, who received from five to seven cargoes each 'season''. These smugglers, 'assisted by a Folkestone man named Dangerfield', supplied the coast from Aberdeen to Montrose. It was believed that when Mitchell went bankrupt he owed 'one James of Folkestone' £5,000. In 1809 some 'fair traders' from Aberdeen 'got up a movement' against the Mitchell and Christie.

In reply Christie placed an advertisement in the Aberdeen Journal dated 11 January 1809: 'NOTICE. - Alexander Christie: notwithstanding - has still on hand for his favourite customers a considerable quantity of anker gin, which cannot in point of quality and flavour be excelled, and a fresh supply daily expected: Also Highland whisky of best quality, and other spirits equal to his neighbours. In these pinched times, a discerning public will find this worth their attention'.

Arrow insisted that he had quashed the smuggling, stating that a man had called at his house one night to say 'I am employed by the smugglers. You know we have had a vessel on the coast the last thirteen nights, and that we want to land near Aberdeen. For the love of God, let her come in, and give us fair play, You take what you can; let us get off with what we can, or she will go away altogether, as she cannot keep on this coast any longer'. According to Arrow the vessel was forced back to sea and was wrecked 'on one of the eastern islands'.

The coastguard inspector produced several testimonials to his success:

- a justice of the peace living near Rattray Head - cargoes were landed in open day between Fraserburgh and Peterhead in 1818 and 1819;

- the Baron-Bailie of Peterhead - many cargoes were run on various parts of the coast between Girdle Ness and Rattray Head before the coastguard was established;

- the Secretary to the Commissioners of General Assembly - for thirty years smuggling was carried on to a very considerable extent at Slains and Cruden;

- a Lieutenant-General and justice of the peace - until lately about two miles from Collieston was the emporium of smuggling. I have often seen one - nay, two - luggers at a time unloaded by twenty or thirty fishboats as regularly and systematically as the disembarkation of an army;

- the minister of Slains - Collieston has been a well-known station for smuggling from time immemorial ... There never has been a year from 1794 to 1819 that there were not three or four cargoes of foreign spirits landed, and some years more than double that quantity;

- the Procurator-Fiscal - before the establishment of the coastguard, smuggled spirits were sold at every tavern between Peterhead and Aberdeen. 'Gin and brandy were presented to visitors in every farmhouse - nay, every cottar's house - in Buchan'.

The Class 4 Aberdeen letter-books, including correspondence from the collector to the deputy collector at Banff [1801 to 1819] and to the officers-in-charge at Peterhead [1823 to 1829], make very few references to smuggling at Collieston. A detailed analysis of the Aberdeen Class 1 and Class 2 letter-books from 1794 to 1823 should prove or disprove Arrow's claims. There is more of the story waiting to be discovered.

APPENDIX I: THE NORTHERN SHORES

Extract from: <u>The Report by Thomas Tucker upon the Settlement of the Revenues of Excise and Customs in Scotland</u> 1656.

Note: Where appropriate, the modern spellings of the place names have been used throughout this extract. Montrose is excluded as it was described in *The Smuggling Story of Two Firths*.

'The port of Aberdeen lies next northward, being a very handsome burgh, seated at the mouth of the river Don, and is commonly called the new tcwn, for distinguishing it from another town hard by, of the same name, but more antiquity, lying at the mouth of the river Dee, some a mile distant from the new town, and is the chief academy of Scotland. This being now a place more for study than trade, hath willingly resigned her interest that way, unto the new town, which is no despicable burgh, either for building or largeness, having a very stately mercat place, sundry houses well built, with a safe harbour before it for vessels to ride in. But the wideness of the place, from the inlet of the sea coming in with a narrow winding gut, and beating in store of sand with its waves, hath rendered it somewhat shallow in a great part of it, and so less useful of late than formerly. But the inhabitants are remedying this inconvenience, by lengthening their quay, and bringing it up close to a neck of land, which, jutting out eastward towards a headland lying before it, makes the coming in so straight. At the end of which foremost neck of land there is a little village called Footdee, and on the other headland, another called Torry, and both nigh the harbour's mouth, and lying very near unto the place where the ships usually ride (being forced to keep some distance from the quay, because of the shallowness of the water), have given opportunity of much fraud, in landing goods privately, but prevented of late, by appointing the waiters, by turns, to watch those two places narrowly, when there are any shipping in harbour. The trade of this place (as generally all over Scotland) is, inwards, from Norway, Eastland, Holland, and France; and outwards, with salmon and pladding, commodities caught and made hereabout in a greater plenty than in any other place of the nation whatsoever.

'In this port there is a collector, a cheque, and three waiters; some of which are still sent into the member ports as often (which is but seldom) as any opportunity is offered, or occasion requires. Those are in number five: Stonehaven, a little fisher town, where formerly goods have been brought in, but not of late, because hindered from doing so by the neighbourhood, and privileges of the burgh of Montrose; Newburgh, where sometimes a few deals and timber are brought; Peterhead, a small town, with a convenient harbour, but spoiled of late by stress of weather; Fraserburgh and Banff, where, in like manner, something now and then is brought in from Norway, but their only trade is coasting, except that from the latter of them some salmon may happen to be shipped out. The vessels to this district belonging are, viz. To Aberdeen: nine, viz. one 80 tons, one 70, one 60, three 50, two 30, one 20; Fraserburgh: four of 20 tons; Peterhead: one of 20 tons.

'The last port northerly is Inverness, lying at the head of the Firth of Moray, not far from Loch Ness, where the town is a small one, though the chief of the whole north, and would be yet worse, were it not for the large citadel built there of late years. This port hath for its district all the harbours and creeks of the shires of Moray, Ross, Sutherland and Caithness, with the Isles of Orkney; in which, although there be many large rivers which, rising in the hills, run down into the sea, and the ocean hath indented many more creeks and inlets, with its stormy waves still beating on the shore, yet few of them are serviceable, and those few much too big for any trade that is, or may be expected in these parts, for as the roughness of the sea and weather lie constantly on the east of them, so on the west they have the hills for their portion. The inhabitants beyond Morayland (except in the Orkneys) speak generally Ober garlickh, or Highlands, and the mixture of both in the town of Inverness is such that one half of the people understand not one another. The trade of this port is only a coast trade, there being no more than one single merchant in all the town, who brings home sometimes a little timber, salt, or wine. Here is a collector, a cheque, and one waiter, who attends here, and looks (as occasion serves) to Garmouth and Findhorn in Morayland, two small places, from whence some 60 lasts of salmon in a year are sent out, for which salt is brought in from France, and sometimes a small vessel comes from Holland or Norway.

'In the shire of Ross there are only two ports, the one called Cromarty, a little town in a bottom, with one of the delicatest harbours reputed in all Europe, the tide coming in a great depth betwixt two stately rocks (called the Sutors) through which the water passes into a large bay, where the greatest ships of burthen may ride in safety; and the other Tain, a small town lying near the mouth of a river of that name. To the former of these nothing comes more than a little salt to serve the country, and to the other it may be a small barque once a year from Leith, to fetch deals, which are brought down thither from the hills.

'In Sutherland there is only Dunrobin, and some two small creeks more, where some barques use to come for carrying the Earl of Sutherland's corn for some other parts of Scotland, according as he finds his best market. In these two shires it was never thought worth the charge of appointing an officer; but the collector keeps a correspondence with some in the place for giving him intelligence when any barques come in or go out.

'In Caithness there is a waiter constantly resident for looking after Thurso and Wick, two small ports, from whence good store of beef, hides, and tallow are usually sent to the coast; his work is rather preventive, for hindering those commodities from being sent into foreign parts, than profitable by anything he is likely to receive there. The like also is practiced at Kirkwall, in the Isles of Orkney, where there is another officer for looking after those Isles, whence they send corn, fish, butter, tallow, hides, and sometimes some timber is brought in from Norway, or else a Dutch vessel may happen to touch there in her passing out.

'As for Shetland, (thought to be the Ultima Thule, so much spoken of and reputed by the ancients to be the furtherest part of the world) it lies over against Bergen in Norway, and very difficult to get thither but in some certain months of the summer. There was never yet officer either sent or that would adventure thither till of late, when the farmer of the inland commodities of those parts having prevailed with one to undertake his affairs there, the commissioners did commission the same party likewise as to customs and foreign excise also; but what success this enterprise may have, must be left to the discovery of some further time. Report speaks the place to be frequented about May with some Dutch, who come to fish there, bringing beer strong waters, and tobaccos with them. The vessels or barques of this district belonging, are: viz. To Inverness: one of 10 tons; Garmouth: one of 12; Cromarty: one of 16; Thurso: two of 30; Orkney: three, viz. one 15 chaldrons, one 13 and one 12. 'There were lately some ten barques more belonging to those Isles, which have been taken or lost by storm, this and the last year.

'Being advanced as far as the furthest coast of Britain, I shall pass over Strathnaver, Assinshire, and the Western Isles, (places mangled with many arms of the Western Sea, embosoming itself within many parts thereof, and destitute of all trade, being a country stored with cattle, craggy hills, and rocks, and planted with the ancient Scots or wild Irish, whose garb and language they do still retain amongst them,) and return southerly as far as Glasgow'.

APPENDIX II: AN ALPHABETICAL LISTING OF VESSELS
(with only Q and Z missing)

This listing includes a cross-section of smuggling vessels and should be studied in conjunction with the appropriate chapters in the book.

Anne of Aberdeen

On 28 January 1747 the snow *Anne* of Aberdeen, James Ferguson master, arrived at her home port. She was boarded by Mr Ogilvie, tidesurveyor, who found 'a great many prohibited and high duty goods'. He placed six officers on board. The master reported that he was from Oporto and Rotterdam bound for Aberdeen and Bergen 'but that he had no bills of loading, having thrown them overboard at sea for fear of privateers and had nothing but his charter party from Holland, which he produced. The surveyor searched for papers but could find none'. While the goods for Aberdeen were being discharged, the officers seized 'twenty half pieces cambrics out of the heart of a matt of undressed flax and forty dozen strings glass beads, twenty-two dozen hanging locks, eighteen gross bone combs, 1 lb saffron, sixteen dozen spectacles, twenty-four dozen pieces unwrought nickel and twelve dozen brass thimbles out of the heart of a cask of unrated toys, together with the flax and toys'. As the vessel was 150 tons burthen no hovering bond was required and she was allowed to sail on 18 April - all other outports were forewarned. On 21 May Kirkwall informed Aberdeen that the *Anne* had 'unload the prohibited and high duty goods reported for Bergen in their country'.

Bacchus of Aberdeen

Alexander Davidson was master of the *Bacchus*, described as 'a beautiful sloop of 40 tons burthen'. On 20 April 1730 the collector at Aberdeen forewarned Harry Elphinstone, landwaiter and acting tidesurveyor at Peterhead [see Appendix III], that 'having (as we are credibly informed) wine and brandy on board [she] came before this harbour on Saturday night last and endeavoured to run some goods ... But being prevented she is, as we are very well informed, gone to the northward having her cargo still on board. We desire therefore that upon receipt of this you will look after this vessel at Peterhead or Fraserburgh and other parts of our district ... in case you find her you are to take an account of the goods aboard, as near as you can, and to put as many officers on board her as you have at the creek where she may happen to be or can fetch from the neighbouring creeks. Remain at the place where you find her yourself until you advise us and have received our return. In the meantime require the master to come into this port and enter into hovering bond ... We expect your diligence and industry in this service'. Elphinstone found the *Bacchus* at Fraserburgh with only ballast in her hold. According to information received by the collector, some of her cargo of brandy had been run just north of Aberdeen. But because of the bad weather, the remainder of the brandy and all the wine were landed at Fraserburgh [the three tidesmen on duty at the time were subsequently dismissed]. As the merchants now faced the risk of transporting their goods thirty miles by land, 'for fear of being catched' the vessel returned to Fraserburgh and reshipped the wine and brandy. Having hovered unsuccessfully off the coast for several days, the *Bacchus* 'proceeded to some foreign country'. In June 1730 she arrived at Aberdeen from Holland with a cargo of tow flax, iron etc.

Christian of Inverness
The *Christian*, Alexander Watson master, with a cargo of tobacco and spirits and seven boxes of damaged apples, pretending bound from Dunkirk to North Faro, was seized in November 1784 and taken to Fort George, where on 8 December George Greig, riding officer at Fortrose, and other customs officers were forcibly put under confinement and part of her cargo carried off. The remaining cargo was lodged in the king's warehouse, where it was guarded by a sergeant and twelve privates. The sloop was condemned in the exchequer court and sold in October 1785 to be broken up. However, the purchaser 'fled the country in bankrupt circumstances' and she was resold the following February. Two of the deforcers, Alexander Dunbar and Aeneas Barclay, were apprehended in July 1785 but in February 1786 the collector was informed that no further criminal prosecutions were intended against them.

Doctor of Lerwick
On 28 July 1800 the *Doctor* of Lerwick, Thomas Gilbertson master, from Bergen laden with deals for her home port was sent into harbour by Captain Collier of His Majesty's sloop of war, the *Victor*, as he had found some half ankers of geneva on board and a paper of instructions from Andrew Grierson 'directing a part of the cargo to be smuggled and a part entered'. Grierson was owner of the *Happy Return* of Lerwick [see Chapter Five].

Endeavour of Aberdeen
The *Endeavour* of Aberdeen (60 tons), Kenneth Irvine master, arrived at Aberdeen from Rotterdam on 13 June 1730 with a cargo of tow flax, wainscot boards and other goods. Two days later the collector received information of 'several hogsheads of wine shipped privately by some other merchants on board this vessel'. The master 'solemnly affirmed that such wine had been put

on board without his knowledge or connivance and that most of the time he was in Holland he was so unrested with the ague, which continues yet with him, that he was not able to take a regular account of the loading and was forced to trust his mate's account'. The wine was seized and the ship condemned in the court of exchequer.

Fortune of Aberdeen

John Souter, master of the *Fortune*, smuggled six hogsheads red wine and a quantity of calf skins in Newburgh Bay on 18 May 1777. This could be proved by William Alcock, late apprentice to John Souter, and John Roy, mate on board the *Fortune* for that voyage [and later a revenue boatman] and the two boats' crews who landed the wine and skins. The goods belonged to Robert McGilligan, merchant in Newburgh, who helped his servants William Duthie and Robert Napier take the goods on carts from the waterside to his cellars [Robert McGilligan also appears in Chapters Four and Eight]. Souter died on 10 October 1777 but the prosecution continued. In April 1785 the *Fortune* of Aberdeen, William Brown master, was wrecked at Harwich with a cargo of wine from Oporto.

Galley of Down

George Lawtie, landwaiter at Banff, secured the *Galley* of Down (35 tons), Thomas Irvine master, in August 1775 on information that spirits and tobacco had been run on the coast and she had then hovered to take on board tow and broadcloth for her outward cargo. The main purpose of the prosecution was to dissuade other merchants from loading goods for exportation this way.

Helen & Wally of Portgordon

In May 1824 the coastguard seized the *Helen & Wally* of Portgordon, a small sloop of 21 tons, registered at Banff in 1822, and a fishing boat which was helping to run 12 lbs manufactured tobacco, 5 lbs unmanufactured tobacco, 40 square yards printed paper and 11 gallons gin. The *Helen & Wally* had cleared from Banff on 17 February with seventy barrels herrings and fifty sacks flour for Inverness and she had not been heard of since. But according to the Banff collector, the idea of her having been to Holland in March or April was 'quite absurd'. The goods must have come from one of the Dutch fishing vessels recently on the coast or through the Caledonian canal from the West.

Industry of Portsoy

Charles Dawson, merchant in Portsoy, 'has been carrying on a contraband trade for some years in the west islands of Scotland'. In March 1785 he boarded the *Industry*, Alexander Wiseman master, from Oporto and sold fifty hogsheads of port wine along the Sound of Mull, one hundred hogsheads in the Isle of Skye and adjoining places and a further twenty hogsheads at Burghead. The witnesses were Alexander Paterson, sailing master, who had left Aberdeen on 3 September 1785 for Sunderland to load coals for Inverness, where the *Industry* was to take on board a cargo of salmon for exportation; George Duncan (who was currently with Paterson) and John Livency, sailors at Sandend, near Portsoy; and the purchasers of the wine: James McDonald of Portree, Isle of Skye, Angus McLaughlan of Lochdon and Mr McCarter, innkeeper at Portmore, Sound of Mull. [see Chapter Three - tailpiece]

James & Ann of Portsoy

On 12 January 1750 the *James & Ann* of Portsoy (60 tons), Alexander Ferguson master, arrived at Portsoy in ballast from Morlaix in France. The master had not made a report by 17 February but William Reid, tidesman at Cullen, had information that wine and spirits had been run, including five hogsheads of wine lodged in Mr MacKie's cellar at Portsoy. Mr Gellie, landsurveyor, went to Cullen and from the declarations of James Hay, John Findlay, George Hay, Alexander Wood, James Smith, James Kelman and Peter Wood, all fishermen in Sandend of Cullen, George Robertson, James Imlach and John Farquhar, merchants in Portsoy, were concerned in the fraud. [see Chapter Six]

Katherine of Aberdeen

James Erskine, master of the *Katherine* of Aberdeen, made a double report from Malaga and Campvere on 6 February 1750. He had on board eighteen hogsheads of wine, fourteen half hogsheads of wine, seven ankers of spirits, seven casks of fruit, one tierce of wine vinegar and one bale of paper for Bergen. Patrick Souper, merchant and owner of the goods from Holland unloaded out of the *Thomas & Mary* of Peterhead, James Wood master, the previous December loaded these on the *Katherine* as well. The master took out a hovering bond for the whole cargo and sailed on 16 March. Only five days later she was in the bay again with only ballast on board. It was clear that her cargo had been run, especially as two fishing boats had been employed to load the ballast on board as she came into the river, 'not being in a condition to keep the sea'. Her hovering bond was put in suit.

Lady Charlotte

In May 1784 the *Lady Charlotte* went into Spey where the waterside officers suspected that ten of the seventeen hogsheads of red wine entered as Portuguese were in fact French. Two samples were sent to Leith, where the one marked 'French' was identified as 'really a French wine'. The ten hogsheads, plus two half hogsheads of port wine belonging to the master, were seized. This wine was still in the warehouse in January 1786 'unsold in danger of spoiling'. The owner, James Gordon, merchant in Portsoy, refused to pay £128 7s 2½d, the composition of the duties. The wine was advertised for sale 'but no offer was made'. In May 1786 Captain Laurence Brown was given orders to take it to Leith to be sold.

Mary & Jean of Aberdeen

The *Mary & Jean* of Aberdeen, Thomas Tosh master, from Rotterdam was taken by a privateer off Peterhead on 7 June 1747 and ransomed for £250. The vessel went into port the next day where the master reported for Aberdeen and Bergen. The collector took a hovering bond of £300 and forewarned the other outports etc. On 1 July she was brought back into port by Mr Ogilvie, tidesurveyor, 'wanting of the goods manifested four casks, eighteen ankers, five half ankers, one box, two caves, two bags, two hampers and thirty-four stone jars and three casks cordage'. On 10 July the bond was prosecuted. A week later the collector reported that Ogilvie had used his 'utmost endeavour to procure evidence of this ship's having run part of her cargo on the coast and particularly to examine the crew of the boat wherein he found a small cave ... they say they took the cave on board from the rocks and at present he says he can not get a proof of anything else'.

Nelly & Increase

Mr Thomson, tidesurveyor at Aberdeen, boarded the *Nelly & Increase*, Thomas Wetherall master in October 1765. During the rummage he found and seized nine kegs of spruce beer. Afterwards, upon an information, he discovered under a parcel of coals six half ankers and twelve small kegs containing 45 gallons spirits. When he went into the hold, John Brand, partner of William Brebner, merchant, ordered 'the hatches to be shut upon him, which was done accordingly'. Later, at the custom house, William Brebner 'abused him'.

Otter

In April 1785 iron and other goods were seized out of the *Otter*, Joseph Ball master, for having no coast dispatches. The goods had been transshipped from the *Susan*, Alexander Thomson master, with dispatches from Aberdeen for the Moray Firth. But because they had been landed at Portsoy and Fraserburgh they remained a seizure. In September 1786 Archibald Chisholm, acting coastwaiter at Findhorn, secured eighteen boxes of tea out of the *Otter*, brought coastwise from London without the correct clearance papers.

Pretty Peggie of Fraserburgh

The *Pretty Peggie*, Alexander Houller master, arrived at Portsoy in September 1748 with wine and spirits from Bergen, pretended bound for Rotterdam. 'The master acknowledges that he was at an anchor upon Sunday last in the bay of Fraserburgh but that he was forced there by a hard gale of wind'. No evidence could be found of her having broken bulk. On 23 May 1765 Captain William Duncan of the *Wharton* excise yacht brought the ship *Pretty Peggie*, William Short master, from Gothenburg into Aberdeen. He had seized 130 lbs of tea in the cabin, concealed in false bulk heads and contained in paper parcels, except for two small canisters. There had been 'a large parcel of tea run out of this ship, part of which was seized by Duncan Aire, after its being landed near Slains Castle'. On 21 June 1765 the vessel was seized by the tidesurveyor.

Robert and Christian of Fort William

The sloop *Robert & Christian* of Fort William, Donald MacDonald master, from Mandale in Norway, principally laden with deals, was detained by Captain Daniel Reid of the *Prince Ernest Augustus* off Cape Wrath on 17 July 1786. She had on board eight ankers containing 29 gallons brandy and three and a half ankers containing 32 gallons geneva. She was allowed to proceed to Fort William with Murdoch MacKenzie and Alexander Mathieson from the cutter on board to be returned as a seizure, including two yawls not in her manifest. The crew was still on board as they could not enter into reconnaissance at Stornoway.

Swallow of Aberdeen (formerly the *John & Barbara*)

On 5 November 1775 the *Swallow* of Aberdeen, Robert Wilson master, arrived at Montrose from Christiansands with a cargo of wood for Aberdeen. A few days afterwards the collector was informed that on 4 November fifty-two casks and boxes of tea had been smuggled out of her at Catterline. 'We are very credibly informed that the master and his employers have been and still are old and atrocious smugglers and thereby have acquired a considerable sum of money'. In September 1776 it was reported that the master was now employed in the coasting trade between Aberdeen and London in another vessel and 'we are informed is in good circumstances'. Other members of the *Swallow*'s crew included James Robertson, now on the Crail revenue boat, James Naaden from Aberdeen, 'sometimes a merchant and sometimes a sailor', and Thomas Robertson, mariner of Aberdeen, now on board a Flushing cutter. 'The crews of the two boats which brought ashore the tea [the two Alexanders and the Bridgefords from Catterline] ... are trustees of the supposed proprietors ... and are always employed by them, when any smuggled goods are to be landed on that part of the coast out of any vessel wherein they had a concern and in particular are well acquainted with the sloop ... having been often on board of her. One of our witnesses [Andrew Dunward, now on board Captain Kyd's yacht] sailed on board of her as mate in the voyage when this fraud was committed. Besides we have another witness, a skipper of a sloop, another witness who pointed out the [vessel] ... then lying in Montrose harbour and the fishers that saw the fraud committed out of her being then at the fishing at a small distance from the sloop'.

Two Sisters of Montrose
On 14 April 1773 the sloop *Two Sisters* of Montrose, George Barclay master, from Holland ran geneva and tobacco stems off Bervie. She sailed directly for Sunderland or Newcastle for coals to carry to Holland 'for another cargo of such like goods ... and is expected on the coast again in a short time'. She was described as 'square-sterned, painted with a stroke of a dirty red colour with a standing topmast and bowsprit'.

Unity of Stornoway
In May 1785 the *Unity* of Stornoway, David McKay master, from North Faro with a cargo of rum, brandy, geneva, white wine, tea and tobacco was seized by William Scott, commander of the *Prince Ernest Augustus* revenue cutter and taken into Stornoway. The goods were lodged in the collector's dwelling and office houses 'the same being properly enclosed but as the cargo ... belongs to Stornoway merchants as far as we can learn ... [the collector wondered] whether a party of military for the protection thereof should be applied for, there being none in these Islands'. On 28 December the collector was taken into the Clyde by the *Prince Ernest Augustus* en route for the trial at the exchequer court scheduled for 26 January 1786.

Vrow Catharina
On 1 March 1785 James Farquhar, landsurveyor, and James McLean, acting comptroller at Aberdeen, on their way to make enquiries about the *Flying Fish*, 'observed ... a small sloop, seemingly foreign built, riding at anchor in the bay of Stonehaven. Upon their arrival there, having made enquiry at the tidesmen who had been on board, they in consequence of this information, being afraid to board her for want of a sufficient party, judged it proper to return as soon as possible from Stonehaven to Aberdeen in order to inform Mr Blair, tidesurveyor, that he and his crew might instantly set off, the wind being favourable, to make seizure of the ship and cargo'. Mr Blair found the *Vrow Catharina* of Ostend, Carolus Philow master, at anchor in Stonehaven bay, loaded with six ankers and six half ankers geneva, twenty casks salt, ten casks onions and a lot of empty casks. She was taken round to Aberdeen. 'Mr

Alexander Brebner, merchant here, brought the master and crew ... to the custom house to make proof of the destination and intention of the voyage ... from which no proof of distress appears in the smallest degree'. She was returned as a seizure.

William

On 15 November 1787 Captain John Robertson, sailing master of the sloop *William* of Kirkwall, stated at Burghead that 'upon the 10th current about four o'clock in the morning he sailed from Shields bound for Kirkwall with the sloop in good condition, well-manned and victualled in ballast and a few goods on board; wind then at south-west. Upon Sunday the 11th current about ten o'clock at night, the same being very dark, the representer continued his course and about four o'clock in the morning of the 12th current it then turned quite calm. Then about six o'clock the wind veered about to the north-north-east and north-east with a most violent gale, when the representative consulted with the mate and rest of the crew what was best to be done. The island of South Ronaldsay being then in sight and only about two leagues distant the representer ... set the ... mainsail and storm gib with a view and sole intention to reach the island ... or any other of the Orkney Islands. But the gale still increasing it was condescended upon by the representer ... to bear away for the harbour of Wick in Caithness. Upon arriving there it was found so hazardous, the sea running high, that it was impossible to get in. The weather growing quite tempestuous it was thought proper and expedient to bear away for Cromarty Bay, there being little room to lay the sloop too in for the greatest part of the short day and long night. Accordingly a proper course was shipped but as the distance was shortened the weather became so thick and the wind so violent that the sloop could not be confined to an exact course nor any land seen above a few cables length distance so that every man on board was on the strictest lookout not only for the sake of the sloop but particularly for their own lives. About seven o'clock at night land was seen, which at last turned out to be Burghead in the Moray Firth, and the vessel close in with the breakers and so close that no manner whatever could pretend to weather it ... at which time the representer ... let go their best anchors and cables for the safety of the sloop and the sailors' lives. One of which cables with the anchor the vessel parted with in a few minutes and thereafter the other cable being quite new and fresh she hung upon the same for a few minutes and then owing to the impetuosity of the weather and roughness of the sea she also parted from the same. All which the representer having seen and that there was no preservation of the vessel (though every person on board did their utmost endeavours both for the sloop and their own lives) he repaired to the mainmast and there protested against wind and weather and took instruments in the hands of

George Brebner, mate of the vessel, that whatever damage might ensue to her or the cargo on board was not owing to the negligence or fault of Captain John Robertson, the representer, but the violence of the weather and sea ... before three witnesses: George Eunson, shipmaster in Kirkwall [passenger], and James Scolater, sailor on board the sloop'.

X (No name)

A smuggling cutter, appearing to be waterlogged and in distress was seen in Peterhead Bay during November 1785. She was 'about the size of the *Experience* cutter lately commanded by Alexander Cook, all dark with a small yellow stroke, deep waisted and with a high up gallan mast, mounting two carriage guns with twenty men on board loaded with a smuggling cargo supposed to be from Copenhagen and said to be commanded by one Allan belonging to Greenock, and bound to that coast. She had got provisions from Peterhead and addition of some sailors ... there are no cutters at present on this coast. We suppose she has suffered considerable damage in the late gales of wind and that she would be an easy prize'.

York

The *York*, Peter Ellis master, was brought into Aberdeen in May 1785 by the mate of the *Osnaburgh* cutter. She was loaded partly with kelp and had ten pipes of wine on board, 'pretending bound for London'. The collector examined the crew except Martin Devonshire, who refused to attend. The master could not be examined until he had returned from Edinburgh and then he refused to sign his statement 'although he made oath to it in the most solemn manner in the presence of the comptroller and collector's clerk before the collector' unless he was given a copy 'which we thought improper'. They suspected that the wine was part of the cargo of the *Union* of Aberdeen, Robert Bruce master, who arrived at Aberdeen on 1 April 1785 from Lisbon with her hold in confusion and only three quarters loaded, 'which may have been taken in in the Highlands, as we have some hints given us to that effect'. Peter Ellis was already under exchequer prosecution for a considerable fraud against the revenue in England. On 14 June Thomas Bannerman paid the wine duties for Pierce Joyce, the proprietor, and £66 the duty on 80 tons of kelp was pledged against delivery of the kelp in London.

APPENDIX III: JACOBITE CONNECTIONS

Previous attempts have been made by the author to understand the connections between the 'smuggling' merchants and their customers [see *George Moore and Friends*]. According to both his letter-book and to the *List of Persons Concerned in the Rebellion* produced by the excise in 1746, bailie John Steuart and his friends were Jacobites.

On 17 August 1716 Steuart wrote to John Steuart [Commissary of Inverness and the Earl of Moray's legal adviser in Edinburgh] 'I am desired by the relations of the miserable prisoners [highland Jacobites taken in 1715] in the castle of Edinburgh to advance them 20s, which I entreat you may do per first and place to my account, and if [you] can send some receipt from them for the money it will be better. There is, I think, four of them'. In December 1716 he sent £20 to the 'poor gentlemen' in prison at Carlisle. On 18 September 1745 in a letter to his son, John, he mentioned 'some impending clouds'. There are no further letters from him recorded until 14 October 1748, when Steuart was in Inverness again.

What happened to him in the meantime is noted in the List. 'John Stewart, late bailie of Inverness, a volunteer in said Rebel Army and very active [is] now at Newtown, Mid Lothian'. The biographical notes add 'A cousin of the noted rebel leader, John Roy Stewart. The bailie was a leading merchant in Inverness ... His daughter Ann was married to Richard Hay Newton of Newton, Haddingtonshire, with whom he found refuge after Culloden'.

Several of Steuart's correspondents were also Jacobites, including the Marquis of Seaforth, Sir James Stewart of Burray, William Gordon of Farskane, near Cullen, Charles Smith of Boulogne, Charles Stewart of Ardshiel and Donald McDonlad of Kinlochmoidart.

According to the biographical notes, after he was attainted Ardshiel 'remained in hiding, in a cave upon his own estate, until, on 17th September 1746, he and four other gentlemen got on board a French vessel, and escaped to the continent. Shortly after Culloden the estate was plundered by the royal troops. Major-General John Campbell, who commanded in the district, was humane enough to show kindness to the wife and children of the fugitive, as appears by a letter from him to the Lady, dated Appin, 25th May 1746, in which he says: MADAM, - Your misfortune, and the unhappy situation Ardshiel has brought you and your innocent children into, by being so deeply concerned in this unjust and unnatural rebellion, makes my heart ache. I know the King to be compassionate and merciful. I know the brave Duke, under whose command and orders I act, to have as much humanity as any man on earth; from which, and my own natural inclination, I have taken the liberty of ordering back your milk cows, six wethers, and as many lambs; the men who pretend a right to them shall be paid. I have taken the freedom at the same time of ordering two bolls of meal, out of my own stores, to be left here for you, which I desire you to accept for the use of yourself and little ones; and if what I write can have any weight, I most earnestly entreat you to bring up your children to be good subjects to His Majesty. I wish your husband, by surrendering himself to the Duke of Cumberland, had given me an opportunity of recommending him to His Majesty's mercy. I feel for you, and am, Madam, your most obedient and humble servant, John Campbell.

'It would appear that General Campbell misjudged the humanity of the Duke, for in December following Ardshiel House was sacked, and the Lady compelled to flee for refuge to a hut. From this also she was driven, the very night after her confinement, to seek, with her newborn infant and five children, another shelter from the falling snow. These cruel details are inscribed upon the stone erected to her memory in Northampton, where she died in 1782'. No record of her death has been found in the Gentleman's Magazine for that year nor has the stone been located in Northampton, yet.

Donald McDonald of Kinlochmoidart fought at Sheriffmuir and in the '45 was aide de camp to Prince Charles. According to the biographical notes 'When the rebel army was marching to England, this officer was taken prisoner by Mr Linning, a minister, at Lesmahagow, in Lanarkshire. He was brought to trial at Carlisle, in September 1746, and being found guilty was executed'.

On the other side, Roderick McCulloch, town sergeant in Aberdeen, John Thomson, also town sergeant, and James Sutherland, merchant, gave evidence to the excise that Henry Elphinstone senior, 'late a landwaiter at Aberdeen', [see pp 184 & 185] had been concerned with the rebels.

BIBLIOGRAPHY

Primary Sources
Custom House Letter-books (CEs) and the Watt Collection (D3)
In this section of the Bibliography the material studied has been listed in terms of letter-book/letters reference numbers. Each archive or record office consulted possesses a 'keyed' copy of this book with the exact references quoted written in the margin. Any further query should be referred to the author direct c/o the Publishers. For more information on Customs records see *Scottish Customs & Excise Records* by Frances Wilkins.

The Archive and Record Centre, City of Dundee District Council
CE53 Montrose: Class 1: 1/1, 1/2, 1/3, 1/4, 1/5, 1/6, 1/7, 1/8, 1/9, 1/10, 1/11, 1/14, 1/15, 1/16 Class 2: 2/1, 2/2, 2/5, 2/6
West Search Room, Scottish Record Office, Edinburgh
CE54 Thurso: Class 2: 2/2
CE62 Inverness: Class 2: 2/1, 2/2, 2/3, 2/4, 2/5, 2/6, 2/7, 2/8
CE64 Banff: Class 2: 2/1
CE65 Peterhead: Class 1: 1/1
CE75 Oban: Class 1: 1/1 Class 2: 2/1, 2/3
CE86 Stornoway: Class 1: 1/1, 1/2 Class 2: 2/1, 2/2, 2/3, 2/4, 2/5, 2/6, 2/7, 2/8, 2/9
CE87 Aberdeen: Class 1: 1/1, 1/2, 1/3, 1/4, 1/5, 1/6, 1/7, 1/8, 1/11, 1/12, 1/13, 1/16, 1/21, 1/22, 1/26 Class 2: 2/8, 2/80, 2/81, 2/82, 2/83, 2/84, 2/85, 2/86, 2/88, 2/93, 2/94 Class 4: 4/3, 4/4, 4/5 Class 6: 6/1 Class 7: 7/1, 7/2, 7/9, 7/10, 7/11 Class 9: 9/3
Orkney Archives, Orkney Library, Kirkwall
CE55 Kirkwall: Class 1: 1/1
Watt Papers: D/3:70, 71, 72, 82, 85, 93, 104, 110, 141, 158, 207, 229, 329, 368, 369, 370, 377, 378
Shetland Archives, Lerwick
CE85 Lerwick: Class 1: 1/1, 1/2, 1/3, 1/4, 1/7

Other Primary Sources
Manx National Heritage Library Atholl Papers: X11/14
PRO Kew CUST90 Whitby

Secondary Sources
Adams, Norman *Malcolm Gillespie* Leopard Vol 1 No 11 July/August 1975
Atton, Henry & Holland, Henry Hurst *The King's Customs Vols I & II* London John Murray 1908 & 1910

Chatterton, E Keble *King's Cutters and Smugglers* 1700-1855 George Allen & Co Ltd 1912

Cochran, L E *Scottish Trade with Ireland in the Eighteenth Century* John Donald Publishers Ltd 1985 ISBN 0 85976 096 0

Dalgarno, James *From the Brig o'Balgownie to the Bullers o'Buchan* W Jolly & Son Aberdeen 1897

Fraser, Duncan *The Smugglers* Standard Press Montrose 1978

Hewison, W S *Smuggling in Eighteenth Century Orkney* Orkney Miscellany No 3

Masterton, William E *Jurisdiction in Marginal Seas with special reference to Smuggling* Macmillan 1929

The Ordnance Survey Gazetteer of Great Britain 2nd Ed *All Names from the 1:50,000 Landranger Map Series* Macmillan Reference Books 1989 ISBN 0 333 49999 9

Pratt, J B *Buchan* quoted in Platt, Richard *Smugglers' Britain* Cassell Publishers Ltd 1991 ISBN 0304 340650

Scottish History Society *A List of Persons Concerned in the Rebellion transmitted to the Commissioners of Excise by the Several Supervisors in Scotland in Obedience to a General Letter of the 7th May 1746 and a supplementary list with evidences to prove the same.* Printed from a manuscript in the possession of the Earl of Rosebery, President Scottish History Society No 8 1890

Scottish History Society *Letter-book of Bailie John Steuart of Inverness 1715-1752* Ed William Mackay Second Series No 9 1915

Smith, Hance D *Shetland Life and Trade 1550-1914* John Donald Publishers Ltd 1984 ISBN 0 85976 103 7

Report by Thomas Tucker upon the settlement of the revenues of Excise and Customs in Scotland A D MDCLVI The Bannatyne Club Vol 7 1825

Vyse, Charles *A New Geographical Grammar: containing a comprehensive system of modern geography after a new and curious method* London 1779

Wilkins, Frances *The Smuggling Story of Two Firths* Wyre Forest Press 1994 ISBN 1 897725 06 X

Wilkins, Frances *George Moore and Friends* Wyre Forest Press 1994 ISBN 1 897725 07 8

Aberdeen Press & Journal January & February 1994

The Gentleman's Magazine 1780, 1782

Note: All the archive material used by the author in researching the Scottish smuggling histories etc is to be held by the Merseyside Maritime Museum so that it is associated with the HM Customs & Excise National Museum and is available for study by those visiting the museum.

INDEX OF PEOPLE